£25.00

**This book is to be returned on or before
the last date stamped below or you will be
charged a fine**

Reflections on How We Live

Reflections on How We Live

Annette C. Baier

OXFORD
UNIVERSITY PRESS

OXFORD
UNIVERSITY PRESS

Great Clarendon Street, Oxford OX2 6DP

Oxford University Press is a department of the University of Oxford.
It furthers the University's objective of excellence in research, scholarship,
and education by publishing worldwide in

Oxford New York

Auckland Cape Town Dar es Salaam Hong Kong Karachi
Kuala Lumpur Madrid Melbourne Mexico City Nairobi
New Delhi Shanghai Taipei Toronto

With offices in

Argentina Austria Brazil Chile Czech Republic France Greece
Guatemala Hungary Italy Japan Poland Portugal Singapore
South Korea Switzerland Thailand Turkey Ukraine Vietnam

Oxford is a registered trade mark of Oxford University Press
in the UK and in certain other countries

Published in the United States
by Oxford University Press Inc., New York

British Library Cataloguing in Publication Data

Data available

Library of Congress Cataloguing-in-Publication Data
Baier, Annette.
Reflections on How We Live/Annette C. Baier.
p. cm.
ISBN 978-0-19-957036-2 (hardback: alk. paper) 1. Ethics. I. Title.
BJ21.B35 2009   170–dc22
2009034145

Typeset by Spi Technologies, Pondicherry, India
Printed in Great Britain
on acid-free paper by
the MGP Books Group, Bodmin and King's Lynn

ISBN 978–0–19–957036–2 (Hbk.)

10 9 8 7 6 5 4 3 2 1

und forzugehn: wohin? Ins Ungewisse.

(Rainer Maria Rilke, "Der Auszug des
Verlorenen Sohnes")

Preface

This book is about ethics in a broad sense. Some of its later chapters are essays in the old sense, rather than professional philosophical papers. David Hume, after turning to essay-writing when his long, three-book *Treatise* failed to gain appreciative readers, wrote a short piece on essay-writing, which he later withdrew, as in it he had appealed to women, as the leaders of the "conversible world," to read essays like his and Addison's, rather than romances. He can be seen, in this piece, as taking up Swift's "Hints for an Essay on Conversation," since Hume's essay is as much about conversation as about essay-writing. He had good reason to withdraw it, but, before his offensive gallantry to the ladies, he had said a little about what he thought the essay genre was suited to. It would indulge "an Inclination to the easier and more gentle Exercises of the Understanding, to obvious Reflections on human Affairs, and the Duties of common Life, and to the Observation of the Blemishes or Perfections of the particular Objects, that surround them."[1] This is not a bad summing up of the themes of the essays I have included in this volume, though the duties of common life may have been somewhat neglected.

When I was a schoolchild, I wrote essays on all sorts of topics, usually provided by my teachers, and I enjoyed doing this. Then I became a philosophy student, and learned to write with an eye to professional assessment, so some fine literary flourishes had to be given up. In one of my final MA exams I was given a choice of topics for a three-hour essay, chose "mysticism," and examined the principle that like knows like. Arthur Prior was external examiner, and although he had little time for mysticism, he liked what I had written, so that I ended with a scholarship to Oxford. There I wrote a B.Phil. thesis, under J. L. Austin's eagle eye, on precision in poetry, so my love of fine writing continued, even if it took the form of a thesis about the precise and the accurate. It was mainly metaphors I looked to, for examples of precise poetic expression, and indeed I had earlier tried my

---

[1] David Hume, *Essays, Moral, Political and Literary*, ed. Eugene F. Miller (Indianapolis: Liberty Classics, 1985), 534–5.

hand at poetry. The first thing I published was an encyclopedia entry on nonsense, written for Arthur Prior (and Paul Edwards), and later much mocked by graduate students at the University of Pittsburgh, who would recite it aloud as if it were a comic opera. It was very concise, and sounded quite good, aloud. It took me quite a while to learn how to write a philosophical paper, how to get a topic of the right size, with sufficient links to what others had recently written about to make them have some interest in what I had to say. I eventually became all too adept at that. At first I was reactive, querying what others had said on action and intention, but eventually I did venture to introduce new topics, and with what I said about trust I could almost be said to have begun a whole new industry.

I had always preferred those philosophers whose texts were a pleasure to read, so Plato, Descartes, and Hume had from the start been my favorites. I tried, when I myself wrote, to achieve clarity and also some literary polish, though I have always benefited from sympathetic copy-editors, as well as from critical input from colleagues and former students, and I continue to get great benefit from that. Some of the essays in this volume have been read in draft by writers such as Alastair Galbraith and Jeffrey Moussaieff Masson who are not philosophers (Alastair writes songs, and Jeffrey writes books about animals and commentaries on Sanskrit vedas), and I was especially pleased to have their approval, since I, like Hume, am delighted if I have a readership beyond my own profession. The essays on faces, friendship, and alienating affection are more solitary meditations on how I have lived than engagements with other philosophers. Others, such as those on honesty, on self-knowledge, and on hope and self-trust, engage more with other philosophers, though that on self-trust engages most with my own past views, but also with the views of others, including those who have reacted to mine. Some of the essays are enquiries into much discussed moral issues such as what we owe future people, and what toleration we should have for killing, and some of them may sound a slightly hectoring note. But as Anthony Ashley Cooper, third Earl of Shaftesbury, pointed out in his "Soliloquy: Advice to an Author," the only person there is any point in advising is oneself. Other people are unlikely to take our advice, and we make offensive displays of superiority if we offer it unasked. The essays on faces, on friendship, and on alienating affection are personal reflections, not theoretical conclusions on how anyone else should live. And "Other Minds," the last essay, is, like this Preface, unabashedly autobiographical. All the essays are reflections on our human condition, and our proclivities, good and bad. My earlier book of essays on ethics, *Moral Prejudices*, contained much about trust, and when I surveyed what I was first intending to include in this book, I found that only one, Essay 10, directly concerned trust. If I had been right that trust is at the heart of ethics, then how could I write about ethics without bringing it in? This was the beginning of Essays 11 and 12, for I still believe our capacity for trust, and where necessary for distrust, is basic to the way we live, and live together.

I am indebted not only to the many people who helped in the original writing of the essays, but also to those former students who have expressed special preference for some of the republished ones. Rob Shaver liked the honesty essay, Chris Williams the friendship one, while Donald Ainslie thought those on future generations merited republication. I thank Jeffrey Moussaieff Masson for encouragement with the recent essays on patriotism and on faces, and Livia Guimaraes, Herlinde Pauer-Studer, and David Wiggins for help with that on killing. For that on sympathy and self-trust, I thank Anik Waldow, with whom I have recently been considering sympathy, and also Rebecca Holsen, who long ago criticized my tendency to apologize. (Dare I apologize, Rebecca, for this acknowledgment?) I also thank Victoria McGeer, who provoked my rather sour reflections on hope. And I thank those at OUP who have worked with me on this book, Peter Momtchiloff, for his encouragement, and Laurien Berkeley for her sympathetic copy-editing.

The dust cover image of Courbet's grain sifters, which I saw when the Hume Society met at Nantes, was chosen because it expresses both our active life, in finding and separating out what we think will sustain us, and also our more restful and reflective absorption of that.

This book is for my daughter, Sarah, who seems to know better than most of us how to live and what will sustain us (and certainly did not learn it from me, since she was adopted at birth, and we met again only when she was 33), and who seems to have passed on that knowledge to my four grandchildren. Sarah, you have shown me what matters.

Dunedin   A.B.
March 2009

Contents

1

The Rights of Past and Future Persons

No one doubts that future generations, once they are present and actual, will have rights, if any of us have rights.[1] What difference is made if we say, not that they *will* have, but that they *do* have, rights—*now*? I see two main points of difference: first, that those rights will then give rise to obligations on our part, as well as on their contemporaries' part; and, second, that what they have a right *to* will be different. In addition to whatever political and civil rights they have or will have, they will also each have a right to a fair share of what is then left of the earth's scarce resources. If they *now* have rights, they have rights to a share of what is *now* left of those scarce resources. To believe that they have rights is to believe that *we* must safeguard those rights and that, where the right is to a share, that we must share with them, and that the size of our share is affected by their right to share.

Should we believe that future persons not merely *will* have rights, but that they presently *do* have rights? To decide this I shall first consider whether any conceptual incoherence would result. Having eliminated that threat, I shall turn to the question of what rational or moral grounds there might be for the belief. I shall argue that some of the reasons for recognizing obligations to future persons are closely connected with reasons for recognizing the rights of past persons and that these reasons are good ones. In addition, there are the obligations that arise from our responsibility for the very

---

[1] I do not take it for granted that any of us do in any morally significant sense have rights. We do of course have legal rights, but to see them as backed by moral rights is to commit oneself to a particular version of the moral enterprise that may not be the best version. As Hegel and Marx pointed out, the language of rights commits us to questionable assumptions concerning the relation of the individual to the community, and, as utilitarians have also pointed out, it also commits us more than may be realistic or wise to fixing the details of our moral priorities in advance of relevant knowledge that only history can provide.

existence of those future persons, through our support of social policies that affect the size and nature of the human population in the future. I shall argue that we have good reason to recognize these obligations to future persons, whether or not we see them as arising out of their rights.

I turn first to the question of what we are committed to in asserting that a person has a certain right. I take it that this is to assert:

(*a*) At least one other person has an obligation to the right-holder. This obligation may be to refrain from interfering with some activity of the right-holder or to take some positive steps to secure for the right-holder what he or she has a right to. These steps may be ones that benefit the right-holder or some third party, as would be the case if I have promised a friend to feed his cat. He thereby has a right to my services that are intended to benefit the cat. Following Feinberg's terminology,[2] I shall say that the obligation is *to* the right-holder and *toward* whomever is the intended beneficiary.

(*b*) There is, or there should and could in practice be, socially recognized means for the right-holder, or his or her proxy, to take appropriate action should the obligations referred to in (*a*) be neglected. This action will range from securing belated discharge of the obligation, to securing compensation for its neglect, to the initiation of punitive measures against the delinquent obligated person.

I think that this account covers both legally recognized rights and also moral rights that are more than mere "manifesto" rights,[3] since clause (*b*) requires that effective recognition could be given to such rights. Such effective recognition can of course be given only to a set of non-conflicting rights, and so I assume that to claim anything as a right is to claim that its effective recognition is compatible with the effective recognition of the other rights one claims to exist.[4] To claim a moral right to something not effectively recognized as a right is to claim that it could without contradiction

  [2] J. Feinberg, "Duties, Rights and Claims," *American Philosophical Quarterly*, 3/2 (Apr. 1966), 137–44.
  [3] J. Feinberg, *Social Philosophy* (Englewood Cliffs, NJ: Prentice-Hall, 1973), 67. The term "manifesto rights" is from Joel Feinberg, who writes, "[I am] willing to speak of a special 'manifesto sense' of 'right,' in which a right need not be correlated with another's duty. Natural needs are real claims, if only upon hypothetical future beings not yet in existence. I accept the moral principle that to have an unfulfilled need is to have a kind of claim against the world, even if against no one in particular. . . . Such claims, based on need alone, are 'permanent possibilities of rights,' the natural seed from which rights grow" (p. 67).
  [4] I assume that while it makes sense to speak of prima facie and possibly conflicting obligations, statements about rights gave final moral decisions, so there are no prima facie or conflicting rights.

to other justifiably recognized rights *be* given recognition, that only inertia, ignorance, greed, or ill will prevent its recognition.

This account of what it is to have a right differs in another sense from the account that is more commonly given. The point of difference lies in the extension of power to claim the right from the right-holder to his spokesman, vicar, or proxy. This extension is required to make sense of the concept of rights of past or future generations. I think we already accept such an extension in empowering executors to claim the rights of the deceased whose wills they execute. The role of executor is distinct from that of trustee for the heirs. We recognize obligations both *to* and *toward* the legal heirs, and *to* the person who made the will. Where the legal heirs are specified only as the "issue" of certain persons known to the will-maker, we already accept the concept of an obligation, owed by the trustees, to look after the interests of such not-yet-determinate persons.

Can those who protect the rights of future persons be properly regarded as their spokesmen, claimants of their rights in the present, when they, unlike executors of wills, cannot be appointed by the original right-holder? The rights of past persons, claimed by their recognized spokesmen, are person-specific rights to have their legally valid powers exercised, while the rights in the present claimed for future persons will be general human rights. No one needs to be privy to the individual wills of future persons to claim their right to clean air. Already recognized spokesmen for known past persons, claiming their particular rights, need knowledge of them, their deeds, and their wishes, and so are sensibly required to have a special tie to the original right-holder, initiated by him. Spokesmen for future persons, claiming general rights, need no such tie.

If future generations have rights, then we, or some of us in some capacity, have obligations to and presumably also toward them, and their spokesman should be empowered to take action to see to it that we discharge those obligations. I see no conceptual incorrectness in attributing such rights. Admittedly we do not now recognize any person as the proper spokesman, guardian, and rights-claimant for future generations. But we could, and perhaps we should.

The fact that future generations are not *now* living persons is irrelevant to the issue, if, as I have argued, we are willing to speak of the rights of those who are no longer living persons. The fact that we do not and cannot have knowledge of the special characteristics and wishes of future generations is,

I have claimed, also irrelevant to the recognition of their rights to basic non-special human requirements, such as uncontaminated air. Our dependence on fossil fuels may be, compared with the needs of past generations, quite special, and there may be good reason not to extrapolate that need into the distant future. But there is no reason to think that the need for air will be lessened by technological progress or regress in the future. Our ignorance of precisely *who* future generations will be, and uncertainty of how numerous they will be, may be relevant to the priority of our obligations to them, compared with obligations to the living, should conflicts arise; but it is not relevant to the reality of obligations to future persons, nor to the moral priority of such obligations over our tastes for conspicuous consumption or our demands for luxury and for the freedom to waste or destroy resources.

As lawful heirs of specific past persons, some of us may have a right to what those persons intended us to possess, should there be sufficient moral reason to recognize the disputed right to pass on private property and to inherit it. By contrast, we all inherit a social order, a cultural tradition, air and water, not as private heirs of private will-makers but as members of a continuous community. We benefit from the wise planning, or perhaps the thoughtless but fortunate conservation, of past generations. In so far as such inherited public goods as constitutions, civil liberties, universities, parks, and uncontaminated water come to us by the deliberate intention of past generations, we inherit them not as sole beneficiaries but as persons able to share and pass on such goods to an indefinite run of future generations. It was, presumably, not for this generation in particular that public-spirited persons in past generations saved or sacrificed.

Rights and obligations are possessed by persons not in virtue of their unique individuality but in virtue of roles they fill, roles that relate to others. For example, children, *qua* children, have obligations to and rights against parents *qua* parents. My obligations as a teacher are owed to my students, whoever they may be. When I discharge obligations to them, such as ordering textbooks, I do not and need not know who those students will be. As long as I believe that determinate actual persons will fill the role of students, will occupy a position involving a moral tie to me, my obligations are real and not lessened by my ignorance of irrelevant details concerning those role-fillers. As long as we believe there will be persons related to us as we are related to past generations, then any obligations and rights this relation engenders will be real. Whether there will be such persons is something about which we can have well-based beliefs, especially as it is to some degree up to us whether to allow such roles to be filled.

The ontological precariousness of future generations that some see as a reason for not recognizing any rights of theirs is not significantly greater than that of the future states of present persons. In neither case does ignorance of details about the future, or the possible non-existence in that future of those who would benefit from discharge of obligations in the present, affect the reality of our obligations. To make sacrifices *now* so that others may benefit in the future is always to risk wasting that sacrifice. The moral enterprise is intrinsically a matter of risky investment,[5] if we measure the return solely in terms of benefits reaped by those toward whom obligations are owed. Only if virtue is its own reward is morality ever a safe investment. The only special feature in a moral tie between us and future generations lies in the inferiority of our knowledge about them, not in the inferiority of their ontological status. They are not merely possible persons, they are whichever possible persons will in the future be actual.

So far I have found no conceptual reason for disallowing talk of the rights of future persons. Neither their non-presence, nor our ignorance of *who* exactly they are, nor our uncertainty concerning how many of them there are, rules out the appropriateness of recognizing rights on their part. The fact that they cannot now claim their rights from us puts them in a position no different from that of past persons with rights in the present—namely, a position of dependency on some representative in this generation, someone empowered to speak for them. Rights typically are *claimed* by their possessors, so if we are to recognize rights of future persons, we must empower some persons to make claims for them.

Another thing that can be done with a right is to waive it. Past persons who leave no will waive the right that they had to determine the heirs of their private property. Since nothing could count as a sign that future generations waive their rights against us, then this dimension of the concept of a right will get no purchase with future generations, unless we empower present persons not merely to claim but also to waive rights of future persons. Waiving rights and alienating them by gift or exchange are both voluntary renunciations of what a right puts in the right-holder's secure

---

[5] I have discussed this in "Secular Faith," *Canadian Journal of Philosophy*, 10 (Mar. 1980), 131–48.

possession. However, waiving rights, unlike alienating them, does not involve a transfer of the right. Since the rights that are transferred are always special rights, and the rights of future persons that we are considering are general ones, there can be no question of transferring such rights. But might a proxy waive them? Guardians of present persons (children, incompetents) do have the power to waive some rights on behalf of their wards, but the justification for this practice, and any exercise of it, depends upon the availability of special knowledge of what will and will not benefit the right-holder. It is barely conceivable that we or any official we appointed could have such knowledge of the special needs of some future generations. If we were facing the prospect of a nuclear war and foresaw that any immediate successor generations would live in the ruins of civilization as we have known it, we might judge that there was no point in trying to preserve, say, the Bill of Rights for one's successors, although they had a prima facie right to inherit it. One might on their behalf waive that right, in extreme conditions, and bury the Constitution, rather than prolong our agony to fight for it. But such scenarios are bizarre, since it is barely conceivable that those who would bequeath to future generations the effects of a nuclear war would care about the rest of their bequest, about the fragments that might be shored against our ruin. The benefits that might be gained for future generations by empowering any of their ancestors to waive some of their rights seem minimal. Still, this is a question not of the conceptual absurdity of waiving a recognized right of future generations but of the practical wisdom of giving another this power.

I conclude that no conceptual error is involved in speaking of the rights of future generations. The concept of a right includes that of the justified power of the right-holder or his spokesman to press for discharge of obligations affecting his particular interests, or to renounce this power. The concept has already shown itself capable of extension to cover the rights of past persons and could as easily accommodate the rights of future generations if we saw good reason thus to extend it.

What might give us such a reason? I have already spoken of our position in relation to past generations whose actions have benefited us, either by planning or by good luck. The conservative way to decide the *moral* question is to ask whether we ourselves claim anything as a matter of right against past generations. Do we feel we had a *right* to be left the relatively uncontaminated water we found available to us, as a generation? Do we feel that the Romans, whose cutting down of forests left barren, eroded hillsides, violated a right of later generations? I think that we do not usually attribute to past generations the obligation to save for us, we do not accept their savings as only our just due, we do not usually condemn past generations where their actions have had bad effects in the present. But the reason for this may be that we are reluctant to attribute obligations where we are uncertain of the ability to meet them. Past generations, unlike ours, were rarely in a position to foresee the long-term effects of their actions, so are rightly not blamed by us for any harm they caused. Where what they did had good consequences for us, we accept these not as our due but as our good fortune. Where past generations deliberately saved or conserved for us, we accept their savings not as something they owed us, even when they may have believed they did owe it, but as something they chose to give us, where the "us" in question includes future generations.

It is possible that we stand to future generations in a relation in which no previous generation has stood to us; so that, although we have no rights against past generations, future generations do have rights against us. This is a possible position one might defend. Our knowledge and our power are significantly different even from that of our grandparents' generation, and might be thought to give rise to new moral relationships and new obligations. Before turning to consider how we might determine what those new obligations are, and how to find for them a common ground with old obligations, I want to look more closely at our relations to past generations and to ask if there is anything they might have done that would have given us a reason to blame them for failing in their obligations to us.

I take as an example of a benefit made possible by the actions of earlier generations my own education at the University of Otago in New Zealand. This university was founded extraordinarily early in the establishment of the colony because of the high priority the Scottish colonists gave to education and to its free availability. The existence of a distinguished university, and of the institutions supporting and financing it, was due to the efforts of people in my great grandparents' generation. Had they not made that effort, or had they or later generations established a university that only the wealthy could attend, I would have had no ground for complaint against them. They did not owe me a university education. But had an intervening generation allowed the university and its supporting institutions to founder, and done so from unwillingness to spend on its upkeep the resources that could be used for personal profit, I and my generation *would* blame those who failed to pass on the public benefits they themselves inherited. One obligation that every generation has toward subsequent generations is to leave "as much and as good" of the public goods previous generations have bequeathed them. This obligation arises as much from a right of past persons to have their good intentions respected as it does from any right of future persons, but I think there *is* a right to have passed on to one those public goods that, but for ill will or irresponsibility, would have been passed on. If I had been deprived of an education because a previous generation had destroyed an already founded university for the sake of its own greater luxury, I would feel that *my* rights, as well as those of the university's founders, had been overridden. It is interesting to note that the rights of past benefactors and their future beneficiaries give rise to one and the same obligation. Indeed, if we consider the motivation of the university's founders, who were heirs to a Scottish tradition of investment in public education, we find that they saw themselves as *preservers* as much as creators, as passing on, in new and difficult conditions, a heritage they had themselves received. As one of their hymns put it:

> They reap not where they laboured,
> We reap where they have sown.
> Our harvest will be garnered
> By ages yet unknown.

The metaphor of seed and harvest is the appropriate one where what is passed on, sown, is the same good as was received or harvested from the earlier sowing by others. The obligation that each generation has, which is owed equally to past and future generations, is the obligation to preserve the seed crop, the obligation to regenerate what they did not themselves generate.

That this obligation can be seen as due, indifferently, to past or future persons shows something of considerable importance about obligations in general and about the moral community. Earlier I said that rights are possessed not in virtue of any unique individuality but in virtue of roles we fill. The crucial role we fill, as moral beings, is as members of a cross-generational community, a community of beings who look before and after, who interpret the past in the light of the present, who see the future as growing out of the past, who see themselves as members of enduring families, nations, cultures, traditions. Perhaps we could even use Kant's language and say that it is because persons are *noumenal* beings that obligations to past persons and to future persons reinforce one another, that every obligation is owed by, to, and toward persons as participants in a continuing process of the generation and regeneration of shared values.

To stress the temporal continuity of the moral community is not to deny that accumulating knowledge and increasing power make a difference to the obligations one has. Earlier I said that the reason we do not morally condemn earlier generations for those actions of theirs whose consequences are bad for us is the reasonable doubt we feel about the extent to which they knew what they were doing. If the overgrazing that turned grasslands into deserts were thought by us to have been a *calculated* policy to increase a past generation's non-renewed wealth, at our expense, we would condemn them for it. Any obligations we have to generations future to us that find no exact analog in obligations past persons owed us arise, I believe, both from special features of our known control over the existence and the conditions of life of future generations and from our awareness of what we owe to past generations. We are especially self-conscious members of the cross-generational community, aware both of how much, and how much more than previous generations, we benefit from the investment of earlier generations and of the extent to which we may determine the fate of future generations. Such self-consciousness has its costs in added obligations.

Another sort of obligation we may have to future generations arises out of our failure to discharge other obligations to them. We, unlike earlier generations, are in a position to control population growth and to attempt to gear it to the expected supply of essential resources. Where we are failing to use this ability responsibly, we incur obligations to compensate our victims in a future overcrowded world for the harm we have thereby done them. Special efforts to increase, not merely to conserve, needed food and water resources are the appropriate accompaniment to our neglect of the obligation not to overbreed.

Our special position, relative to previous generations, in the procession of human possessors of knowledge and power gives us the ability to end the sequence of human generations as well as to be self-conscious and deliberate in our procreative or regenerative activities. It is a consequence of my version of the cross-generational moral community that this power to end the human community's existence could justifiably be exercised only in conditions so extreme that one could sincerely believe that past generations would concur in the judgment that it all should end. I do not think that anyone, past, present, or future, has a right to exist, and certainly no merely possible person has such a right. But we do not need the rights of possible persons to restrain us from bringing about the end of human life; the rights of past persons and the very nature of membership in a moral community rule that out in all except the very direst circumstances. Just as we have no *right* to use up all scarce resources in our generation for our own luxury or whim but, rather, an obligation to renew what we use, to pass on what we received, so we have no right to decree the ending of an enterprise in which we are latecomers. To end it all would not be the communal equivalent of suicide, since it would end not only our endeavors but those invested endeavors of all our predecessors. Only if they could be seen as concurring in the decision not to renew human life, or not to allow it to be renewed, could such a decision be likened to suicide.

I have said almost nothing about the theoretical basis for the obligations and rights I have claimed exist. Indeed, I am not sure that theories are the right sort of thing on which to ground assertions about obligations. In any case I shall not here go into the question of which moral theory would best systematize the sorts of reasons there are for recognizing the rights and obligations I have invoked. Kant's moral theory, if it could be stripped of its overintellectualism, Burke's account of a cross-generational community, if it could be stripped of its contractarian overtones, Hume's account of the virtues recognized by us humans who see ourselves as "plac'd in a kind of middle station betwixt the past and the future" who "imagine our ancestors to be, in a manner, mounted above us, and our posterity to lie below us,"[6] Rawls's idea of social union, of a continuing community in which "the realization of the powers of human individuals living at any one time takes the cooperation of many generations (or even societies) over a long period of time."[7] If this could be used, as he does not use it, to give an account of the right as well as the good, all these give us assistance in articulating the

[6] David Hume, *A Treatise of Human Nature*, ed. L. A. Selby-Bigge and Peter Nidditch (Oxford: Clarendon Press, 1978), 437.

[7] John Rawls, *A Theory of Justice* (New York: Oxford University Press, 1971), 525. Rawls uses this idea of a cross-temporal social union to explicate the concept of the good, but in his account of justice he restricts the relevant moral community, those who make an agreement with one another, to contemporaries who do not know their common temporal position.

reasons that we should recognize obligations of piety to past persons and responsibility to future ones. I do not think that either utilitarian theories or contractarian theories, or any version of any moral theory I am familiar with, capture the right reasons for the right attitudes to past and future persons. Perhaps we need a new theory, but the "intuitions" it will ground are, I believe, very old ones. I have relied, rather dogmatically, on those intuitions that I think are fairly widely shared, but before attempting to summarize in broad outline the factors relevant to our obligations to future generations I need to make clear a few points about the community in which such obligations arise.

First, it is not a community to which one *chooses* to belong, but one in which one finds oneself. By the time any moral reflections arise, one is already heir to a language and a way of life, and one has already received benefits from those particular older persons who cared for one in one's initial extreme dependency and who initiated one into a way of life. This way of life typically includes conventions to enable one voluntarily to take on obligations as well as to renounce and transfer some rights; but not all obligations are self-imposed, and those that are arise from institutions, like that of promising, which depend for their preservation on other obligations that are not self-imposed. As Hume said: "We are surely not bound to keep our word because we have given our word to keep it."[8] We may, and usually do, "agree," as Hume put it, or go along with the customs we find in force, including the custom of promising and demanding that promises be kept, since we see the benefits of having such a practice; but any obligations there may be to support existent practices depend not on the prior consent of the obligated but on the value of the practice to all concerned and on their reliance on it.

Reliance creates dependency, and the second point I wish to make is that the relations that form a moral community, and which, once recognized, give rise to obligations, all concern dependency and interdependency. Some of these dependency relations are self-initiated, but the most fundamental ones are not. The dependency of child on parent, for example, is a natural and inevitable one, and the particular form it takes is socially determined but certainly not chosen by the child. Socially contrived dependencies shape,

---

[8] David Hume, *An Enquiry Concerning the Principles of Morals*, ed. L. A. Selby-Bigge (Oxford: Clarendon Press, 1935), 306.

supplement, and balance natural and unavoidable dependencies. Rights and duties attach to roles in a network of interdependent roles, which if it is wisely designed will conserve and increase the common store of goods, and if it is fairly designed will distribute them equitably. Some morally significant and interrelated roles are ones we all occupy in sequence: the dependent child becomes the adult with children in his care, those who care for the dependent elderly themselves become old and in need of care. Similar to these roles in their reference to earlier and later persons, but unlike them in that we do not occupy them in temporal succession, are the roles of inheritor from past generations, executor and determiner of the inheritance of future generations. In filling these roles one both receives and transfers goods, but the transfer involved is of necessity non-reciprocal, only a *virtual* exchange, and the taking begins to occur too early to be by choice.

The third point is that the cross-temporal moral community in which one finds oneself is not restricted to those who share one's own way of life, but extends to all those with whom one stands, directly or indirectly, in dependency or interdependency relations. Although a seventeenth-century Scotsman may have had no ties, social or economic, with Maoris in New Zealand, or even any knowledge of them, he has indirect ties if his descendants have economic and social and political relations with them. Interdependency is transitive, and so relates me to all those with whom either earlier or later participants in my particular way of life have stood in interdependent relationships.[9] Thus, the tie linking "those who are living, those who are dead, and those who are yet to be born"[10] is a cross-cultural one and brings it about that (at least) no one human is alien to me.

What facts about our own dependency relations to past and future generations are relevant to deciding what rights and duties those relations should entail? As far as our own duties to past and future generations go, the relevant

---

[9] This transitivity of dependency and interdependency does not imply any strong cultural continuity; but I do assume that, where the dependency is recognized and so is obligation-engendering, there is sufficient common culture for some sort of understanding of intentions to be possible. Even if, as those like Michel Foucault believe, there is radical discontinuity in human culture, so that we are deluded if we think we can understand what Plato or Hume meant, it is nevertheless a significant fact that we try to understand them and that we get insight from those attempts. Indeed, part of the intention of any writer, artist, or producer of other meaningful human works may be to provide something that can be reinterpreted. We do not need to see the heritage of the past to be fixed in form in order to value it, nor see future persons as strict constructionists, finding only our intentions in our works, in order to work for them.

[10] Edmund Burke, *Reflections on the Revolution in France* (London: Macmillan, 1910), 93–4.

facts are these: first, our relatively privileged material position, compared with that of most members of most previous generations; second, our dependency for this on past generations as well as our own generation's efforts; third, our power to affect the lot of future generations; fourth, our comparatively extensive knowledge of the long-term effects of our policies; and fifth, the fact that when past generations conserved or saved deliberately for the sake of future generations (in creating parks, writing and fighting for constitutions), there is no reason to think that it was for us in particular, but rather that it was done on the assumption that we would pass on the inheritance. To sum up, the chief facts are our indebtedness to the past and our dangerously great ability to affect the future. We, like most of our forebears, are the unconsulted beneficiaries of the sacrifice of past generations, sometimes seen by them as obligatory, often in fact non-obligatory. If we owe something in return, what is it, and what can we do for those who benefited us? The most obvious response is to continue the cooperative scheme they thought worth contributing to, adapting our contributions to our distinctive circumstances. What is distinctive is our increased ability to plan and foresee the future (and to recognize the dangers of overplanning). If we say that all generations have owed it to the moral community as a whole, and to past generations in particular, to try to leave things no worse than they found them, then we too have that obligation. In addition, as far as past generations, by supererogatory effort, left things *better* than they found them, we owe it to them to pass on such inherited benefits. We must not poison the wells, even such wells as we have deepened.

We, unlike our ancestors, are better able to judge and control what will benefit and harm our descendants, so our obligations are correspondingly more determinate. Does our special position warrant speaking of the rights of future generations and not just of our obligations toward them? I have argued that past generations have rights against us, that we not wantonly waste or destroy what they made possible for us to have, not intending it for us only. It would therefore be appropriate to recognize spokesmen for their rights. Should spokesmen for future generations, as well as for past generations, be empowered to ensure that we discharge our obligations, take our "trusteeship" seriously, and should we see our obligations as arising out of the rights of future generations?

When we speak of obligations as arising out of rights, we do several morally pertinent things. First, we put a certain emphasis on determinate interests that these rights protect and individuate our obligations by reference to these individual interests of persons. Second, we give a certain guarantee of moral priority to the protection of these definite central interests over negotiable goods. Third, we give the person whose interest a right protects a certain power of individual initiative to claim or demand or waive the right.[11] In all three aspects the concept of a right goes along with that of a certain individualist version of respect for persons and involves seeing obligations as arising out of this respect.

I have argued for a convergence of important interests of past and future persons, so that obligations to future persons do not stem from consideration of their interests alone. But their interests are of undeniable importance and merit a high priority, so that the first two dimensions of rights apply here. The third ingredient, respect for the right-holder's initiative in claiming a right, could only be fictionally present in the case of future generations, if we recognized a spokesman for them. I see no reason in principle why we should not speak of rights of future generations as well as of our obligations to them, but on the other hand I see nothing very important to be gained by doing so. As long as we recognize our obligations to consider the good of the continuing human community, it matters little whether we speak of the rights of future persons. Whether an official agency to execute our collective obligations were seen as a guardian of the interests of future persons or as a spokesman for their rights would make little difference to the responsibility of such an agency. To speak of their rights would be to commit ourselves to the priority of whatever rights we recognized over our own lesser interests. Until we are clear exactly what priority we are willing to give to the interests of future persons, and to which of their interests we will give this priority, it would be less misleading not to use the language of rights. We should first recognize that we have obligations, then devote ourselves to clarifying the precise content of these. If when that is done we find that we do believe we should give priority to certain definite individuated rights of future persons, we can then recognize and itemize such rights.

I have not detailed the content of our obligations to future persons, but have addressed myself only to the general question of whether there are any. I shall end by repeating the features of our own relationship with future

[11] H. L. A. Hart stresses this element in the concept of a right in "Are There Any Natural Rights?", *Philosophical Review*, 64/2 (1955), 175–91, and in "Bentham on Legal Powers," in Hart, *Oxford Essays in Jurisprudence*, 2nd ser., ed. A. W. B. Simpson (Oxford: Clarendon Press, 1973).

persons that I have claimed to be relevant to these obligations. Future persons stand to us in several morally pertinent roles that give rise to obligations on our part:

1. As those who, like us, depend upon naturally self-renewing resources like air, soil, and water, which none of us produced, they are owed the use of these resources in an unpoisoned state.

2. As intended heirs, with us, of the public goods past generations created, often at great cost and sacrifice, they are owed their share in these goods.

3. As those whose existence we could have prevented, but which we owe it to past generations not to prevent wantonly or for our own increased luxury, they have a right to a tolerable and so to a not too crowded existence. Our duty to the past is to ensure that, short of catastrophe, there be future persons. Our duty to those persons is to ensure that there not be too many of them.

4. As victims of our probable failure to meet the last-mentioned obligation, they are owed some compensation from us. This means, for example, that we as a society should be working on methods to increase food supplies beyond those that would be needed should our justifiable population policies succeed.

I have claimed that there is no conceptual counter-reason, and that there is good moral reason, to recognize obligations to future generations, to recognize that either they, or past generations, or both, have a moral right to our discharge of such obligations. I agree with Golding that "if obligation to the past is a superstition, so is obligation to the future,"[12] and I have tried to suggest that, if both these are superstitions, then all obligation is superstition.

[12] M. P. Golding, "Obligations to Future Generations," *Monist* (Jan. 1972), 91.

2

For the Sake of Future Generations

1 Introduction

Moral philosophers have only quite recently worried over the question of what we are morally obliged to do, or not to do, for the sake of persons who will live after we are dead. Classical moral traditions give us little help with this question. Though ordinary common sense moralities have usually regarded waste as immoral, and have recognized a vague general obligation to leave our camping places as clean as we found them, such popular moral beliefs are not specific about exactly what our duties to future people are, nor about the ground of such obligations—whether, for example, their basis lies in the rights of our successors to a fair share in what we might squander, to a camping site no dirtier than that enjoyed by their predecessors. We do not find most older moral theorists addressing the questions of what is due to future persons, why it is due, nor how any such moral dues link up with what is due to those persons whose lives overlap with our own.

1.1 Seeing into the Future

Several explanations might be offered for this recent emergence of the question of obligations to future persons. The increase in our ability or sense of our ability to foresee the long-term effects of our policies might be thought to explain it. As long as persons could not see how their actions affected later

Several friends and colleagues have helped me during the writing of this essay by their helpful suggestions and criticisms of earlier drafts. In particular I am indebted to David Gauthier and to Alan Meltzer for help with Sect. 3.3, although of course its faults are all my own. From Tom Regan I have had much help in simplifying and clarifying the argument of the essay. I am aware of some of its oversimplifications, and some of its evasions of hard and important questions.

'For the Sake of Future Generations' was originally published in *Earthbound: New Introductory Essays on Environmental Ethics*, edited by Thomas Regan and William Aiken (Random House 1984) and is reproduced with permission of The McGraw-Hill Companies.

generations, they could not be expected to feel any obligation to bring about good rather than bad effects. Our recently won confidence that we do control the fate of future persons brings with it a moral burden, responsibility for what we knowingly do. As long as our ancestors did not know what they did to us, and could not reasonably be expected to have known it, they cannot be blamed for any ill effects they produced, nor praised for any good effects. We, rightly or wrongly, feel we can estimate the effects of our policies; we think we know just how our great-great-grandchildren's teeth will be set on edge by the sour grapes we eat.

My use of this biblical metaphor shows that this hypothesis to explain the lack of classical discussions of our topic cannot be quite correct—people have always believed they could foresee *some* long-term cross-generational effects of actions, and have engaged at least in praise of ancestors for their lasting mighty works, if not so often in condemnation of ancestors for their less welcome legacies. "Let us now praise famous men, and our fathers that begat us. The Lord has wrought great glory by them through his great power, from the beginning…Their bodies are buried in peace, but their name liveth for ever more" (Ecclesiasticus 44: 1–14). It has been a normal human wish that future generations will not curse their predecessors, but rise up and call them blessed. This repeated wish, however, has not been accompanied by any clear doctrine about just how much it is reasonable to expect from previous generations, about just what we must avoid doing to avoid meriting the curses of our successors, nor about the ground for such intergenerational obligations. There has always been a willingness to pass moral judgment on past persons for meritorious or wrongful actions of theirs, some of these actions by which we are affected, but the exact link between the recognized merit or demerit of those actions, and their foreseeable consequences for us, have not been so clear. Maybe the "great glory" for which ancestors were praised were glories of piety, exemplary obedience to a divine law, rather than glorious world building for later persons. Indeed the preacher who invited us to praise ancestors cited them as "giving counsel by their understanding and declaring prophecies" (ibid.). They bequeathed to us their counsel and prophecies, not any more mundane bequest.

1.2 Laws and Consequences

Consequentialist moral theories see the moral status of actions to depend on their good or bad effects. But as long as doing the right thing is equated with doing what one believes God requires, one does not need to know about the long-term consequences of one's actions to discern right and wrong. One can leave it to God to see to it that our doing the right thing does some good to someone or something, at some time or other. The immorality of, say, willful waste will be thought to lie not in its causal link with woeful want, but in divine prohibition of wasteful policies. A belief in divine goodwill toward human beings will lead the believer to expect that there is *some* link between the content of the divinely ordained moral law and human welfare, but not a link we need to discern in order to know what is right. Then it would make sense to praise past persons for their great acts, from which we do in fact benefit, without thereby praising them *for* benefiting us. We might praise them because they did what was right or virtuous, and praise God that the consequences of their virtuous action for us are beneficial rather than harmful. For a non-consequentialist moral theory, it is possible that there are duties whose discharge does benefit future generations, yet which are not duties *to* those future generations. They might be the beneficiaries of our obligations, without being either those to whom the obligations are owed, or those for whose sake the obligatory action must be done. "Against thee only have I sinned," said David to God, not thereby denying that his sinful action (arranging the death of his ladylove's husband, Uriah) harmed another human, nor even that God prohibits such acts *because* they harm other humans. If our duties are to God and His law, our moral task would not be to fathom God's reasons, but to obey, trusting in the goodness of the will whose word is law. For such a religious non-consequentialist, it might be wrong to squander resources, poison air and water, and the like, not because future generations would thereby suffer (although this consequence of wrongful action is foreseen) but simply because God and His moral law forbids it. Future persons could condemn us for such wrongful action, action which in fact hurt them, but would do so not because it hurt them but because it was wrong, contrary to God's will and so to the moral law.

1.3 From Religious Ethics to Secular Ethics

One does not need to equate morality with the revealed content of God's will or God's law in order to be a non-consequentialist in moral theory. The philosopher Immanuel Kant (1724–1804) believed that human reason could discern the moral law, and that we need know neither about God's will nor about the actual long-run consequences of individual right and wrong acts in order to recognize this law. Just as it is in the power of human reason, in its scientific employment, to discern regularities or laws which hold good in physical nature, so reason in its practical employment can recognize law—indeed can *make* law to govern human behavior. The moral lawmaker, Kant claimed, was the individual acting as if setting an example all other persons would follow. For us to know what acts to perform, what example to try to set, theoretical predictive reason often has to help practical legislative reason, in order to work out what would be involved if everyone followed a particular example. But once we are satisfied that we can will that everyone follow our example of, say, ceasing to make nuclear weapons, then we have established that policy as morally right, and are not to consider as morally relevant the *actual* consequences of this policy in the real world where others may not and often do not all follow our example. The right thing to do must be seen to have acceptable consequences *were everyone to do likewise*, but may not have good consequences when done only by some. "Let justice be done, though the earth perish," or, in this case, although the just person or just nation perishes.[1]

This complex moral theory of Kant's both gives our power to envisage consequences of various policies an important role to play in moral reasoning, yet does not identify the right action with that which will in the actual state of things have the best consequences. Kant still needs and keeps a divine power in the background of morality, a power who is to see to it that the discrepancy between ideal and real world consequences is somehow compensated for, some day, so that obedience to the moral law does not, *in the end*, prove destructive to those who do what is right or to the world they would will into being. Kant's is a non-consequentialist moral theory where the test of moral rightness is the rational acceptability of hypothetical *universal* conformity to a policy, and of the consequences over time of such conformity. We are to do the act which we can will as universal law in "a system of nature," that is, in an ongoing world with interaction and feedback.

This ethical theory holds out some promise of applicability to the question of our duty to future persons, since any practice like dumping toxic

---

[1] Actually Kant seems to mean that we should not discontinue the administration of justice, such as punishing wrongdoers, even if the world is perishing, not that our just acts themselves may lead to that perishing of the world. However, nothing in his account guarantees that unilateral just acts, especially punitive ones, will not destroy the world.

wastes where they will poison soil, air, or water seems forbidden by Kant's test. We cannot conceive of a system of nature in which all humans regularly do this, yet survive as a species; it is not a coherently universalizable practice. Some, such as the Australian philosopher John Passmore,[2] who taught me, have seen Kant's ethics as addressing the question of our obligations to future persons, and there is no doubt that Kant's test of moral rightness can easily be applied to condemn many current practices, and also that the very form of his *test* for rightness (Can I will this as a law in a system of nature?) forces us to think about the long-term implications of policies. But, as far as I know, Kant did not himself actually draw out the consequences of his theory for this issue. He did make some claims about our *motivation*—he believed that we cannot help but care to some degree about future persons and the sort of life they will have—but he did not spell out what our duty to such persons is, or even if there are any special duties we owe them. To find out whether we do wrong if we refuse to help our contemporaries when they are in need, Kant's test forces us to consider what our world would be like, over time, if such refusal were the universal rule; so to discern our duty to anybody, we must in a sense think of everybody, future persons included, according to Kant's test. Future persons therefore come into his theory implicitly, but not as ones whose interests give rise to any *special* problems about duties on our part. Future persons themselves, and the fore-seeable consequences of our actions for them, come into Kant's theory only indirectly. His theory is usable only by moral agents capable of seeing the long-run implications of policies for whole systems, natural and social, and he believed that we moral agents do in fact care about the future of the human world, but he did not spell out any particular obligations we have, or, for that matter, which we fail to have, to future persons.

1.4 Modern Moral Theories and the Person-Affecting Principle

Post-Kantian moral theories, both utilitarian and some *rights* theories, have focused attention very strongly on the *effects* of right and wrong actions on the good of human persons, often making this the decisive test of their

---

[2] For a discussion of the implications of Kant's philosophy for our duty to future generations, see John Passmore, *Man's Responsibility for Nature: Ecological Problems and Western Traditions* (New York: Scribner's, 1974), ch. 4. Passmore quotes Kant's statement, in *The Idea of a Universal History*, eighth thesis, that "human nature is such that it cannot be indifferent even to the most remote epoch which may eventually affect our species, so long as this epoch may be expected with certainty."

rightness or wrongness. They see human moral agents, not some supervising God,[3] as responsible for the foreseeable effects of their actions. Modern moral theorists, while agreed on seeing morality as promoting our human good, disagree over what precise effect on human (and perhaps animal) good determines the moral rightness of an action: utilitarians see the crucial thing to be the effect of an action or policy on people's *happiness*, others emphasize the effect on *interests*, while those who hold a theory of rights (either rights arising from a hypothetical agreement, or so-called natural rights) see the crucial question to be the effect of an action on people as rights' holders.

The violation of a right is, of course, a special sort of effect on a person and on his or her good. It cannot be equated with making that person unhappier, or less able to get what she in fact wants. If I don't want to vote, then the violation of my right to vote by the removal of my name from electoral rolls will not hurt me—it may not even be noticed by me. Nevertheless, someone else on my behalf might correctly protest the violation of my right, and correctly say that my position is worsened by this inability to do what in fact I have no wish to do. I might even myself protest, and insist on my rights, then never exercise them. Once we see ourselves as right-holders, the violation of our rights becomes an injury, even if it makes no *other* difference to our lives. The violation of my rights affects my position among right-holders, even if that position is not very important to my particular goals in life. I shall return to this question of the relation between what affects our happiness and what affects our interests and our position among persons in Section 2.6. For the moment I want merely to draw attention to the agreement between most utilitarians and most of those who hold a rights theory that the moral wrongness of an act consists in some sort of bad effect it has on people.

The principle which they agree upon (but which religious moralists, or even Kantians, need not accept) has been called the *Person-Affecting Principle*, which says that *for any action to be wrong, it must affect some person or persons (usually other than the agent) for the worse.* This is a minimal requirement of wrongness: the principle does not say that all acts which have any bad effects

[3] See Jerome Schneewind, "The Divine Corporation and the History of Ethics," in Richard Rorty, Quentin Skinner, and Jerome Schneewind (eds.), *Philosophy and History* (Cambridge: Cambridge University Press), for a discussion of the effect on ethical theory of loss of faith in a divine world manager.

on others are wrong, but only that, if an action has *no* bad effect on anyone, it cannot be really wrong.

Versions of this principle, sometimes called the principle of *No Wrongs Without Victims*, were used by the nineteenth-century English social philosopher John Stuart Mill (1806–73), and by many reformers since then, to distinguish "real" wrongs from those traditionally frowned-upon actions which seem in fact to have no victims, to do no harm to any (non-consenting) person. The principle seems to sort moral prohibitions into those soundly based on the requirements of human good, and mere taboos and expressions of culturally fostered distaste or disgust. It was used by the framers of Britain's controversial Wolfenden Report (1957) to distinguish "moralistic" bad legislation, which created "victimless crimes," from those parts of the criminal law which protect persons from becoming, in a variety of ways, the victims of other persons.

The Person-Affecting Principle directs us always to think of the consequences of our actions for other people, when making a moral decision. It is natural, if one finds the principle plausible, to think of consequences for future people as well as for our contemporaries, and to see a moral agent's responsibility as extending to the foreseeable effects of our actions on future and distant as well as present and close persons. I suggest, then, that one reason why it is only recently that the question of our duty to future persons has been discussed is that it is relatively recently that ethical theory has seen the responsibility for consequences to fall on human agents, and only recently that the Person-Affecting Principle has come to seem acceptable. It took so long for the question of our duty to future persons to come to our attention because it took so long for ethics to free itself from theology, and to make morality concerned primarily and directly with the human good. It took the same long time for us to accept the related, sometimes frightening, fact that, if we do not consider the consequences of our policies for future people, no one will—that neither gods nor hidden hands will arrange things for us so that doing anything we for any reason believe to be right will in fact advance the human good not only now but also indefinitely into the future. This increasing secularization of moral theory, and with it the increasing acceptability of the Person-Affecting Principle, along with our increasing ability to trace consequences and our increasing power to perform acts with dramatically great foreseeable consequences for future persons, has forced this moral issue on our attention.

Paradoxically enough, however, that same Person-Affecting Principle which seems to direct us to think about future persons has been invoked by some recent thinkers to reveal a problem in the very idea that future people could possibly be our victims. I turn next to that worry.

2 The Futurity Problem

2.1 Our Knowledge of Future People

There are several features of future people, in relation to us, which can make the idea that we have duties to them seem problematic. I shall consider their *unknowability*, their *indeterminacy*, and their *contingency*.

We do not know much about all those children who will be born during the next seven months, although their genetic makeup is now quite fixed and determinate. For people further in the future, not only *do* we not know details about them, those details are not yet fixed, so are unknowable. Such lack of knowledge, especially when due to the not yet determinate status of future people, does, I think, rule out our having to them one kind of duty which we can have to our contemporaries. For example, some people now living are accustomed to a particular diet, and *could* not easily adapt to a different one. There would be no point in shipping canned pork and beans off to avert a famine in a Muslim country—the people could not eat it. We know, or can find out, this sort of special need, when we are considering the effects of our policies on our contemporaries, but we cannot know this sort of fact about distant future people. Since they are not yet determinate people, their special requirements are as yet unknowable. *Some* wrongs we can do to our contemporaries, those harmings which depend upon their special needs, we cannot knowingly do to future persons. Their indeterminacy protects us against the charge of doing them that sort of wrong.

But such wrongs, although real, are only one sort of wrong we can do people, and there are plenty other wrongs which depend not upon the victims' special needs, but upon their common human nature. However little we know about future people, however much about them is not yet fixed, as long as they are human people they can be expected to need air, water, some fruits of the earth to eat. They will be vulnerable to poisons, just as we are, and we can, it seems, affect the availability to them of the unpoisoned air, water, soil, undestroyed naturally self-renewing or self-cleansing basic physical resources, which we as a species need. By the Person–Affecting Principle, then, as far as we have seen, there can be wrongs to future persons despite their indeterminacy and our ignorance of their special needs. The principle will not itself tell us how bad the effects of our action must be for future persons to have been wronged, but it allows room for the idea that we really can wrong future persons. So far so good.

There is, however, the third characteristic of future persons to consider, namely their *contingency*. Not merely is their identity now indeterminate, but what will eventually fix it are a host of causal factors including the actions and inactions of their predecessors. It is *this* fact, the *contingency of future people on their predecessors*, which generates what has come to be seen as the worst philosophical "problem of futurity,"[4] one which might seem to cancel all duties we may have thought we had to future persons. I turn to that problem.

2.2 *The Ontological Precariousness of Persons*

A thing is ontologically precarious, precarious in its very being, to the extent that its coming into being is dependent on other things. To appreciate just how precarious we all are, or were, we need merely think of the many possible things our parents might have done which would have led to our own non-being, to our total absence from the human scene. Not merely do deliberate parental actions of family planning determine which children come to exist, but all sorts of outside factors determining the precise time of conception also play their role—such things as owl hoots or train whistles which wake potential parents in the night. The English philosopher Derek Parfit, who has in a number of influential papers[5] explored this problem thoroughly, asks how many of us could truly claim that we would have existed even if railways had never been invented. A recent electricity blackout in the city of New York was followed nine months later by a significantly increased number of births. As times goes on, the number of

---

[4] See Gregory Kavka, "The Futurity Problem," in Richard Sikora and Brian Barry (eds.), *Obligations to Future Generations* (Philadelphia, Pa.: Temple University Press, 1978), 180–203, and id. "The Paradox of Future Individuals," *Philosophy and Public Affairs*, 11/2 (Spring 1982), 93–112.

[5] See Derek Parfit, "On Doing the Best for Our Children," in Michael Bayles (ed.), *Ethics and Population* (Cambridge, Mass.: Schenkman, 1976); id., "Future Generations: Further Problems," *Philosophy and Public Affairs*, 11/2 (Spring 1982), 113–72; id., "Energy Policy and the Further Future: The Identity Problem," in Douglas Maclean and Peter Brown (eds.), *Energy and the Future* (Totowa, NJ: Rowman and Littlefield, 1983).

descendants of these "blackout babies" will probably become larger and larger, so that factors such as trains and blackouts come to figure in causal ancestry of a larger and larger proportion of the population.

Philosophers have long been aware of this radical contingency of particular existent things on earlier happenings, of the reverberating effects of seemingly trivial events, given a long enough time. In metaphysical discussions of causal determinism, and in theological discussions of divine predestination, the implications of this dependency of future on past realities have often been explored, and moral philosophers have often worried about the implications of this interrelatedness of things for our free will and moral responsibility for what we do or fail to do. Recently the implications for our responsibility for and to future people have been drawn out by Parfit and others.

2.3 Wanting the Past to Have Been Different

If anyone's existence would have been prevented by so many thinkable changes in earlier history, it seems to follow that there are severe constraints on seriously judging that it would have been better if some earlier event, no matter how bad it may seem, had not occurred. In particular, one must consider the likelihood that, had it not occurred, one would not have existed at all to do any judging.

I am inclined to judge that the potato famine in Ireland and food shortages in Scotland in the nineteenth century were bad things, and that it would have been better if those in charge of agricultural policy in Britain had made different decisions which would have averted those hard times. Then I reflect that my great-grandparents left Britain for New Zealand because of those very hard times. Had they not done so, they would not have met one another, married, had the children they did. Had the famine been averted, their great-grandchildren, if any, would have been *other* possible people, and I would not have existed. So do I *sincerely* judge that it would have been better had the past been different, had those persons who, as things actually turned out, did have me as a great-grandchild had a less difficult life, had not been faced with famine? I will sincerely make this judgment only if I can sincerely say that it would have been better, all things considered, that I not have existed. (Alternative interpretations of this judgment are examined below, in Section 2.5.) So it is not easy as one might have thought to judge that it would have been better for the past to have been other than it was. Even to wish that one's own parents had been richer, or more fortunate, or healthier than they were in youth becomes hard, since any change in their lives before the time of one's own conception probably would have brought with it one's own non-existence.

2.4 The No Obligation Argument

Let us now see how this presumed fact, the extreme ontological precariousness of persons (and indeed of all other particular things), and the consequent difficulty of wanting the past to have been different, can be made to yield the conclusion that we have no obligations to future persons. We need to add, to what I shall call the *precariousness* premise (P), a version of the Person-Affecting Principle which I will call the *victim* premise (V), which says that a person has not been wronged by another unless he has been made worse off by the other's act, unless, that is, he is thereby the other's victim. Now we can construct a simple argument from P and V, to give us the conclusion (C) that nothing which we do can wrong future persons unless what we do is so bad that future persons wish they had never been born. To spell it out more fully:

(V)   We do not wrong a person by our current action or policy unless it would have been better for that person had we not acted that way.

(P)   For any actual future person F, the outcome had we not done what we are doing would (in all likelihood) have been that F not exist at all, rather than that F exist and be better off.

(C)   Unless it would have been better for F not to exist at all, we are (in all likelihood) not wronging F by what we are doing.

This argument, if it works, works whatever our actions are—however wasteful, depleting, or polluting. As long as future persons are not so affected by our actions that they can make a charge of "wrongful existence"[6] against us, they have no complaint against us, since they cannot claim to have been

---

[6] "Wrongful life" is recognized in some legal jurisdictions as a tort—that is, a harm for which one may sue for damages. The California Appellate Court, in *Curlender v. BioScience Laboratories*, allowed a wrongful life cause of action on behalf of an infant born with Tay–Sachs disease after the parents had been falsely assured that they were not carriers of the recessive genes. See Maxine A. Sonnenberg, "A Preference for Non-Existence: Wrongful Life and a Proposed Tort of Genetic Malpractice," *California Law Review* (Jan. 1982), 477–510. In such legal cases a problem parallel to that expressed in the No Obligation Argument is whether a case for legal action exists when the plaintiff has in any way benefited from the defendant's act. The proper application of the so-called Benefit Rule in such cases is an issue

wronged by what we did. The only wrong, it seems, that we can do future persons is to allow them to exist in an intolerable world. As long as that world is tolerable enough for them not to regret existing, they are not wronged by our world-spoiling activities. No future person will be able to say to us (or to our ghosts), "If you had acted rightly, *I* would have had a better life."

This is a very troubling argument. What troubles most of us about it is that the conclusion seems at odds with our moral intuitions on this matter. For, once the issue has been raised, most of us do feel that we would be wronging our successors by unrestrainedly depleting and polluting the earth even if that did not render their lives intolerable. We may be unclear exactly what we must, in decency, do for the sake of a future person (I take up this problem in Section 3), but most of us do feel not only that it is wrong to pollute and deplete, but also that it is "future people," in some sense of that phrase, who are the ones who are wronged if we act wrongly in this regard. The contemporary American political philosopher Thomas Schwartz, when he propounded an early version of our argument above, concluded not that we were free to do what we liked, as far as the consequences for the world future people will live in goes, but rather that *we owe it to one another*, to our *contemporaries* who do happen to care about humanity's future, to restrain our earth-ravaging activities. If Schwartz is right, we will have sinned only against our contemporaries if we poison the wells of the future; we will not have sinned against the persons who suffer the poisoning.

Now although it is good to have our conviction that we are not morally free to pollute the earth endorsed and given some basis, despite the troublesome argument we are examining, I think that we still are apt to feel that Schwartz's proposed basis for our obligations is not the right one. Many of us also care about the future of various precious artworks, or other nonsentient things. If we have a duty to preserve such things, it is a duty to our fellow art lovers, not to the artworks themselves. It seems wrong to put our concern for our successors in the same moral boat as our concern for the future of anything else which happens at present to have a place in our

---

which raises in law the same problems as the No Obligation Argument in ethics, but philosophers have not yet appealed much to the legal literature for help in getting a solution to it. In the case of *Berman* v. *Allen*, the New Jersey courts rejected the wrongful life claim on behalf of a child with Down syndrome, partly on the grounds that life even with a major physical handicap is better than no life.

affections. Surely it must be in some sense for future persons' sakes, not just for our own sakes, that we consider what sort of existence for them our actions entail? If Schwartz is right, then if we could make ourselves or let ourselves cease to feel concerned about the future of our human communities, then we would be rid not only of a sense of obligation not to pollute but also of the obligation itself. If it is only that "those who would like our distant descendants to enjoy a clean commodious well stocked world just may owe it to their like-minded contemporaries to contribute to these goals,"[7] then if we all cultivate indifference, cease to care, we can come to owe nothing to anyone in this regard. Can this be right? For whose sake, and for whose good, ought we to conserve scarce resources and refrain from putting delayed-action poisons in our common wells—if, that is, we do have a duty to conserve and not to poison? To help us see if it can be said to be for the sake of future persons, despite the troubling argument, we need first to have a closer look at the conclusion, C, and the qualification in that conclusion. When would a person judge that it would have been better, for her *own* sake, that she not have been born?

2.5   Better For One Not To Have Been Born

We have already seen in Section 2.3 how one can become committed to the judgment that it would have been better if one had not been born. One is committed to this if one seriously judges that some event such as a famine (without whose occurrence one would not have been born) was a bad thing, better averted. But such a judgment (if we ever really do make it) is made from an attempted God's-eye view, so to speak, one that takes into account *all* those who are involved. It is not made from one's own self-concerned standpoint, since one might make it although one's own life was pleasant enough, or was until one starts being obsessed with what went into one's own "prehistory," the human cost of one's own existence. To make the issues clearer, we need to distinguish two "objective" judgments from two subjective judgments. The former are judgments about the comparative value of alternative "world histories," made from no particular person's point of view, while the latter are judgments about a particular life history, made from the point of view of the one whose life it is.

---

[7] Thomas Schwartz, "Obligations to Posterity," in Bayles (ed.), *Ethics and Population*, 13.

(O₁)   All things considered, the world history (after some chosen fixed point) where F comes to exist is, given the causal chains which produced F, and the nature of F's life, worse than alternative world histories in which F does not exist.

(O₂)   The world history containing F's life is, because of F's own dreadfully intolerable life, *thereby* a worse world history than alternative world histories in which F's existence is prevented.

We could only make this second objective judgment if we (or F) could make one of two more subjective judgments, ones made from F's own point of view:

(S₁)   For F's own sake, or from her own self-concerned point of view, the sooner her life ends the better.

(S₂)   For F's own sake, or from her own self-concerned point of view, it would have been better if her life had never started.

The qualification in C, the conclusion of the No Obligation Argument, seems to refer only to those cases where the judgment O₂ could be made, and this in turn requires us to make either S₁ or S₂. Which of them does O₂ presuppose?

I think that S₂ is what is needed to support O₂. S₁ is the judgment made by most suicides, but a person need not be driven to suicide in order to judge S₂ and to have a valid claim of wrongful existence against someone. There are powerful forces, religious, instinctive, and altruistic, which may prevent even desperately unhappy people from ending their own lives even when they judge S₂. Nor is it true that one need judge S₂ in order to judge S₁. One's life can *become* intolerable enough to make one judge S₁, although long stretches of it were good and one would not judge S₂. For one to judge S₂, one's life would have had to be continuously intolerable, or some bits so bad that they clearly outweighed the good bits, when weighed not from a momentary but from a "life's-eye" point of view. One does not need to suppose that a suicide's life was as bad as that, bad enough to support S₂, in order to understand how suicide can look the best option. But it is just this very strong judgment, S₂, which F would need to make to charge her predecessors with wronging her by allowing her to exist at all.

The conclusion, C, of the No Obligation Argument, then, presupposes that S₂ makes sense, that it is conceivable that a person could be wronged by having been allowed to come into existence at all. Persons who judge S_2 are victims of previous events or actions in a sense which is *wider*, or different, than that in which our contemporaries are victims of our assault or neglect. In the latter case, we can say that the victim's *life* is worse than it would have been without the assault or neglect. But the victims of earlier events who are driven to S_2 judgments about their own lives are not complaining that they don't have lives better in this or that respect, they are complaining that they are, and ever were, alive at all, given their life prospects. This means that we must interpret premise V in a fairly wide way, to include this sort of victim, if V is to be even *compatible* with giving any sense to C, the conclusion which is supposed to follow from V and P. The argument itself requires us to recognize that not all victims of policies are victims because their *lives* would have been better in some respect if someone had done something different; rather, some people are victims because they are alive—period. This fact will become important in the following sections when I try to diagnose the fault of the No Obligation Argument.

2.6 Varieties of Victims, Varieties of Ills

So far we have seen that there can be victims of events and policies, those who judge S_2, whose claim is not that their lives would have been better had those events not occurred. Earlier, in Section 1.4, we said that one can be affected for good or ill by a policy or action in a variety of ways. One's rights may be violated even when one might not need to exercise those rights to further the interests one in fact has. Similarly, one's interests can be injured, say by loss of a job opportunity, or a pension scheme, even when one would not have wanted that job and does not yet care about one's old age. Normally what advances one's interests *does* help one get what one wants, and getting what one wants does make one happy, but one's interests can be injured without that affecting one's getting what one wanted, and one's wants can be frustrated although getting what one wanted would not have made one happy. Misery, frustration, injury to one's interests, violation or denial of rights, all unfavorably affect a person's good but can do so in different ways. The good of a person is complex since persons are and usually see themselves as bearers of rights, possessors of interests, as well as goal-directed and sentient. To act for the sake of some person or group is to act to advance any of these components of their good. The good of persons, seen prospectively, includes more than what will in fact give them happiness, since they may not be aware of some of their interests, so not be unhappy at their non-advancement, and they may neither know nor care about some violations of their rights. One needs not only to be fully self-conscious but also to have what today we call a "raised consciousness" for one's feeling of happiness to reflect the level to which one's rights and interests as well as one's purposes and tastes are respected.

As I am using the term "interests,"[8] we have an interest in the obtaining *conditions*, or *states of affairs*, such as our own good health, our prosperity, peace in our time, liberty, where these conditions are favorable for our success in satisfying a whole range of particular desires we have and expect to have in the future. The sort of things a parent or godparent wishes for a child are general goods of this sort, conditions which will enable the child to acquire and cultivate ambitions, desires, and tastes which can in those conditions be satisfied, and give pleasure when satisfied. Although it might occasionally turn out that these conditions are *not* needed or even favorable for the satisfaction of the actual desires the child comes to have, as a general rule the furthering of one's interests *does* increase the extent to which one's desires get satisfied, just as normally getting what one desired does give one the pleasure one expected it would. In acting in the interests of a person, we are trying to increase their *prospects* of satisfying their desires, and so, normally, of being happy with the outcome.

As a person grows from childhood to adulthood, and tastes and concerns become formed, these very general interests, shared with almost all persons, become specified in ways which often limit the number of other persons with whom we share them. An interest in peace in our time will become associated with an interest in the success of the political party whose plan for peace one judges the best one. One will have an interest not only in health but in the maintenance of a specific health insurance scheme, not just in prosperity but in the wise policies of certain banks and corporations, not just in liberty but in the removal of some specific threats to liberty. However specific one's interests become, they usually are still specifications

---

[8] See Joel Feinberg's discussion of interests in "Harm and Self Interest" and in "The Rights of Animals and Unborn Generations," in Feinberg, *Rights, Justice, and the Bounds of Liberty* (Princeton: Princeton University Press, 1980). I follow Feinberg in seeing interests as "somehow compounded out of" goals and wants (p. 166), but not to be identified with them. Feinberg's definition is: "A person has an interest in Y when he has a stake in Y, that is, when he stands to gain or lose depending on the condition or outcome of Y" (p. 45). Feinberg, however, does not want to speak, as I shall in Sects. 2.7 and 2.8, of an interest existing before its possessor does.

of interests most people have, interests in livelihood, health, peace, in a decent community which provides scope for public participation and for private friendships, for satisfying work and for the enjoyment both of nature and of a rich, varied, and historically conscious cultural tradition.

Among the interests we share with others are interests we have only because we are cooperating with others in some project. Membership in a nation gives us this sort of interest in the nation's affairs, and gives each of us an interest in the protection of our individual roles as citizens and taxpayers. As a member of the taxpaying public my interests are injured by the tax fraud of my fellows as well as by misuse of public funds by officials. Here my interest is the same as that of any other honest taxpayer, an interest in not being ripped off. Yet this interest I share with many others can clash with more private interests I may have, if for, example, my employer is among those guilty of tax fraud and my job depends on his ill-gotten "savings." My interest as a member of the taxpaying public and my interest as an employee of this employer may be in conflict with one another. Often we need to refer to the *roles* we play, roles relating us to others and to schemes of cooperation, to specify the variety of our interests, and many of the duties and rights we have, and wrongs done to us, also depend upon these social roles. I have duties as a daughter, family member, department member, teacher, university employee, and citizen, and I have rights as all of these, as well as a member of a particular professional association, health insurance scheme, and so on. Since in most of these roles my rights and interests coincide with those of some others, I will protest any violation of rights, and wrongful injury of interests, even if I foresee that my own goals will not be frustrated by those wrongs. For example, I will protest *as* university teacher, if tenure guarantees are broken, even if I am about to retire and so will not be hurt myself.

Let us now try to apply these points about the complexity of a person's good, its inclusion of *interests* to be protected or furthered as well as desires to be satisfied and pleasures to be enjoyed, to the case of future people. Because interests are *always* future-oriented, and because we can know what they are, at least at a general level, without having much if any information about what particular tastes and desires a person has, it seems to me that future persons' *interests* can be determinate even when the persons themselves are not yet determinate, even when the *whole* of what will count as their good is not yet fixed. Of course, in being sure that, whoever they are, they will *have* an interest in clean air, we are also usually assuming that they will *want* to breathe, and be *pained* by inability to do so: some assumptions about their sensitivities and their desires will be included in our claims about their interests. A person whose interest in good health is badly injured will most probably also have frustration and pain, as "ills" which accompany the ill of ill health. We may even feel we know what *particular* desires a future person will have because of grave ill health; for example, in extreme cases the desire to end life. So in concentrating on the *interests* of future people in what follows, I shall not be supposing that in injuring interests we are not usually also frustrating and hurting. I shall, however, be relying on the *possibility* that an injury to a person's interest can (and sometimes should) be averted, although that does *not* bring that person a better life, more satisfaction and less frustration, more pleasure and less pain. Interests are important, and injury to interests is important, *whether or not* averting the injury in fact leads to less frustration and less pain for the one whose interest it is.

Future people, once actual, will come to have specific interests as well as general ones, and will have particular desires and sensitivities, as well as interests, which will need to be taken into account by anyone *then* concerned with their good. We now *cannot* consider their good "all things considered," because all the relevant things are not yet determinate. But we *can* consider some vital dimensions of what will be their good, and do so when we consider those of their interests which are general enough, or, even though specific, predictable enough, to be already fixed. (One specific interest we can be fairly sure that people a few generations after us will have is an interest in the advancement of knowledge of methods of *detoxifying* all the resources we are currently poisoning. This is not an interest people in the past have needed to have.)

What we now need to consider is whether the fact that our acts help to *determine* both the identity of future persons and some of the specific interests they will have means that *those* acts cannot at the same time damage interests of those persons. The No Obligation Argument seems to allow us to injure only one of the interests a future person might have, a rather complex interest, namely the interest in not existing at all if other vital interests, such as health, are to be very badly served. This is a conditional interest—an interest in not existing unless other unconditional interests can be tolerably well served. The No Obligation Argument in effect claims that unless a future person has *this* exceptional interest injured by us, she is not wronged by us by those policies of ours which "select" her for existence. Is it possible, contrary to what the argument claims, for us to wrong a person by injuring an interest she has even though she comes to *be* a person with that interest only because of the very actions which also injure that interest? Can that person say *both*, "If you had acted differently, *my interests* would have been better served," *and* also, "Had you acted differently, I would not have been one of those who exist and have such interests"? I shall try to show that such a complaint makes sense.

2.7 Selecting Populations by Our Acts

Before looking at future people, let us consider present people, and sketch analogous ways in which our actions can injure their interests, perhaps violate their rights. Take a case such as a teacher who writes a course description. It is surely primarily for the sake of the students who will be in the course that such descriptions are written, with whatever care is taken. Yet *who* precisely they turn out to be depends to some degree on the course description itself, if it is an elective course. The description, and the care taken in writing it, both is for the sake of the students, and also helps to select which students are those for whose sake a course plan is produced. The teacher's actions help to fix the class population. Similar sorts of cases arise with immigration policy: the ways in which a nation encourages or discourages immigrants help to determine who comes, but once in a country an immigrant might complain, "You didn't warn me about the high unemployment. Had you done so, I probably wouldn't have come." (Note that it need *not* be claimed that they regret being there for them to have a complaint.) Have we injured and perhaps wronged the class members who suffer once in the badly described course, the immigrants who come with inadequate advance warning of conditions, even if, once in the class or nation, they do not on balance regret being there?

It is important to see that a version of the No Obligation Argument can be used to give a negative answer here too. To any complainer we can say, "If you wouldn't have been in the relevant population (class member, immigrant) had we done what you say we should have done, then you are not a wronged member of that population. You would not have been a *better-off* class member or immigrant had we acted as you think we should have; *you* would not have been a member of that population *at all*. So you have no complaint as class member, as immigrant." Must they then reformulate their complaint, and say that it was the population of those *considering* joining the class or nation, not those actually joining it, whose interests are injured by the poor descriptions and plans? Such wider populations certainly are affected, but it would seem counterintuitive to say that when a teacher designs a course and makes the design known in a course description she is fulfilling a duty only to the wider group of all those who might consider joining, not also to the narrower group who actually join. Any class member (or immigrant) whose complaint is responded to by these moves would, if she had her wits about her, say, "I *as class member* (immigrant) as well as a potential class member have been wronged by the bad advance description. You owe it to all those deciding whether to join, and in particular to those who *do* so decide, to have an adequate plan and to give adequate advance notice of it. Had you done the right thing, I would not have *been* a class member, but you didn't, and I am, and I, like all other members, have been wronged by you."

It seems to me that this response is right. The interests of ours which can be injured include those dependent on the act which does the injury, in this case the act which helped make one a class member. This may sound paradoxical, but the paradox disappears once we are clear about what interests are, and how we can possess them in virtue of roles we fill and come to fill. Sometimes we come to fill a particular role, giving rise to an interest, because of the very act of another person which injures our interest once we are in that role.

Of course, the extent of the analogy between this case and the case of future persons is limited. *They* do not *decide* to become actual persons; it is "decided" for them. But we can find, among injuries to present persons, cases of non-voluntary as well as voluntary membership in some group where the act of determining membership also injures the interests of the members, as members. An annexation of a territory subjects the inhabitants to a new rule, makes them members of a new "population," and may simultaneously make them second-class subjects, a disadvantaged minority. After the Second World War, Transylvanians who had been Hungarians became subjects of Romania, and could complain (as many of them did) that the very act which made them Romanians also injured their interests as Romanians. Adopted children sometimes feel that the very fact that they are adopted gives them a lower place in their adoptive parents' affections than those who are the parents' "own" children in the biological sense. The very act which made the adopted children members of their new family, some feel, injured them *as* members of that family. (They may feel this without believing that it would have been better had they never been adopted, without feeling that they are, all things considered, injured by the act of adoption.) Could future persons, as our successors, be injured by us although the injuring act selected them as our successors? Well, so far we can say that the fact that they didn't *choose* that status does not rule that out. Nevertheless, the fact that our acts determine who will exist, and so do not *shift* them from one "population" into another, but determines their very availability for *any* population, must not be glossed over.

This fact certainly limits the analogy between our relation to future people and our relation to students in our elective courses, to our adopted children, and to members of our annexed territories. We do not by any act literally *select* from a host of already determinate possible people the ones who will become actual, as would-be adoptive parents might survey the row of orphaned babies in a nursery, picking out the one to become their child. If there *are* fully determinate possible people, we cannot distinguish them as such. All we can do is consider similar descriptions of them such as "the next child I shall have," or "my future eldest great-great-grandchild," or "the first future person who may actually formulate a complaint beginning 'Those Americans who had any say over policy in the 1980s are to blame for...'" Although each of these titles is designed to pick out one and only one person, we have little idea what that person will be like, or what their total good will consist in. To discern injuries to people we know, we consider them fully determinate people about whose good-all-things-considered we may have opinions, people whose full range of characteristics enables them to fit many descriptions and fill many bills; then we emphasize the role relevant to the injury we discern: "He was injured *as a parent*" or "*as an employee*." With actual people we do not know, we usually know more of the roles and bills they fill than simply the one relevant to the injury, so that although we do not know much about, say, those who are starving in the Sahara, we can say *something* about who it is whose interests in health and nourishment are so injured. With future people, there may be nothing yet fixed and known about them except the general interests we need to consider to try to avoid injuring them. All there is, yet, are those interests, not yet the actual people whose interests they will be, whose good those interests will help comprise. So we should not pretend that our relation to future persons is not significantly different from our relation to already existent persons, nor pretend that making them existent is simply moving them from the "population" of possible people into the more exclusive population of actual people. Any responses we make to the No Obligation Argument should avoid that confusion.

Nevertheless, we ought also not forget that any act which injures an actual person's long-term interests is one which looks ahead to the not-yet-fixed *older person* the injured one might become. If I now lose my retirement pension rights, I am injured, even though, as far as I know, the older person of retirement age is not yet fixed in her needs or wants. There are many possible future mes. I may become rich enough not to need any pension, or become a beachcomber and not want one, or I may not live long enough to reach retirement age. All these uncertainties for the future are always there, and my interests lie in being somehow prepared for any of them. My interests are injured if I today lose my pension rights, even if I come into an unexpected inheritance or drop dead tomorrow. We must steer clear, then, not only of blurring the difference between future not yet actual people and actual people, but also of exaggerating it, of treating the interests it is wrong to injure as always the interests of people with determinate sets of concerns, wants, tastes. Only the dead are *fully* determinate, and the very finality, fixedness, of the nature of their wants and the character of their lives severely limits the interests they can have.

2.8 Past, Present, and Future Persons

Although a past person cannot any longer suffer, nor want anything, some interests and rights of past people can still be protected or neglected. If I tell malicious lies about some dead persons, their interests in having and keeping a good name is injured. I can do things for the sake of past persons, although they neither know nor feel the effects of what I do. Once we are dead, the range of things which it is possible for others to do for our sake, or to do us ill, shrinks. But we may still, for the dead person's sake, protect his reputation, do what he wanted or would have wanted (especially with his estate), and we may even do things like putting flowers on his grave, thinking that to have some link with what pleased or would have pleased him. (If we put flowers on the grave of someone who hated flowers, it certainly is not done for that one's sake.) The very finished fixed character of the past person's life history puts him beyond most of the harms present and future persons can suffer: he cannot be hurt or frustrated, nor has he any longer many of the interests and rights living persons have. He is safe from much but not all ill.

Future persons too seem safe from being harmed by us in certain ways in which we may harm our contemporaries. We cannot deny them their marital rights, nor any contractual rights, nor libel them, nor take an unfairly large share of a good to which they too have *contributors'* rights. (But we *may* take, for ourselves, too large a share of what earlier people "bequeathed" to an indefinite run of future generations, or ruin a "bequest" which could have been enjoyed much longer but for our spoiling activities.) Just as there are many harms and wrongs we *cannot* do past people, so there are many harms and wrongs we *cannot* do future people.

Future people will, whoever they turn out to be, have a good, but only some components of that good are yet fixed. Must we say the same of the interests which help comprise that good, that they *will be* their interests, but are not yet their interests? We have seen how some interests, like that in not being spoken ill of, last longer than does the person whose interest it is. I have argued that some interests preexist the person whose interests they are. Common predictable human interests, such as the availability of unpoisoned soil as a resource, seem to depend in no way upon that combination of specific interests, concerns, wants, tastes that comprise the concrete *individuality* of persons, which possible people lack, and which future people do not yet have. Whoever becomes actual will have such common interests and we know they will, so I see nothing wrong in saying that those already existent interests are now *theirs*. We do not need to know exactly who "they" are to recognize the reality of their common human interests. Whomever we allow to become actual, those ones have the interests all people have and we can also see what specific form some of those interests will take, since it depends on our policies. Of the interests people claim as their interests, some were predictable before the person's conception or birth; others come into being only because of particular unpredictable facts about them and choices they make. It is the interests which are fixed and predictable in advance which we can say preexist the person of whose good they form a part, and usually it is other less predictable and more specific interests of theirs, such as the success of a particular book they wrote, which last once they are dead. People cast shadows in the form of interests both before them and after them.

We can, then, speak of acting *for the sake of* a person not merely when we act to promote that one's all-things-considered good, as an actual living person, or act to prevent injuries to their *individual* and perhaps eccentric interests, but also when we protect the general interests they have, *in advance of their existence*, or do things for them *after they are dead*. We can even prevent a person's existence, for that person's sake, when we think that, if she were born, she would judge S_2. The concept of a person's sake is the most flexible and so the best concept for us to use to cover all the ways in which what we do can be *better for* a person. If, contrary to what the No Obligation Argument concluded, there *are* things we can do which are better for future persons, in addition to preventing their coming to exist to judge S_2, then they will be things we do *for their sake*.

2.9 *The No Obligation Argument Rejected*

We can now see what is wrong with the No Obligation Argument. The Victim Premise, V, did not spell out all the ways in which a person can be a victim, and only if some of those ways, especially ways of injuring interests, are neglected or denied does the conclusion, C, really follow from V and P. To see this we should expand V, mentioning all the ways we have distinguished in which something can be worse or better for a person's sake.

The revised version, V_r, will read

(V$_r$) We do not wrong a person by our action or policy unless it would have been better, for that person's sake, not to have acted that way because our present actions bring

(1) more suffering than the person would have had, had we acted differently;

or (2) more frustration than the person would have had, had we acted differently;

or (3) greater injury to the person's interests than would have occurred had we acted differently, where such interests include the interest in not existing at all, if other interests are to be very badly injured;

or (4) greater violation of the person's rights than would have occurred had we acted differently.

What do we get when we add the original precariousness premise to V_r? I think we need first to add a premise we can derive from the preceding account of the nature and variety of our interests, namely,

(I)   Among the interests of a person which can be injured are interests which are fixed before the identity of those whose interests they are is fixed, and includes interests which a given person comes to possess only because of the very act which injures those interests.

When we add I to P and V_r, I think we can get a revised conclusion, C_r, which is very different from the No Obligation conclusion.

(C_r)   Therefore the wrongs we can do a future person are usually restricted to injuries to interests fixed before the identity of future persons are fixed (and to such frustration and pain as is consequent upon the injury to such interests), and cannot include injury to interests not yet fixed or frustration of wants and concerns not yet fixed or hurts to sensibilities not yet fixed.

C_r is very different from C since it not merely allows the wrong of "wrongful existence," now included as injury of an already fixed conditional interest of all persons, but it also allows those *injuries to other already fixed interests* where the act which does the injury at the same time helps settle who it is whose interest it is.

We have avoided the No Obligation conclusion, C, by allowing the concept of an effect on a person to include "*effect*" *on interests*, including interests which come to be possessed only because of the "affecting" act. Parfit regards such interpretations of the Person-Affecting Principle as a "cheat," and himself avoids the No Obligation conclusion by renouncing the Person-Affecting Principle in favor of a vaguer principle which says, "It is bad if those who live are worse off than those who might have lived,"[9] a principle explicitly allowing comparisons between *different* possible people, not just comparisons of the possible fates of people of fixed identity. I think that once we come to see what sort of things interests are, and how indirectly injury to them is linked to worsening of the determinate life history of a person, then it is no "cheat" to allow the Person-Affecting Principle to include effect on interests, including those of the future people whose very existence to possess interests is due to the act which perhaps adversely affects those interests. So although no future person may be able to say to our ghosts, "If you had acted differently and rightly, I would have had a better life," plenty of the future people might well be able to

---

[9] Parfit formulates this principle in "Energy Policy and the Further Future," 171. He called solutions similar to mine a "cheat" in "On Doing the Best for Our Children," 103, 111.

say, "Interests which are, as it turns out, *my* interests, have been injured by what you did, and would have been less injured had you acted differently."

All we have done, so far, is to try to show that there is no good reason to think that the only wrongful injury we can do future people is to inflict "wrongful existence" upon them. We can now admit other injuries to their interests, other things we can, perhaps wrongfully, fail to do *for their sakes*. But which of these other injuries to the interests of future persons *should count as wrongs*? That is a question we have yet to consider, and different moral theories will give different answers. All would agree that our duties to future people are what can in reason be demanded of us for their sake, that wrongs to future people are neglectings of these duties, but there is no agreed way of determining *what* it is reasonable to demand of any of us for others', including our successors', sakes. In what follows I shall rely largely on widely shared intuitions rather than upon any (of necessity controversial) moral theory. To *really establish* the content of our duties and obligations would take a lot more space, a lot more thought, and knowledge of what happens when communities try to practice and pass on such versions of our obligations.

3 The Content of Our Obligations

3.1 Population Control

One of the obvious ways in which future person F will be affected by previous generations' policies is in the size of F's generation. Utilitarians believe that we should maximize happiness. If it is the total amount of it which is to be maximized, then they must recommend that we increase the world's population, even when that brings a lowered standard of living. As long as the larger population is composed of persons who, despite the over-crowding, do not regret existing, then the total amount of human happiness can be greater in the world with the lower quality of life than in the less crowded world with a higher quality of life. This conclusion, which most people find repugnant, can be avoided by making what is to be maximized average, not total, happiness. It can also be avoided by rejecting the utilitarian claim that wrong acts are those which fail to maximize happiness. The position defended so far in this essay is not utilitarian, and allows us to say that a person F may be wronged, because that one's interests are injured, where such injury can occur both by making that one a member of a grossly underpopulated world, and by making him or her a member of an overcrowded world. At this juncture, it is overpopulation and not under-population which is the ill we are most likely to inflict on our successors—unless, of course, our weapons policy leads to the death of the majority, and problems of underpopulation for the survivors.

In an earlier article on this topic, written before the recent discussion of the Futurity Problem we have just tried to solve, I said, "Our duty to future persons is to see to it that there are not too many of them."[10] Suppose that F is a member of a much too large generation, living in a very overcrowded and famine-threatened world but not wishing he had not been born. If he makes a complaint of the form "There are too many of us. Our forefathers did too much fathering. They should not have allowed so many of us to exist," then he will, if he accepts the precariousness premise, have to allow that, had his forefathers acted as he believes they should have, he might not be there to commend them for their population control policies. But if what we have said above is correct, he *can* in consistency say, "I do not regret my existence, but my interests are injured by the size of the population of which I am a member, a population which should have been controlled in size by earlier generations. I realize that if they had done what they should have I probably would not have existed at all. As it is, I do exist, with the same interests in suitable population size as every other member actual and possible of my or any generation, and this interest was injured by the poli-cies of previous people." There is nothing incoherent in this charge, as we now can see. If F were pressed on the question "Do you *really wish* that your predecessors had done what they ought, and so deprived you of your unre-gretted existence?", F may reasonably say, "What I on balance wish or do not wish is not decisive as to whether or not my interests have been injured."

It would seem, then, that among the obligations we can plausibly be claimed to have to future generations, especially those in the near future, is the obligation to adopt policies designed to limit population growth. Such policies will, of course, have to weigh the rights and interests of present people against those of future people, and so avoid unnecessary coercion, and recognize the interest most people have in reproduction, an interest

---

[10] "The Rights of Past and Future Persons" (Ch. 1 in this volume), 15.

which should ground some reproductive rights. One of the most urgent tasks of applied moral philosophy is to work out just what are properly construed as a person's reproduction rights, just what population control measures are compatible with recognition of such rights.[11]

3.2 Fair Shares: Another Problem

Since the sorts of things we can and should do for the sake of future generations are limited to safeguarding already fixed interests of theirs which, like the interest in reproduction, are mostly common human interests and rights, one might expect that among these is the right to a fair share of whatever no one has a special title to, or a fair share of what they have as good a title to as do we. Do we have duties of *distributive justice* to future generations? Should first come be first served?

Here we encounter another problem. We cannot judge whether or not we have taken more than our fair share of some cake unless we know how many others there are who want a piece. This is a problem whether the "cake" is the earth's supply of fossil fuels, or some humanly created benefit "bequeathed" by some earlier benefactor to successors.

In the village of Lindos, on the Greek island of Rhodes, is a fountain, with a water system, designed and built in the sixth century BC by the local "philosopher" Cleovolus, and still functioning well. Suppose that recent use of some chemical as a fertilizer in the water catchment area will not only overtax the system's natural filter capacity but eventually lead to the clogging, cracking, and eventual destruction of the conduits in the system. Suppose that the prediction is that, unless the fertilizer use is regulated, the water system will be irreversibly destroyed in 200 years. Does that mean that, unless something is done, twenty-third-century inhabitants of Lindos will be done out of their rightful inheritance from Cleovolus? If a regulation were introduced which, if observed indefinitely, would postpone the system's predicted demise by another 200 years, or even another 1,000 years, would that be enough? For how long must we preserve, and with how many others must we share, for distributive justice to have been done?

When we turn from the Lindos water supply to questions of world supply of essential human resources, this problem is magnified. We simply do not

---

[11] See Mary Ann Warren's helpful discussion of this in "Future Generations," in Tom Regan and Donald VanDeVeer (eds.), *And Justice for All* (Totowa, NJ: Rowman and Littlefield, 1982), 139–68.

and cannot know what size the population of the earth will be in 200 years, since we do not know and cannot control, although our policies may influence, the policies of the previous generation, those living say 180 years from now, and they are the ones who will have the greatest say about that. Nor do we know how long the human race will continue, how many generations it is for whose sake we should be regulating our own policies. How can we work out what our share of the earth's exhaustible resources is, if we cannot know and have no power to decide how many we are, in the end, sharing those resources with? (Of course, there is one way in which we can control that, namely by arranging that we be the last generation, easily enough done if we use our stockpiles of nuclear weapons. I assume that we rule out this theoretical option—that we do not deliberately make ourselves the last generation.[12]) Our *power* to determine how many more people there will be is shared with all the future people, so is small, and our *knowledge* of how many more people there will be seems just as unimpressive. How, then, can we act for the sake of distributive justice to future persons, ignorant as we must be about how many of them there will be?

Faced with this daunting vision of an endless procession of faceless successors, all clamoring for our consideration, we might well be led to moral despair. Is it not a hopeless task to try to give them all their due, when, for all we know, there are indefinitely many of them, with indefinitely diverse needs, wants, and abilities? Surely we must somehow narrow the moral task, if it is to be a manageable one. David Hume (1711–76), speaking of human beneficence, said, "It is wisely ordained by nature that private connections should commonly prevail over universal views and considerations, otherwise our affections and actions would be dissipated and lost, for want of a proper limited object."[13] Even if we should have a view to more than "private connections," Hume is surely right that our moral concerns, including our concerns for justice, need a limited object if they are not to be dissipated and lost, or worse still, if our moral will is not to be paralyzed by the hopelessly large scope of our moral task. To take as our moral burden putting the world to rights for the indefinite future is to all but guarantee that we will *do* very little. If we not merely can but do have obligations of justice to future generations, we must find a way of limiting those obligations.

<hr>

[12] I discuss this in Chapter 1, "The Rights of Past and Future Persons."

[13] David Hume, *Enquiries*, ed. L. A. Selby-Bigge and P. H. Nidditch (Oxford: Clarendon Press, 1975), 229 n.

3.3 Discounting for Distance in Time

Hume drew attention to our natural tendency to give preference to that which and those who are "close" to us, over those who are more distant, whether that distance is in blood relationship, in space, in time, or even in political opinion. Even within our own lives we tend to treat the present and near future as counting for more than our own more distant future: we postpone unpleasantness, as if pain next year is not as bad as pain tomorrow, let alone pain today. Of course, on reflection, we would agree with Hume that distant future ills are "never the less real for being remote"[14] and that this holds good for all varieties of remoteness. The suffering of strangers is as real as that of our loved ones, that of strangers half a world or half a century away as real as that of our neighbors. Our unreflective attitudes, however, do give preference to what is close to us, in all these senses of "close." What is out of sight tends to be out of mind.

If we could morally endorse this natural tendency, then our obligations to future people would shrink dramatically. We could concentrate on our own descendants and, among those, concentrate more on those closer in time to us. While accepting a duty to be our brother's and perhaps our nephew's keeper, we would accept less responsibility for the welfare of grandnephews, and perhaps none at all for the friends and contemporaries of great-grandnephews. Or, even if we did accept some responsibility for non-kin, we would weaken it as those generations get remoter in time from us. We do apparently endorse some version of this preference for those close to us. We would be shocked, for example, if a mother refused to give to her own child any special attention above and beyond what she thought due from her to all the world's children. Why do we think it not merely natural but best for each to recognize special duties to close relatives? Presumably for the reason Hume gave, that this ensures better chances of care for each than each would have if everyone cultivated an impartial benevolence to everyone, so to no one in particular. Division of the moral labor is the more efficient way to get the moral work done, and kinship is an obvious and easy way to apportion the child care labor. Other ways have been tried, for example in kibbutzim, but it is not yet clear if the gains exceeded the costs. The important thing for our purposes is that there always are costs: kinship

---

[14] Ibid. 535.

as a way of allocating responsibility for others has its costs, and so does any alternative method. To direct people to take responsibility for what is "nearest" them at least reduces the "transport" costs of getting the assistance from the giver to the receiver.

But we do not on reflection endorse all versions of preferential treatment for what is close. When this takes the form of "living for the present," of giving priority to today's over tomorrow's pleasures, we give only qualified endorsement. We encourage people to make prudent provision for their own future, to think ahead. If such prudence is a virtue of individuals, it surely is also of nations and other collectives. As the English economist Sir Roy Harrod said, pure time preference is "a polite expression for rapacity."[15] Those who are charged with responsibility for the community's welfare must think ahead, and should make prudent provision of some sort for the presumably indefinite future of the community, just as a wise person makes provision for a personal future of unknown but limited duration. In this case, however, we encounter a complication. Whereas it costs more of our present resources to, say, feed the starving in Bangladesh than to feed the same number of starving in our own country, it costs much less of our present resources to feed that same number fifty years hence, provided we can profitably invest that lesser amount and let it yield an increase proportional to the time it is invested. Whereas there are "transport costs" of caring for the spatially distant, there seem, as long as productivity is increasing, to be transport *benefits* when the resources are "transported" through time. So a little, when invested, goes a long way, and goes a longer way the longer it is invested. Just as when I now, in my fifties, want to provide from my current resources for my own life from now on into my sixties, seventies, and eighties, I need to invest less for my eighties than for my seventies, and less for my seventies than my sixties, and keep most of all for my (present) fifties, so, even if we wanted to be as evenhanded with future generations as I wish to be with my older self we would need to sacrifice less of current resources for those who are more distant in time from now than for those who are closer, to yield the same returns for all.

How much less? Economists do not agree about what this "social discount rate" is, nor even on what factors should determine it.[16] In the individual

[15] Sir Roy Harrod, *Towards a Dynamic Economics* (London: Macmillan, 1948), 40.

[16] See, for example, Stephen A. Marglin, "The Social Rate of Discount and the Optimal Rate of Investment," *Quarterly Journal of Economics*, 77/1 (Feb. 1963), 95–111; William J. Baumol, "On the Social Rate of Discount," *American Economic Review*, 58/4 (Sept. 1968), 788–802.

case it is fairly clear that the "time discount" rate should be determined by the projected rate of return on investment. This in turn will depend upon tax considerations, the future of the economy, the risks involved in the particular investment made. For public decision-makers, however, investment decisions are made by the ones who *control* tax and monetary policies, whose decisions influence the state of the economy, the risk of foreign wars or other disturbances, and so on. So we get considerable disagreement about how governments should make long-term investment decisions, how they should measure the opportunity costs of postponing the receiving of a benefit, that is, of long-term investment. Whatever we may come to agree on about what we should be *aiming* to do for future generations, economists will disagree about how best to set about fulfilling those aims.

What should we be aiming at? On the individual level it is fairly clear that a person who lives to be 80 will regret *not* having saved earlier, and may also regret having sacrificed too much earlier, may come to realize that her individual time discount rate was too low. Indeed, taking into account the chances that one will not live into one's eighties, it may be quite sensible to sacrifice very little now for the sake of one's 80-year-old self: not only will a little have gone a long way by then, but that amount may accrue to one's heirs rather than to oneself. If one's investment decisions are purely self-interested, one might sensibly discount very heavily for futurity. But public bodies, if they represent an ongoing public interest, need not be concerned with the chances that the society not survive to reap the returns on long-run investment. (There are no actuarial tables for nations.) They must assume that their other decisions, in foreign policy and environmental policy, will not lead to the death of the nation they represent, so must assume that the returns of long-term investments will be in fact received. The only question they need worry about is the complex question of opportunity costs, if it is assumed that they *should* think ahead for all future generations.

Should they? Should we, in our capacity as citizens? Or is there an argument parallel to that which leads us to recognize special duties to close relatives which would lead us to suppose that it is better if, at each time, a government *restricts* its responsibility to a few generations ahead, rather than trying to plan for all time? Is neglect of the interests of distant future generations benign neglect, just as my "neglecting" your children, and your "neglecting" of mine, may be benign neglect in a society which recognizes parental duties?

To think clearly about such moral matters we have to consider what (if any) sacrifice is involved in the various alternatives and what each sacrifice yields to others. If it is indeed true that we can with a tiny sacrifice now confer considerable benefits on distant future people, that would itself be a good reason to accept the duty to make that small sacrifice. If, however, an unreasonable sacrifice is demanded of us, both absolutely or compared with what is being demanded of others, we might well see reason to recognize a moral right not to make such a sacrifice. Have others made long-term investments from which we benefit, as future people would benefit from any we made on their behalf? It seems that the answer is yes. Past generations *have* "saved," have invested in parks, water reservoirs, waste disposal systems, and so on, designed to outlast the investors, and from which we benefit. The degree of sacrifice needed by the present generation to make parallel investments in disposal of new forms of waste, in maintenance of water supply systems, and so on, seems no greater than past persons have already fairly steadily made for people future to them. So, unless the degree of sacrifice demanded of us turns out to be disproportionately great, we should accept a duty to invest for a future we will not live to see, leaving it to the experts to argue over the details of that investment portfolio.

What of our sacrifice compared to that to be made by future people? If, as must be assumed for the earlier claims about dependable returns on investment to be true, the national wealth steadily increases, then future people will be better off than we are anyway, so can afford more easily than we can now to set their own world in order. Two things need to be said about this. First, unless we continue doing some investing, at a cost of forgone present consumption, the assumed growth will not take place. Second, this sort of comparison of how much better off the "beneficiaries" are, compared to their "benefactors," can be made to our moral disadvantage as beneficiaries as well as to our advantage as benefactors. If it is *unfair* to expect us, poorer than they will be, to invest on their behalf, it was unfair that our predecessors, poorer than we are, sacrificed on *our* behalf. We could take a tough line and say, "The more fools they. We won't repeat their foolishness. From now on, save for yourself." But this would be hypocrisy or foolishness on our part. Unless from our predecessors we had inherited not only an advancing technology and a growing economy, but also some unpoisoned land, air, and water, it would not have done us much good. Unless we pass these on to our successors, at whatever sacrifice is needed to do so, it will not do them much good to have their projected greater wealth.

This is an obvious point, and one which does not depend upon the intricacies of controversial economic theories. Even economists who argue for a relatively high social discount rate, that is for relatively small public investment in long-term projects, make an exception for those "public goods" which, if lost, are impossible or extremely difficult to regain. Concluding an article arguing for a relatively high social discount rate, the American economist William J. Baumol writes,

> However this does not mean that the future should in every respect be left to the mercy of the free market. There are important externalities and investments of the public goods variety which cry for special attention. If we poison our soil so that never again will it be the same, if we destroy the Grand Canyon and turn it into a hydroelectric plant...all the wealth and resources of future generations will not suffice to restore them.[17]

Where we are in doubt whether a certain change for the worse is or is not irreversible, it would seem the prudent thing to suppose the worst. Few of us happily incur the risk of cancer (from, say, cigarette smoking) on the grounds that by the time we fall victim to the disease a cure may have been found for it. Similarly with responsible thinking on behalf of future people: we should not *count* on their finding ways to detoxify what we are poisoning. The sacrifice required of us to stop the poisoning seems much less than the burden placed on them if we bet wrongly on their ability to undo what we are doing.

What we have considered in this essay is whether there is any good reason to endorse our natural tendency to let the more distant future count for less than the close future, supposing each to be equally real. We have found no reasons to do so. At most there may be arguments for a certain division of labor between generations, as the best means to see to it that all are well served, but even these arguments do not apply to public goods, especially to those goods which no individual, nor any one generation, can supply for themselves, but where dependency on earlier people is unavoidable, and where there is danger of irreversibility. One of the goods we enjoy is that tradition of receiving benefits from past persons and contributing to

---

[17] Baumol, "On the Social Rate of Discount," 801.

the maintenance and provision of such public goods for future people. To destroy that tradition might well be itself irreversible. All the economic rationality we bequeath to future people would not itself suffice to restore lost trust in such a cross-generational cooperative scheme.

3.4 Better Ways to Determine Our Obligations

Discounting for futurity is not the right way to get a definite limited content to our obligations to future people. Nor can we work out what those duties are by trying to see what is their fair share of some divisible shareable good to which each person has a right, perhaps a contributor's right. For one thing, we cannot be sure that future people *will* contribute, and even if we assume that they will, we do not know how *many* of them there are or what their contribution is, or therefore what their fair share is. We know neither the size of the cake nor the number of those who deserve a piece. What, then, *are* we obliged to do for future people? What duties do we have if not duties of distributive justice?

From what has already been argued, it seems reasonable to say that our duties are to avoid endangering future persons' vital interests by reckless action now, by creating, or failing to try to remove, clear dangers to those interests. This sort of consideration for people's interests is not dependent on our knowing exactly how many people there are who are threatened. I think I have a duty to remove dangerous objects like broken glass from the sidewalk in front of my house, even though I do not know how many people are endangered. I will *want* to do it,[18] for the sake of myself, my family, and my friends, and I have an obligation[19] to do it for them and for

---

[18] For a discussion of whether we can be got to *want* to do things for future people, see Norman Care, "Future Generations, Public Policy, and the Motivation Problem," *Environmental Ethics* (Fall 1982), 195–213.

[19] In this essay I have discussed mainly the way we can injure others, and some bad ways of selecting which injuries to others to treat as morally allowable. I have *not* said much about the sound basis on which we *should* select which injuries to others are moral wrongs. I incline to a theory which is neither utilitarian nor natural rights, nor contractarian, but resembles the last in holding, with Hume, that a morality deserving of respect must be a transgenerational cooperative scheme of rights and obligations from which each participant can, over a normal lifetime, expect at least that he/she is "a gainer, on balancing the account" (*A Treatise of Human Nature*, ed. L. A. Selby-Bigge, rev. P. H. Nidditch (Oxford: Clarendon Press, 1978), 497). This requires, at the least, that one not have been "duped," and at best, "infinite advantages." It is extremely difficult, however, to judge whether a particular person in a particular scheme *is* a gainer thereby, difficult even to answer the question "gainer compared with what?" Even when we have answered that question, and perhaps found our own morality failing to pass this test, found that it does make some people dupes of others, it is very difficult to know if any proposed change

any strangers. Since *what* I should do is not affected by how many people are endangered, my ignorance of numbers is no obstacle to my knowing what my duty is.

There are many dangers which seem to face us and our successors which are dangers *however* many people we all are, and where what should be done is the same however many we are. Radiation will affect us, however thinly or densely we are spread over the affected area. A poisoned river or lake is useless to those living near it, whether they be few or many. Of course, if there are *other* rivers and lakes, which people may move to and "use up," then numbers will count. Numbers count when the good is one which is both divisible and consumed. In recent times more and more of our activities *have* "consumed" the goods used in those activities. Cleovolus' water system was not "used up" by its use over the centuries, but will be "used up," at a faster or a slower rate, if the water flowing into it is contaminated with conduit-clogging chemicals. Whereas agriculture practiced in some ways does not "use up" the land or the water supply, practiced in some modern intensive ways with pesticides and chemical fertilizers it does. Some of our policies are ensuring that more and more problems *become* ones where numbers count. Once the numbers count, we do need estimates of numbers to determine both our "fair share" of burdens and benefits and to determine exactly what dangers face us. In those cases we must simply do the best we can to estimate numbers. But there are still many dangers which face us where *what* is endangered is not (yet) a supply of to-be-consumed goods, but a source or "mother" of potentially endless such supplies—seas, forests, rivers, soil, atmosphere. Our obligations then are clearest, since not dependent on fallible estimates of numbers. They are obligations not to arrange the future death of the goose that lays the variety of eggs we and future people can be reliably expected to need and want.

John Locke (1632–1704), to whom the Founding Fathers of the American nation looked for a formulation of the moral and political principles on which the nation was founded, said that among our duties to others in a prepolitical "state of nature" was to leave "enough and as good" of whatever one used of those resources of the earth to which mankind has a "common

---

would really be an improvement by the same criteria. To have any well-based opinion about that one would need knowledge or imagination of the range of viable options, and knowledge of the fate of societies which tried them.

title." We are in a state of nature toward distant persons, even to our own distant descendants, since no one political order can be known to forge ties of common citizenship between us and them. There are grave problems about knowing how much of the divisible and exhaustible goods are "enough" for future people, but to know what counts as leaving "as good" an earth as we enjoyed is not as difficult. Our obligations to future people, then, can reasonably be seen to include everything this general obligation entails, the passing on of unruined self-renewing sources of the satisfiers of basic human needs and wants, the providers of human enjoyment. These self-renewing sources include not just physical ones like seas, forests, and land, but cultural ones such as art and science (and products of it such as Cleovolus' water system), social institutions including ones which help us to take responsibility for the consequences of our policy for future people, and moral ideas themselves. To people in the near future, those in the generations whose size and fate we more directly control, we owe in addition responsible planning—planning aimed at seeing that they inherit not merely basic resources "as good" as ours, but also the means to get "enough" of the divisible exhaustible goods we know they will need. To enable them to get enough, control of population size as well as of size of our depletion of nature's resources is needed.

Our obligations to future people, then, do vary depending on whether they are close enough in time to us for their *particular* needs and abilities to be foreseeable, and for us to have control over how many of them there will be, what opportunities they will have, what supply problems they will face. To people in the *next* few generations we have extra obligations, obligations over and above those owed to all future people. To all future people, however distant and unknowable in numbers, special abilities, special opportunities, special needs, we are obligated not knowingly to injure the common human interests they like all of us have—interests in a good earth and in a good tradition guiding us in living well on it without destroying its hospitality to human life.

A good tradition is one conscious of its roots in the past and of its influence on the future. From past thinkers we have inherited the basis for that scientific knowledge which has enabled us to create, for future people, both great opportunities and great dangers. It seems fitting that to this bequest we add some attempt at an understanding of the moral issues that we face, and that they too will face, issues requiring us to clarify our ideas about our moral relations to past and to future people. Such attempts will build on the moral ideas and practices we have inherited, but we have seen how much more work still needs to be done before we can "give counsel by our understanding." Not only should our population, and our agricultural, industrial, and defense policies, be ones we would praise or at least not condemn if we could change places with our descendants, but our thinking about these policies also ought to set a good example. Even if such thinking by philosophers and reflective people fails to have the effect on current public policy which some of us hope for, it can nevertheless do useful work in getting the right discussions launched, the right questions posed. Even if future people, looking back at us, can say no better than "Well, at least they *worried* about what they were doing to the world we were to inherit," that worry may itself be a fitting legacy.

3

Discriminate Death–Dealing: Who May Kill Whom, and How?

David Wiggins speaks of "our primitive aversion from acts that appear as a direct assault by one on the personal being of another, acts such as murder, wounding, injury, plunder, pillage, the harming of innocents…"[1] Are we really so averse to killing and injuring each other, and, when we do show some such aversion, is it primitive? Wiggins sees "the deontological core"[2] of morality to be a prohibition of such acts, accompanied by revulsion at the thought of them, but he knows that we permit abortion, and train our military troops and our police in the use of deadly force. Nations invade and kill their neighbors. Genocide has occurred, and is still occurring. Young men get into fights fairly easily, and do not seem reluctant to injure each other, and most children seem prone to body contact with each other, often to "horseplay" which sometimes becomes a rough and tumble. They are not like Simone Weil, who instinctively moved out of the way of others around her, and spoke, in her *The "Iliad," or, The Poem of Force* (1939) of the "indefinable influence that the presence of another has on us," an influence lost if "in a moment of impatience" one attacks the other. If there is a primitive aversion to attack, it shows itself very unreliably. We do not seem to have found it against the grain to fight and kill, even if we prefer to kill from a

---

[1] David Wiggins, *Ethics: Twelve Lectures on the Philosophy of Morality* (Cambridge, Mass.: Harvard University Press, 2006), 246.

[2] Part of what Wiggins means is that the category of the forbidden is more basic, so more "primitive," than that of the permissible, and the required. See ibid. 248 n. 22. But he also means that we do not have to be taught what is thus forbidden, and that the content of one, perhaps the first, of these basic deontological prohibitions is of assault and killing. He does not tell us what others, if any, are in this "core." This seems to me to amount to a claim that we have innate knowledge of the core of morality, that we all have a "moral sense" which agrees in its deliverance of the basic taboos. As I see it, the category of the forbidden could not be primitive, since it implies a forbidder, be that God, one's parents, or the state. I agree with Hume that any deontology is "artificial," not natural or primitive.

distance, rather than with bayonets. Our ancestors believed the gods would smile on us more if we made the occasional human sacrifice. That may be a case of a special breaking of the usual rule, which anthropologists tell us is typical of the sacred. Religion can demand ritual cannibalism, as in the Mass, so perhaps one should not generalize from what goes on in churches and on altars to what is allowed in ordinary life. Still, human sacrifice has been thought not only allowed, but demanded. Infanticide has been allowed, and young men sent to the front line in battle.

The recently popular trolley problem, where one is killed to save five, is just an updated meditation on the willingness to sacrifice some, as cannon fodder or as human sacrifice, in order to save more. The Christian religion makes such a requisite human sacrifice central to its teaching. Can the core of our morality be a prohibition on killing, while the core of the religion established in England, and providing the background culture in many other places, has human sacrifice at its core? Maybe this discrepancy is not atypical, if altars and churches are places where the usual rules do not hold good, if they are places of sacrifice and sanctuary. If, as I have claimed in other places,[3] our moral rules tend to tell us who may kill (or disappropriate, deceive, etc.) whom, by what means, and with whose permission, rather than tell us simply not to kill or steal or deceive, then human sacrifice, and the ritual rebreaking of a human body and pretend-eating of it, in the Mass, could be cases of such privileged acts. Some see the form of our moral demand to be "Do not kill, unless..." but whether the allowed killings should be seen as exceptions to a general prohibition, or perhaps as specifications of a sort of division of labor, in which some (the military, executioners, priests) are directed to kill while others are denied this right, perhaps instead directed, like physicians, to keep alive rather than to kill, depends on just how many allowed killings, and types of allowed killings, there are. It is not that a monopoly on killing is kept for the state and its troops. A society that allows abortion allows non-official killings. It may not, by substituting abortion for infanticide, thereby sacrifice fewer human lives, but does try to stop the spread of the willingness to kill fellow human beings by denying the fetus the status of a human being, so not giving it the rites of burial. To have funerals for all aborted fetuses would proclaim too loudly our willingness to

---

[3] "Poisoning the Wells" and "Violent Demonstrations," in Baier, *Moral Prejudices* (Cambridge, Mass.: Harvard University Press, 1994).

kill the innocent. In India today, female fetuses are aborted on a grand scale, and this may be an improvement on earlier infanticidal practices, but it shows how our attitude to killing depends a lot on who is killed by whom. It is indiscriminate killing of fellow already born human beings by other human beings that we forbid, and even that can become obligatory rather than forbidden, in wartime, by those wearing military uniform. Or is killing enemy troops, like genocide or ethnic cleansing, still a case of discriminate killing, of killing only some declared targets?

T. M. Scanlon in his recent book *Moral Dimensions*[4] considers how strategic bombing which kills civilians, during a war, differs from terrorist bombing, and finds the main difference to lie in the intent with which the killing is done. Civilian deaths in, say, Hamburg can be regarded as regretted side effects of the main goal, destruction of the port and military power of a nation with whom one is at declared war, whereas the terrorist bombers in Manhattan relied on civilian deaths for the impact they aimed at. Scanlon invokes the doctrine of double effect, originally invoked by Aquinas to show why killing in self-defense can be excusable, partially to exonerate the military bombers, while blaming the terrorists. But Al Qaeda had done the equivalent of declaring war on the West, so that difference (having declared war) cannot be what is crucial. The bombing of Dresden killed more civilians than the terrorist attack on Manhattan. Is it that the terrorist killers wore no military uniform? Would it have made a difference if they had donned some uniform, perhaps Muslim headgear, before taking over the planes? The group they claimed to act on behalf of is not a nation state, but that was the case in every revolutionary or civil war, so can scarcely be a condition of permissibility of large-scale killing. And they could claim that their intent was to draw attention to their grievances, using their own deaths, and those of their victims, to achieve this goal. As I put it in "Violent Demonstrations" (published well before 9/11), they used themselves and their victims as a living flare, to get our attention. They certainly succeeded in that aim.

Our attitude to killing the very young seems inconsistent. Abortion is seen as excusable since it kills one whose lifetime has not yet begun, so it does not cut short an already launched lifetime. A similar excuse may be given for infanticide. Yet killing a 5-year-old is often deemed worse than

---

[4] T. M. Scanlon, *Moral Dimensions* (Cambridge, Mass.: Harvard University Press, 2008).

killing an adult, since so much of a normal lifetime is denied the victim. Yet if it is the amount of lifetime taken away which determines the severity of the crime, then the younger the victim, the worse, so abortion and infanticide would become the worst forms of murder. We seem to have a very baroque rule about how the age of the victim affects the severity of the crime. Only if a life, outside the womb, has begun and lasted a month or two is it clearly wrong to end that life, but ending it when it is only just begun is worse than ending that of a very old person, soon to die anyway. Do we think this makes sense?

Is it that we endorse rules that serve to minimize the killing? We are the descendants of hunters and warriors, and of herders who killed and butchered the animals they had looked after. They had to develop the ability and willingness to kill animals for food, and kill human beings who attacked them. The willingness to assault and kill living things is part of our species nature, so a primitive aversion to it is unlikely.[5] We may now feel uncomfortable at this fact, so try to protect ourselves from facing it, by talk of human solidarity,[6] and pretending that the high rate of assault, domestic violence, gang violence, and murder, in our societies, is a falling off from a civilized condition we had attained, rather than a fairly constant part of the human condition. Human solidarity is an ideal, not an actuality. Of course, decent humane people will try to avoid being part of any killing squad, and will try to design institutions at both local and international levels that reduce the likelihood of war or other widespread death-dealing. We will try to ensure that baby food does not contain melamine, that air is not badly polluted, that waterways remain clean, that the roads and passenger airplanes are fairly safe. That we have a bad conscience about our species' record is understandable. That we should hope to improve is only proper. But we do not improve by pretending we feel a revulsion that clearly many do not feel, and which we count on their not feeling, or on their easily overcoming, when we train them to kill in wars.

---

[5] The film *Earth* shows very graphically how eating and being eaten is the norm for life on earth. The polar bear, not his prey, is the tragic hero of this film.

[6] Wiggins cites both Philippa Foot and Simone Weil in appealing to this concept. Richard Rorty also appeals to it. Of course none of them deny the facts about the killings that occur, but Wiggins and Weil see them as done at the cost of overcoming a near-instinctive aversion to assault. My claim is that such an instinct is highly unlikely, in descendants of predators, and not obviously in evidence in today's society.

Most of us depend for food on someone else killing the animals we eat. Prohibitions on diet vary. We do not eat cats and dogs, but the Chinese do. Many do not eat pig-meat, and some do not eat cattle flesh. We are horrified when we hear of the hunting and eating of monkeys, chimpanzees, and gorillas. Is that because they are our cousins? Do we refuse to eat pets, relatives, and anything as omnivorous as we are? (Cannibals report that human flesh tastes like pork, and the monkey meat sold in Cameroon is called bush-pig.) Our eating habits are as discriminating as our killing habits, and the two, for flesh-eaters, are of course connected. The people in Cameroon who hunt and eat monkeys, chimpanzees, and gorillas would go hungry, perhaps starve, if this were prevented. Do we want to save the gorillas at their expense?[7]

Every decision about how scarce medical resources are to be used involves saving some, while not saving others. There are not enough organ donors for the need for them, so many die for lack of a transplant. We have come to regard letting die as not quite as bad as killing, but this distinction, like that between what we aim to do and what we know we are thereby doing, seems at best a salve to our bad conscience about the equanimity with which we decide who shall die. Such decisions are unavoidable, as long as we live in conditions of scarcity. We let millions starve, we let triage decisions give the aged second place to the young, when it comes to prolonging life, since it makes good sense to spend our limited resources extending lives by decades rather than years or months. Honesty demands that we acknowledge this. The best we can do is kill or let die as few as we can, and if we have to decide whom to save, to do so on fair and agreed principles.

Hume saw justice as the virtue that responds to scarce resources, and to some defects in our nature (our "limited generosity"). But, alas, he did not say how we should respond to the aggression in our nature, and to the scarcity of our life-protecting resources. He noted in his *Enquiry Concerning the Principles of Morals* how sports like boxing, and also war, have transformed aggression into rule-governed conduct, a bit like the way property rights and transfer by contract transform our avidity for possessions. "War has its laws as well as peace; and even that sportive kind of war, carried on

---

[7] According to a Reuters news report (*Otago Daily Times*, Sept. 23, 2008) the trade in bush-meat across central Africa is worth $200 million annually, and in the Amazon basin, $175 million. In the markets of Yaoundé, Cameroon, 70–90 tons of it is sold monthly. This is mostly the smaller apes, but if restaurant patrons want chimpanzee or gorilla, it can be obtained, despite laws against hunting.

among wrestlers, boxers, cudgel-players, and gladiators, is regulated by fixed principles" (*Enquiry*, 4. 20). Not until he wrote his *History of England* did he take fully into account just what a bloodthirsty, quarrelsome, and cruel species we are, and he did not go back to revise his ethics to say how we should respond to these ugly features of our innate endowment. Laws of nations try to mitigate the destructiveness and horror of war, and the civil law includes complex distinctions when it comes to assault, self-defense, and homicide. Hume was quite firm in his belief that no ethics is of any use unless based on a sound knowledge of human nature. But his own ethics do not say much on how we should cope with anger, envy, the desire for revenge, the easy ability to strike and kill, and with the awareness of our species' nasty past. Gentleness and humanity are virtues for him, but just how they can be cultivated when our nation is at war, or neighboring nations are starving, or epidemics stalk our cities, is less than clear. Realism about what we are in fact doing, and condoning, is a first step in working out how we might become gentler and less ruthless in our attitudes to the death of others, wiser and less selfish in our attitudes to our own precious lives. The trolley problem, discussed at such length by Thomson, Kamm, and Scanlon, when it considers whether it is permissible to push one person off an over-bridge to save the five on the runaway trolley, would do better to ask whether one should throw oneself down, rather than whether one can push another. Self-sacrifice has always been allowed. It is the sacrifice of one's neighbor that is dubious. Self-defense is one agreed excuse for killing, so if one's neighbor on the over-bridge suspects he is about to be sacrificed, and so preemptively throws the would-be other-sacrificer, he may be within his rights. We need to think more about our past practices of human sacrifice, about how the victims were chosen (virgins, unblemished lambs, sinless only sons), and how it would be fairer to choose them. In China criminals, once executed, have their organs used for transplants, and this seems efficient, as long as that is not the reason why execution is their punishment. But what gods would want criminals, or the old and infirm, on their altars? To please the gods we must offer up our best, not our worst. But for other purposes, the selection of who is to die need not single out the young and unspoiled. We have regularly sent our young men to fight and be killed, but that is because we thought they would fight better than the old. Who should be let die, if there is not enough food or medicine or skilled surgeons, or body parts, for all who need them? Medical ethics could serve to make our thinking about death-dealing more realistic than it is in some moral philosophers' pronouncements about human solidarity, and about the ban on killing being at the heart of our morality. That is, at best, a huge oversimplification, at worst, self-saving hypocrisy.

As the SS discovered, it is easier on the psyche of the killers to kill people en masse, in gas chambers, than to shoot them one by one. And intuitions on the trolley problem show that we are more willing to sacrifice one to save five by throwing a switch diverting the runaway trolley into the path of the one, than by throwing one from the over-bridge. The modality of the killing seems to matter to us: bombing cities, or blockading them, is done with less revulsion than the hand-to-hand slaughter of civilians in an invaded city, when the killer has to face her victims. (I discuss this in "Faces, and Other Body Parts," Chapter 15 in this volume.) Is this pickiness about modes of attack because, as young children, we were all taught not to bite, poke, strike, or kick our siblings, nor to aim our toy bows and arrows at them, but were understandably not instructed in the ethics of railtrack control, nor of bombing, nor of blockade? As Hume says, every parent has to enforce some rules to keep peace among her children, and it would not be surprising if such acquired inhibitions of direct bodily attack on others remains with us in later life, as long as we were not ourselves, when we were children, subjected to beating, as discipline.[8] Is Wiggins's point about a "primitive aversion" to bodily assault really a misstated point about the acquired inhibitions of well and gently brought-up people? Women who are trained in self-defense are instructed to poke the eyes and knee the genitals of sexual attackers, and some find this to go very much against the grain. But the grain may be not so much primitive as acquired in infancy. Wiggins quotes Simone Weil's claim that only impatience or thoughtlessness would allow us to ignore the usual influence that the presence of another person has on us, inhibiting disrespect or attack, and cites Philippa Foot's reference to the "moral space" surrounding each person. But many killings are neither hotheaded nor thoughtless. When Henry VIII had the schoolmaster John

---

[8] British schoolboys were until 1999 subjected to beatings, so it would be surprising if they ended up unable to strike another, since the abused tend to become abusers. In New Zealand, as I write, we are to have a referendum on whether or not to repeal a recent law making it a criminal offense to strike a child, and the level of support for the repeal makes it very evident that the time-honored right of parents and teachers to hit children is a treasured one. Some of the worst horrors we have perpetrated have been in the name of punishment and discipline.

Lambert burned especially slowly to death, to show what happened to those who disagreed not just with their bishops but with their king about the real presence, it was neither an impatient nor an unthinking killing. It was calculated and cold-blooded, as was the "final solution" in Nazi Germany. It is true that it may be easier for most of us to kill from a distance than to use a bayonet. Research has shown that we do show a preference for less direct modes of killing.[9] It is lack of imagination that makes it easier for the bomber to set cities on fire from the air than to set fire to them when he invades on the ground, and can see the faces of some of his victims. But lack of imagination is not uncommon, and knowing what they do when they do it from afar could be paralyzing in air force bombardiers. The terrorists who died in the twin towers were spared the sight of those who jumped to their death to avoid the flames, and they knew they would be spared this sight when they embarked on their mission. No suicide bomber sees what she is doing, and this, not just the promise of paradise, makes it possible for her to do it.

Our tradition of moral philosophy has little helpful to say about death-dealing. Hume is not the only one who neglected the topic. Aquinas is often appealed to, for example by Wiggins and Scanlon, but his account of the right to self-defense presupposes, rather than clarifies, a prior divine prohibition on intentional killing. "Thou shalt not kill" is taken as given. Montaigne on cannibals, Grotius on war, Swift's "Modest Proposal," and Nietzsche's *Genealogy of Morals* are the best we have, when it comes to explicit examination of our attitudes to killing. Butler avoids it. Hutcheson discusses Spartan customs of killing the unfit, and infanticide, and is accepting that the greatest good of the greatest number may require such policies. He expresses qualms about infanticide, resorted to when "parents are sufficiently stocked." This would be done from self-love, he says, and "I scarce think it passes for a good action, any where." But as for the deformed and unfit, if they "can never, by any Ingenuity or Art, make themselves useful to Mankind, but should grow an absolutely unsupportable Burden, so as to involve a whole State in Misery, it is just to put them to Death. This all allow to be

---

[9] Fiery Cushman, Lian Young, and Marc Hauser, "The Role of Conscious Reasoning in Moral Judgment: Testing Three Principles of Harm," *Psychological Science*, 17 (2006), 1082–9. The third principle they tested was "*the contact principle*: Using physical contact to cause harm to a victim is morally worse than causing equivalent harm to a victim without physical contact." Subjects were found to judge in accord with this principle, which, however, they were incapable of defending.

just, in the Case of an overloaded Boat in a Storm."[10] Adam Smith considers murder the most atrocious crime against a person, and thinks we "applaud with ardour" the execution of the murderer. He gives fairly detailed attention in his *Lectures on Jurisprudence* to the murder–manslaughter distinction, various sorts of injury, and the concept of the just war. If his talk of ardor for judicial killings is chilling, Kant is even more so, since he condones the infanticide of illegitimate children (to conceal the mother's shame), and honor killings in duels, as well as requiring, like Smith, the judicial killing of those found guilty of murder. As the convicted murderer has lost the right to life, protected by a society which forbids murder of its legitimate members, so the illegitimate child, born without a license, has never had such a right. The doctrine of the state's right to cleanse itself of those who offend it, and so are denied its protection, is formulated fairly clearly in Kant's *Doctrine of Right*. And it is killing oneself that he believed involves a contradiction in the will, not the killing of those whose existence offends one, such as gypsies, Jews, Armenians, Tutsis, or Kurds. Latter-day Kantians try to play up the formula of respect for persons as ends in themselves, rather than the details Kant gave of the application of his categorical imperative. One respects the murderer as an offending person when one executes him, he teaches us. Does one respect the illegitimate child as a person when one asks it for its license for being born, before condoning its killing? If this demand for proper documents is what respect for persons involves, then one respects the would-be immigrants whose ship one turns away, leaving them to starve or drown. Illegal immigrants have, like illegitimate children, "*eingeschlicken*" ("slipped," or "sneaked") into the commonwealth, and so have no civil rights. And the right to life, to the state's protection of that right, does seem, for Kant, to be a civil not a moral right. Hume too may think that killing is a matter for the civil magistrate to rule on, not a matter of natural right or natural virtue. He at least did see it as proper for us to adopt a moral point of view and judge the artifices we find in place in our society, where necessary condemning them (slavery), even rebelling against evil magistrates and tyrants. His doctrine of social artifice makes all de facto social rules generate only self-interested "natural obligations" unless the artifices in question do pass the moral test, which involves sympathy with all those affected by them.

---

[10] Frances Hutcheson, *An Inquiry into the Original of Our Ideas of Virtue and Beauty*, ed. Wolfgang Leidhold (Indianapolis: Liberty Press, 2004), sect. iv, p. 140.

Only then do they generate moral obligations, and only then does Hume's person of virtue respect such rules. In Kant's Prussia, one might indeed sympathize with the unmarried woman driven to kill her baby to hide her shame, but one would sympathize more with the baby, and have no sympathy at all for the official who decrees that the illegitimate child be denied citizenship and state protection. Not that one would want the mother to be put to death as a murderer: the death penalty itself is part of what appalls one in Kant's version of right conduct. Moral approbation for such a social system would be obscene.

Hutcheson's version of the deliverances of the moral sense, to which Hume is often seen as indebted, not only fails to provide any "deontological core" forbidding killing each other, but also seems to open the door too wide to utilitarian excuses for killing some to make life easier for others. And Hume? I believe his ethics have the theoretical resources to say something both realistic and humane about killing, but he left it for his followers to say it. He did the groundwork, in showing how we need (and do have), in some important areas of life, precise permissions and entitlements which vary from society to society, and may vary on the scale going from "barbaric" to "civilized," and also that such social rules must be subjected to assessment from a moral point of view, requiring extensive sympathy, before we give them any respect. We may fail to protest bad rules, out of fear of powerful magistrates, but we will distinguish this timid conformity from anything deserving to be called moral merit. And we certainly will not call the person who can throw the least fit person out of the lifeboat, to give the rest a better chance of survival, a humane man of virtue. Hume did think that justice came into play only when the scarcity was moderate, so it was not unjust to grab a plank from another to save one's life. But he did not, like Hutcheson, say such self-serving action was just. C. D. Broad, who criticized Hume on this point, and thought we should die together in a shipwreck, sharing the last biscuit and having "the grace to starve decently, and in order,"[11] would have done better to direct his guns at Hutcheson.

One reader of a draft of this chapter, Livia Guimaraes, commented that I am revising Hume's account of human nature, by denying Wiggins's claim that we have a primitive aversion to assaulting others, and by including aggression in our species nature. But it was Hume's own *History* which

[11] C. D. Broad, *Five Types of Ethical Theory* (London: Kegan Paul, Trench, Trubner, 1944), 98.

rubbed my nose in the atrocities that his own *Treatise of Human Nature* had not really led us to expect. It had not denied malice, envy, and the wish for revenge, but had seen sympathy with the distress or joy of others as near-automatic, and had found "kindness to children" to be innate in us. So it had been a fairly rose-colored version of our nature, with little said about our disciplinary and killing customs. Killing was said to be a problem for the rationalist, who condemns parricide in humans but not in trees. The natural thing to conclude from that was that a sentiment-based view of ethics would have no trouble with the ethics of killing. But then none was in fact given. The worst vice is cruelty, so we will condemn cruel slow killings more than quick painless ones, but why do we, as distinct from our laws and our magistrates, condemn many or most cases of homicide? Hume does not really help us articulate the rules of discriminate killing. He does stress that self-defense excuses killing. But what else does? He does not tell us. In "A Dialogue" he raises some questions about the social variability of prohibitions on suicide, infanticide, and assassination. The suggestion is that these, like property conventions and rules about incest, and rules about what one may eat, are all matters of social artifice, governing various sorts of conduct that require definite permissions and prohibitions, so that we may know what to expect. Among headhunters and cannibals, expect to be killed or eaten, just as farm animals, if aware of their fate, would. Clarice Lispector has a story about a chicken who rebels at her fate, and flies onto a rooftop when about to be killed and cooked for dinner. She is recaptured, then surprises her captors by laying an egg in the kitchen. She becomes a family pet, until one day they kill her and eat her. "And the years rolled on."[12] Lispector also has a scary tale of the world's smallest woman, a tiny tree-living black woman, of a near-extinct tribe, a variant of the pygmies, hunted and eaten by the Bantu, as bush-meat. She is entranced with the tall anthropologist who discovers her, the only tall person she has encountered who is not hunting her. She smiles at him, in her happiness not to be hunted and eaten. She was enjoying "the ineffable sensation of not having been devoured yet."[13] "Not to be devoured is the most perfect sentiment."[14] Our inhumanity is not reserved for those who are not human. If we, in our attempt to improve on our ancestors, espouse a morality which takes pride in the

---

[12] Clarice Lispector, *Family Ties*, trans. Giovanni Pontiero (Austin: University of Texas Press, 1972), 52.
[13] Ibid. 93–4.   [14] Ibid. 94.

"sentiment of humanity," we should perhaps humble our pride occasionally and appreciate that "ineffable sensation" which we put an end to in those we kill for food, which Lispector's chicken, on the rooftops, and her little woman, in her treetops, knew, and appreciated, for a while. Then the years rolled on. And still roll on.

When we consider our human record, we, like A. E. Housman, may find it difficult to gaze and not be sick.[15] Hume, when he considered the ancient Roman games, felt sympathy with Caligula when he wished that humanity had but one head, so that at one stroke one could destroy this race of monsters.[16] We must restrain this inhumane collective self-disgust, and instead ask how our better, gentler nature can be assisted to show itself, and what enforced rules in our communities will protect us from our own worst instincts. The sentiment of humanity has to be realistic, and not deny the facts about our known customs. It has to reform those customs, just as parents reform the infant aggression that would bite and scratch, when thwarted in its urgent self-will. How do we teach the young the arts of self-defense, without making them too willing to assault? Not by providing them with violent video games. How do we train our military to fight and kill, and then come home and be peaceable citizens? We have not yet invented the arts of living with one another, reasonably secure from threat of violent death, yet not armed against possible aggressors. Do we need a new Hobbes? A new Grotius? I think what we need is an applied Hume, with a revised version of our nature, such as he would have given after his study of the chain of atrocities that make up English history, had he then returned to his first topic. An ethics of killing for a post-terrorist and historically conscious world, for those of us who know we may well die, directly or indirectly, at human hands, and know that terrorists are not alone in their willingness to kill.

I am a citizen of a country whose native population, the Maori, killed each other in tribal warfare, and often ate their enemy dead (as well as the occasional missionary); whose first European citizens, with their superior weapons, fought and slaughtered the Maori, to get their land. My uncles returned from the First World War with shell shock, and I had a lover who

[15] The 16th of A. E. Housman's *Additional Poems* begins "Some can gaze and not be sick | But I could never learn the trick."

[16] "Of the Populousness of Ancient Nations," in David Hume, *Essays, Moral, Political and Literary*, ed. Eugene F. Miller (Indianapolis: Liberty Classics, 1985), 386 n.

had been at Monte Cassino, when the streets ran with blood. I myself, as far as I am aware, have never struck anyone, and, even in resisting a not so young and already lame would-be rapist, took care not to injure him.[17] That perhaps was foolish non-violence. As a 10-year-old, I took and broke a teacher's cane, to protest the caning of my schoolfellows, and got away with that. The teacher did not replace it, and I was not punished. But I was never in any doubt that I was one of a species who assault and kill each other, on the slightest of pretexts. (It is possible that there is a gender difference, when it comes to capacity for violence, in those descended from hunter warriors, whose women were left at home to tend the children and the gardens, while the men did the killing.) As a young person I read the Old Testament, both the Ten Commandments and the books of Samuel and Kings, with their account of many ruthless killings, especially of contenders for the throne, as well as of some heroic killings, like Judith's of Holofernes. King David may have begun with a heroic killing of Goliath, but his subsequent arranged killing of Bathsheba's husband, Uriah, was not heroic. Nor did his and Bathsheba's son Solomon hesitate to kill his older brother, to secure the throne for himself. "Thou shalt not kill" was honored by King David and King Solomon more in the breach than any other way. Or was it that they claimed a monopoly on the killing? The Old Testament could serve, as much as Hume's *History*, or any history of New Zealand, or of almost any country, to keep our feet on the ground as we formulate any "deontological core" we take our morality to have. But we like to think we are decent people, with civilized morals. Whether we eat chicken or simian bush-meat, most of us try to leave the slaughtering to others. We in effect hire others to do our killing for us. And the years roll on.

---

[17] I may, however, have killed in my mother's womb, as an ovarian cyst which was removed from me in adulthood was said, by the surgeon, to be the remains of a twin I had absorbed in the womb, alarmingly regrowing. This supposed fact horrified me, but then I do confess to an aversion to killing. It is an aversion, however, that I find not so widely shared. David Wiggins must share it, and so may many others, but the facts of our history show that we must have other proclivities which can fairly easily overpower it.

4

Can Philosophers Be Patriots?

Richard Rorty challenged the profession of philosophy to examine its own activities, to avoid false consciousness of what it is that we do. We are not, he claimed, scientists of the mind, nor discerners of eternal moral truths. Ours is not a view *sub specie aeternitatis*, but a view from a given culture at a given time. This challenge is salutary, and has been influential, but largely outside philosophy. The Princeton philosophy department is still doing the sorts of things it was doing when Rorty left and turned his back on the analytic philosophy he had been practicing.[1] I attended a graduate seminar he gave, in the philosophy of mind, as a visitor in Pittsburgh, shortly before he left Princeton, and I was a member of the American Philosophical Association (APA) board on the memorable occasion when he quarreled with his old friend Ruth Marcus, and wept with the anguish of it. I myself came in for some flak, from defenders of analytic philosophy, for my championing of "pluralists," so felt for Rorty in this confrontation. And I too had raised the question of what our professional ethics were for our own profession, what made us think public moneys should support us in our intellectual games. Yet I stayed in a philosophy department, while Rorty ended with only an honorary place in Stanford's. Why did I stay? Largely because I felt that teaching ethics in the way I was doing, and teaching the history of philosophy, was increasing understanding and reflectiveness in my students.

Some small changes from the original have been made in this version of this essay. It is forthcoming in German in Barry Allen, Alexander Groeschner, and Mike Sandbote (eds.), *Pragmatismus als Kultur-politik: Beitrage zum Werk von Richard Rorty* (Frankfurt am Main: Surkamp, 2010).

[1] His own training at Chicago and Yale had not been especially analytic, but once he joined the Princeton department he had more or less practiced philosophy in the way his colleagues there did. During the 1980s he seemed to leave the analytic philosophy to Donald Davidson, and give himself the role of interpreting him, relating his views to those of Wilfrid Sellars, and to his favorite, Dewey. In the index to *Objectivity, Relativism and Truth* (Cambridge: Cambridge University Press, 1991), there are eight lines of references to Dewey and six lines to Davidson.

Rorty had not been an analytic *moral* philosopher, and it is interesting to speculate on what arc his thought might have taken had he begun, not with potentiality and the mind–body problem, but with the moral potential of American democracy, and good reasons in ethics. For he ended as a social and political philosopher, indeed as a patriot philosopher, defending the US ideal of democracy, which he took to have an egalitarian component, believing in moral progress, and looking for the right version of human solidarity. He was very much a patriot, but also a globetrotter, speaking in Tehran and Beijing as well as Frankfurt and Paris.

Rorty raised the question of whether any claim about what does and does not exist can be raised independently of our current cultural and social goals. We interpret what we find to be the facts in terms of their bearing on our hopes and our fears. To say that we currently face dangers from climate change, and from violence from disaffected groups, is certainly to make factual claims, and also to make value judgments. I see social philosophers as having a duty to think about clear and present dangers, and I think that study of such philosophers as Grotius, Hume, Kant, Hegel, and Rawls can help us to do so. At any rate I shall hope that I am doing the sort of philosophy Rorty would have approved of, in what follows, when I consider two grave dangers currently facing all of us. My tone, however, will scarcely be ironical, since I know of no alternative debunking vocabulary for describing these dangers, so I fail Rorty's criteria for an ironist.[2] It is difficult to recontextualize climate change, unless we go back to Noah, and the only way I know to recontextualize terrorism is to attempt to see it from the terrorist's point of view.[3]

I shall be speaking as a critical citizen both of my native country, New Zealand, and of the country where I spent most of my working life, the US. I shall also be speaking as a committed cosmopolitan (who spent over three years in Britain, one in Berlin, and every summer for three decades in Austria), trying to advance the cause of what David Hume called "the party of humankind, against vice and disorder." Travel helps the would-be world citizen, and my double citizenship also gives me, I like to think, an advantage, in that I can see each of my two countries from the standpoint of the other. Just as learning another language instructs one on the peculiarities of one's

---

[2] I refer to his characterization of the ironist in "Private Irony and Liberal Hope," in Rorty, *Contingency, Irony and Solidarity* (Cambridge, Cambridge University Press, 1989), 73.

[3] I tried this in "Violent Demonstrations," in Baier, *Moral Prejudices* (Cambridge, Mass.: Harvard University Press, 1994).

native language,[4] so having double citizenship helps one's vision of each country, recontextualizes one's patriotism. At least I hope double citizenship makes my vision bifocal, and not cross-eyed. (It might even begin to make me into an ironist patriot, seeing each country as the other sees it.)

The notion of leaving footprints behind us is one of those metaphors that, by serving a useful purpose and dying, have become as entrenched in our language as any non-metaphorical talk. Its usefulness is practical and moral. We accuse each other, these days, of leaving dirty footprints. In terms of carbon footprints, the US is the worst world offender, and so far has made no progress on that front, unless making films on the topic is progress, which I suppose it is, or at least as much progress as writing essays on it. The pilgrim fathers did not pollute their environment more than the native Indians, nor worry about any environmental effects they were having. At least today some of us, in many countries, do worry, but it has taken melting icecaps to make us worry. Whether global warming is occurring, and if so how fast, is for scientists, not film-makers or essayists, to tell us. I take it their reports assure us of real danger, and have myself seen the icebergs which last year drifted from the Antarctic to off the Dunedin coast, halfway to the equator. I confess to being an unreformed empiricist, for whom such evidence was absolutely convincing. "Icecap melting" is now part of what Rorty would call my "final vocabulary." The icebergs were unforgettable, both beautiful, and ominous. So now we in New Zealand do worry about climate change. And now the carbon footprints of visiting tourists and exported foods have to be weighed against whatever benefits come from the tourist trade, and from conveying food from where it is most efficiently produced to distant markets. This is of obvious importance to an isolated country, such as New Zealand, which depends on its tourist trade, whose markets for its dairy products are worldwide, and whose own local greenhouse gas problem stems to a considerable degree from its dairy industry, even before the carbon produced in exporting dairy products is taken into account. (No one has measured human methane gas emissions, only bovine ones.) And, of course, as an island nation with a long coastline, we will be among the most affected, after the polar bears and penguins, by rising sea levels.

---

[4] When as a student I learned ancient Greek, I was fascinated with its middle voice and dual number, and felt English the poorer for lacking them. And my experience of living in different countries, with differing climates of trust, certainly affected my appreciation of the importance of trust. So I like to think of my own philosophy as essentially cosmopolitan.

It is proper, I think, to be aware of what we are doing, as tourism promoters, dairy farmers, exporters, world travelers, and consumers, and to consider how that will affect those who come after us. "Peak oil" is another Cassandra cry these days, and that metaphor, of what is peaking, among the supplies that we consume, and what will become less available to those who come after us, is also a popular one among worried alarmists. What should we leave for our descendants, what sort of footprint should we want to leave? What should we conserve, what can we afford to let peak and decline, without feeling we have wronged those who come after us? If we leave the technology to supply clean renewable energy, that legacy will be welcomed, as oil gives out. And if terrorism peaks in our generation, that will be good for those who come later. But unless we find a way to let it decline, to let the grievances of those with strong grievances be expressed in less lethal ways, then we cannot reasonably take its peak to have been reached. Unless we find alternative forms of energy, the peaking of fossil fuel supplies will mean a lowered standard of life for our great-great-grandchildren. And unless it is a clean as well as renewable form of energy, they will face pollution and disastrous climate change.

We are not without some success stories in changing our ways for the better. I lived in Pittsburgh, Pennsylvania, both when it was smog-shrouded, and after its air was cleaned up, and it was transformed for the better as a place to live. But that change for the better in that one place was effected largely by the closing down of the local steel mills, the moving away of steel production to other places, some in other lands. Still, we do have some proven skills when it comes to controlling smoke stack and automobile emissions. The challenge we now face is to somehow increase those skills, to invent new, better ways to move around without polluting the space we move through, perhaps to return to sailing ships, and to learn to produce what we need with forms of energy, such as solar and wind power, that are renewable and non-polluting. We are an inventive species. We are also an adaptable species, and could, if we chose, return to the habits of my grandparents, who did without cars, refrigerators, washing machines, air conditioning, and did not feel their way of life to have been bad. Patriots tend to look back to how their grandparents lived, as well as to look forward. We are aware of our heritage, and take notice both of the faults, and of the potential for improvement, of our own countries, the places whose culture formed us, and where we choose to live and work, retire and die. Being a citizen of two countries, one very powerful, one not, whose relations with each other are less than very close, imposes interesting constraints on my attempts to see clearly the good and bad aspects of my two countries. My grandparents lived in New Zealand, and its culture formed me. I confess I feel more at home in a powerless than in a powerful country. New Zealand will not allow nuclear-powered ships in its territorial waters. Its foreign policy is influenced as much by its memory of nuclear tests in the South Pacific as by its old friendship with England, its more recent friendship with China (dating from the days of Rewi Alley), and its hope to trade with the US. Since we are so powerless, no one much cares what our foreign policy is. We seem at present to concentrate our small military might in peacekeeping forces, in East Timor, in Afghanistan. At present New Zealand is doing better than the US on carbon emissions, but we too have much room for improvement. "Pioneer values" are what we pay lip service to, in New Zealand, mucking in and making do, operating with number eight fencing wire, and we could, if we chose, show that we really can manage with fewer creature comforts. Will we so choose? Time will tell.

One modern luxury I certainly would miss, even if I did my laundry, as my parents did for most of their lives with a boiler, then rinsing tubs and a hand-operated ringer, and kept my perishable foods in a fly-proof meat safe, would be the Internet, and email. The ease of communication, and of consulting experts, which they have brought has transformed our lives for the better, and could help with the sharing of ideas and expertise in coping with current world problems, such as the continent-sized swirl of plastic garbage floating in the North Pacific, or rising sea levels. Hume hailed the printing press as a transformer of human life, and the Internet is just as great a transformer. It can facilitate cooperative efforts to cope with world dangers.

But the physical challenges are not the only ones we face, nor technological inventions the only ones we must hope for, as we attempt to recontextualize our lives and concerns. We also face the more intractable problem of how to prevent desperate and aggrieved people from suicidal massacres, in schools, shopping malls, airports, on airplanes. And with greater ease in knowing how others live comes greater likelihood of indignation at inequality, at exploitation, at neglect. The desperation expressed in violent acts is sometimes private, and so the massacres are as it were domestic to the nation, sometimes public, those responsible for it sometimes foreign. American soil has recently seen several of the former, and one huge, impressively coordinated, three-sited version of the latter. Given the ease for anyone to procure lethal weapons, or to transform a mode of transport into a lethal weapon, the only way we can protect ourselves from such suicidal desperadoes is by defusing their anger and aggression, by persuading them to express their grievances in ways that allow both them and their perceived enemies a chance to survive. For us to do that, we must listen to them, and attend to their grievances. For the desperate young people in our schools, colleges, and shopping malls, private counseling services, and social opportunities for making something of their lives, is where we must hope that new efforts will improve things. The US is not alone in having disaffected young. New Zealand too, although it rated second best on an international "peace index," while the US was low on that list, has a high youth suicide rate, and terrible rate of violence in the home, including violence against very young children. We have not yet had anyone open fire indiscriminately in a children's clothing store where Christmas gifts are being wrapped, nor any school massacres, but some frightful things have been done to little children. No nation can stand in judgment on another in this matter, whatever their place on any list, and we all depend on international agencies to advise us about how we can improve the conditions of life for our children and young people. For relative affluence is no guarantee of contentment, and social discontent arises from many causes. In New Zealand, our colonial past affects the discontents of some of our Maori population, and the very fact that there are several cultures in one territory always presents some problems. When one of them sees itself as the master culture, and does have a history of ruthless mastery, trouble is to be expected. New Zealanders never were slave-owners, but although we began our national existence with a treaty with the Maori, who had arrived several centuries before the Europeans, we did continue to displace and disappropriate them, and had some very bloody Maori wars in the nineteenth century. Alexis de Tocqueville wonders how the fact that three races share American soil, one of them native, one colonizing, the third recently enslaved, would work out in the long run (he did not foresee the Hispanic influx). That, after a civil war he did not foresee, seems to be working out not too disastrously, and in a self-proclaimed melting pot, diversity of origins is surely to be welcomed, not feared.

But has there been all that much melting in the United States? Intermarriage is the best indicator of that. Maybe that has happened between Polish

Americans and Irish Americans, or even English and Puerto Rican, but between the members of de Tocqueville's three races? With us in New Zealand there has been so much that half the self-perceived Maori population[5] in the last census had partners who were not Maori. We New Zealanders are increasingly becoming a monotonously pale brown race, where presence of a facial tattoo, or speaking Maori, is needed to declare oneself a Maori. The word *pakeha* is still used, but almost as a term of abuse. It means "pale" or even "pallid" and was how the Polynesian original New Zealanders saw the missionaries, whalers, and eventually settlers who came to live among them. It is always instructive to see oneself as others see one, and they saw my own Scots and English ancestors as unnaturally pale, almost as anemic. As Seyla Ben-Habib said in her presidential address to the APA in the Eastern Division, in 2007,[6] all cultures are partial cultures, and we all need to look at ourselves from the perspective of other cultures.

The United States had the great good fortune to be carefully observed by de Tocqueville, and would be wise not to ignore other foreign points of view on its own character. From Graham Greene's *Quiet American* (1955), to militant Islamic characterizations, and to those from many nations who booed in Bali, before they had reason to cheer, all should be grist to a self-analysis properly informed by such foreign viewpoints. "O wad some power the giftie gie us, to see ourselves as ithers see us!" Robert Burns said, and the US has been made a great gift in de Tocqueville's *Democracy in America* (1835). He did not foresee either the civil war or the wars on foreign soil that America would wage, but did foresee that its military leaders might be reckless of lives, especially of foreign lives. New Zealand too has had the benefit of some foreign viewpoints about what is good and bad in our society. In 1872 both Samuel Butler, in his satirical *Erehwon*, and Anthony Trollope, in his account of his travels, gave their impressions. More recently Jeffrey Moussaieff Masson,[7] while praising the beauty of our beaches, forests, and mountains, and praising our friendliness and egalitarianism, notes a certain anti-intellectualism, a "tall poppy syndrome," which wants exceptional talents cut down to size. His book has been ill-received by some New Zealanders, perhaps because we

[5] One in seven New Zealanders is Maori, one in ten of Asian descent.
[6] Seyla Ben-Habib, Presidential Address to the APA in the Eastern Division, *Proceedings and Addresses of the American Philosophical Association*, 81/2 (Nov. 2007), 23.
[7] Jeffrey Moussaieff Masson, *Slipping into Paradise: Why I Live in New Zealand* (Toronto: Random House, 2004).

smugly regard ourselves as "God's Own Country" ("godzone") and do not take well to any criticism, especially not from American[8] intellectual tall poppies. New Zealanders are thin-skinned when it comes to our national character. We, like all countries, need more frank reactions to the way we live.[9]

We need to listen to criticism, including the charges of those who are so aggrieved that they resort to violence. As I write, New Zealand has experienced its first domestic plane hijacking, by a knife-wielding unhappy 33-year-old woman refugee from Somaliland, who wanted to be flown to Australia, to get right out of the godzone. Part of her problem was language. We take in refugees, then do too little to make them feel at home, expect them to learn English. We never dream of trying to learn their language. Every English-speaking country is easily tempted to suppose that ours is the lingua franca, so, even if we are cosmopolitans, we can be excused from learning foreign languages. But the true cosmopolitan is multilingual, and the truly welcoming host learns at least a greeting in the guest's language. Our new schools curriculum, in New Zealand, is putting more stress on the importance not just of knowing the native language of our fellow citizens, the Maori, but of knowing at least one foreign language spoken in the Pacific rim. (Somaliland, of course, is not on that rim.) When I was at school, French was the only language (other than Latin) I was taught. Now we in New Zealand teach Chinese and Japanese, as well as Spanish, French, Russian, and German, and, as I write this, my local paper has a photo of an Arabic man showing little schoolchildren how to write "New Zealand" in Arabic. Learning a people's language is a step towards understanding their culture, and increased understanding of other cultures is urgently needed, if fear of the foreign is to be fought. Americans abroad would appear much less ugly if they could show forms of politeness in the language of the places they visit. In how many US schools could anyone learn Arabic, I wonder, before being sent to serve in any capacity in the Middle East? Google tells me that only 1 percent of FBI personnel know even a few words of Arabic, and that there is a conflict between having that knowledge and getting a

---

[8] Masson, since the publication of his book, has also become a New Zealand citizen, but now sees the troubles in Paradise more vividly than when he devoted a perceptive chapter of his book to them.

[9] It was inevitable, I think, that a pastoral country like New Zealand, dependent on its dairy exports, would eventually not prove paradise to a vegan like Masson, and a bookish Sanskrit-reading vegan at that.

security clearance. British diplomats used to learn it, and it should be seen as a valued ability, rather than as a disqualification, in an applicant to the diplomatic service. But until knowing any foreign language is more valued, knowledge of Arabic is likely to remain more feared than welcomed.[10] Another way to decrease the fear of the unfamiliar is to teach comparative religion. Some understanding of Islam, as well as Christianity and the Jewish faith, and other world religions, should be regarded as an obligation, not a peculiar hobby. Religious conflict is one major source of violence, so love of peace must include knowledge of world religions, and their potentials both for peace and for war.

One of the social tools we have evolved to enable us to get along is rights recognition, and rights are enshrined in the US Constitution. To recognize equal rights is to empower those who before the recognition were less than equal in power; it is for the stronger to strengthen the weaker in some respects. As a small state is empowered if it has two senators just like a very populous state, and a humble unknown citizen with a vote has the same elective power as the most famous voter, so whenever we recognize rights we alter the power balance. If we recognize international rights, in bodies like the United Nations, small countries like New Zealand acquire a voice they would otherwise have lacked, and big powers submit themselves to consultation and advice from those who are relatively powerless, when it comes to military might. The presence of the United Nations headquarters in Manhattan signals an acquiescence on the part of the US to the need for a world body to try to contain conflicts between nations, and to coordinate cooperative measures to cope with famine, deforestation, climate change, and other matters where what one nation does affects life for others. National sovereignty *is* threatened by such international bodies, but its sacredness is relatively recent in human history, and always was limited by treaty obligations, and by policies like the Monroe Doctrine, which not merely warned European powers to keep out of the Americas, but was taken by Theodor Roosevelt to license some interference by the US in other countries in what it declared its sphere of influence, the whole of North, Central, and South America. That Mexico and Canada are neighbors, whose borders

---

[10] Richard Rorty in "Representation, Social Practise, Truth," in Rorty, *Objectivity, Relativism, and Truth,* 157, defends those who "explain *true* in terms of *language I know,*" but the defense would be better, and a better answer to charges of insularity, if *language* became *languages*.

with the US are very porous, is one thing. Even that the Caribbean is close and that the Panama Canal affects US interests is a similar thing. But how was what went on in Argentina or Chile the concern of the US any more than what happens in Mongolia, or how did it affect the US more than it affected other equally distant countries? A common past of colonization from European powers would bring a right to intervene, even to prevent recolonization, only if the doctrine had been a joint one, by all American powers. It was not; it was a unilateral proclamation by one such power, and rightly was it mitigated by Franklin Roosevelt's "good neighbor" assurance, which limited the intention to intervene. Now, after the recognition in NATO that there are neighbors across the Atlantic, and now that the US has seen fit to intervene in Asia and the Middle East, the Monroe Doctrine seems quietly buried. But it did contain a grain of truth, that cooperation between nations who share a huge continent, divided into two only by human engineering, is plainly sensible, as long as there are common dangers. The original common danger was colonial aggression from Europe. That was succeeded by the perceived danger of a spread of communism, then by nuclear proliferation. Now the declared war is on terrorism, but, as Grotius pointed out (book II, chapter xxiv, section 9), bringing a matter to issue by "terror and reputation of strength" rather than all-out war can be what Pliny called "the most brilliant kind of victory." Grotius thought single combat to decide a matter was better than pitched battles, and threats of great force with only modest display of killing power better than all-out war. War kills the innocent, and causes terror in its civilian victims, so a war against terror has to take care that it not cause more death and suffering than it prevents. Grotius wrote while wars of religion were ravaging Europe, and we need a new Grotius, perhaps an Islamic one, and, until such a one turns up, more study of the original one, to help us cope with the divisions in today's world. The nominally Christian Grotius sought wisdom from any source, not just his own religious tradition, and had a clear aim of finding the least destructive way to settle quarrels between nations and peoples. Conference, if we speak a common language, arbitration if we do not, even single combat and terrifying show of strength, were, in his eyes, better than going to war, even if one's cause was seen as just.

Sometimes the better part of wisdom is to lay down one's rights, and one's arms. We need some international equivalent of the mutually disempowering handshake, to enable us to approach other peoples in peace, to make and seal deals with them, not attempt to use our stronger arm to force them to the actions that suit us, to give us access to their oil, and to control their uranium enrichment plants. The arrogance of claiming exclusive rights to dangerous forms of power has to be somehow broken, and it is best if it is broken from within, rather than by tempting outsiders to make a spectacular display of how equally vulnerable we all are. The forms of international cooperation and diplomacy which we have evolved can still serve us to help get laws for nations, laws like Hobbes's theorems of peace, ways to safely lay down our arms and give peacemakers safe conduct. The tradition of diplomacy is the one we have to hope will develop new skills. The oldest skill for getting along with foreigners is learning their language, not just expecting them to learn ours, and that is one the US has not laid much emphasis on.

US foreign policy has been dominated by its perceptions of a series of threats from foreign powers, first colonial powers, then communism, then nuclear proliferation, now terrorism and militant Islam. But some real present dangers have their source here on the home soil, as well as elsewhere. Carbon emissions in the US threaten not just the US and its nearest neighbors, Canada and Mexico, but everyone. What happens to Brazil's rainforests is of vital concern not just to Brazil's neighbors, but to all of us. Climate change, air pollution, water pollution, and icecap melting are no respecters of national boundaries, and we must act collectively, not just singly, to address them. Exemplary action by some is a start, but will be wasted unless all join in. The recent Bali agreement[11] is a small step forward, and did demonstrate the willingness of the more powerful, and the worst polluters, to submit to the judgment of the rest, to be booed into concessions. A new inverse Monroe Doctrine, where those who pose the worst dangers agree to act to lessen them, and to cooperate with all those facing the dangers, or a renewed and extended Roosevelt good neighbor policy, is needed now. For who, now, is not one's neighbor?

David Hume mentioned abstaining from poisoned arms as among the recognized laws between nations. And it is obvious why such a law makes sense. For poison is difficult to direct only at one's declared enemies, but tends to drift, both to one's own troops and to innocent third parties. Poisoned water and air, and nuclear fallout, are well nigh impossible to

---

[11] In 2007 in Bali the United Nations adopted a "road plan" to reduced carbon emissions.

confine to one area or one population. One's neighbors should now be seen as any who may be poisoned by what drifts over one's fence. All people, whether or not they are citizens of recognized states, have a right not to be knowingly poisoned. When Hume faced the question of who should be granted rights, once rights are recognized and possessed by some (and it is important to realize that they do have to be recognized, and spelled out; they are not written in the heavens), his answer was: by all who have the power to make their resentment of exclusion felt. This power to make exclusive clubs of right-holders feel the resentment of those who are kept out is possessed not only by small nations, if denied a voice, but by any group, whether or not it amounts to a nation. The Taliban, persecuted groups within Darfur, Palestinians in Israeli territory, all can show resentment in effective ways, if not listened to by those they resent, and this includes not just those in their own country who oppress them, but those who know of but ignore their plight. Hume pointed out to the women of his time, who did not have equal rights with men in marriage or in civil society, that their power to control whether or not men knew which children were their own children was something they could use to get a better deal. Today, with DNA tests, that can no longer be said, but fortunately women in at least his society now do have a better deal. The parenting and care of children is not the only cooperative activity in which men and women are involved. In pioneer societies such as New Zealand and the US were, all hands were needed if the animals were to be tended, the hay made, the crops got in. Colorado and New Zealand were the first to give women suffrage. Both for the continuation of known families, and for the continuing supply of the means to feed them, cooperation is needed, and partners in the activity must be given due recognition. That there has been progress in accepting the equal position of women, in Western societies, is hard to deny. The same need for recognition of all partners is now true, at the level of nations cooperating to ensure the continued supply of unpoisoned air and water. The fact that some have greater military might does not give them any right to exempt themselves from the common task. Theodor Roosevelt, in announcing his extension to the Monroe Doctrine, advised speaking gently while carrying a big stick. Big sticks do not make friends, nor inspire trust. The neighbor one trusts is one who comes with strong right arm extended for a handshake, displaying clearly that he carries no weapon. And big sticks are too easily acquired to impose much of an advantage. They should be left to aggrieved and excluded groups, who have to make threats to get recognition. Those with the monopoly of power can afford to speak firmly, while leaving their hands free of weapons.

Hume, that naturalist and empiricist, wrote of the role of what he called social "artifices," what we invent to remedy our natural inadequacies: "By the conjunction of forces our power is augmented: By the partition of employments our ability increases: And by mutual succor we are less exposed to fortune and accidents. 'Tis by this additional *force*, *ability*, and *security*, that society becomes advantageous."[12] Conjunction of forces, and federation of states within one nation, have given the US force enough to threaten weaker nations, both near and far. That, of course, was not the use of force that Hume had in mind, except for purposes of defense. He saw a need for cooperation not just within but between nations, both in the form of free trade, and also in observation of "laws of nations." Security is not increased by aggressive use of force, but only, on Hume's story, by "mutual succor." Such mutual help can go on between nations as well as within them, and can take the form of exchange of expert advice. Some countries do better than others, whatever the field one specifies. Costa Rica does a lot better at lowered greenhouse gases than the United States. Iceland takes the prize for books purchased, per head of population, and New Zealand is not far behind. New Zealand leads at curbside recycling. If those who do well in some area were invited by those who do less well to come in and advise, in a sort of expanded and targeted Fulbright exchange scheme, then all could benefit. Or the existing Fulbright scheme could be adapted, so that those who come to the US from other places be invited to give their reactions, both favorable and less favorable, to life in the US and those Americans who study abroad be encouraged to bring home lessons for the home scene. Guests usually feel they must not criticize their hosts, but we all need to see ourselves as others see us, especially those others who have had a chance to have a good look at us. We need a rethinking of the duties of host and guest, so that guests can share their observations. Hume noted that although most nations show politeness to guests by an "after you" gesture, when leaving a dwelling, Spanish hosts deliberately leave the guest to follow, as if leaving them briefly in charge. To leave our guests in charge of our homes is to trust them, to relinquish control of the situation, for a token moment, to grant

---

[12] David Hume, *A Treatise of Human Nature*, ed. L. A. Selby-Bigge, rev. P.H. Nidditch (Oxford: Clarendon Press, 1978), 485.

temporary special rights. The right to be the last to leave a dwelling is not the only right we sometimes freely grant, nor need courtesy be a mere masking of who really is in charge. The old habit of doffing one's hat and bowing to an acquaintance, on meeting, or offering a handshake, are other cases of a voluntary putting of oneself at a temporary disadvantage. Baring one's head or extending one's strong right hand to be taken by another are other cases of renouncing protection.

Why would anyone make herself vulnerable, relinquish any protection or superiority she possesses, by granting others, even briefly, equal or superior rights in some matter, in cases where she is not vanquished, so is not bowing to the other in submission? Because anyone, however strong, wants to be trusted by others, and knows she will not be trusted if she relies on superior power to get her way. Some measure of equality must be secured if we are to have any mutual trust. I return to the handshake as symbol of that voluntary mutual disempowerment which makes cooperation possible. When a strong man approaches another weaker one with his right hand outstretched, showing he has no weapon, nor intention to strike, the weaker can afford to take that hand in his own. The Romans grasped each other's elbows, making sure the whole lower arm was put out of dangerous action, but right hands are good enough. We take the handshake to seal a deal, and of course, like any agreement, it can fail to secure performance, but the handshake can also initiate a meeting, make the very possibility of a deal possible between strangers.

Alternative accounts of the origin of the handshake show it as the inadvertent outcome of two people each trying to take the other's hand to the lips, for a kiss. If neither wants to be in the position assumed by those who offer their hands to be kissed, so each tugs the hand away from the one who tries to lift it, a handshake of a sort will result. As one who has been subjected to the Austrian hand kiss, when not expecting it, and whose hand tended to be inky, I rather like this account of the handshake—a mutual "better not try to kiss my hand!!" It builds the equality in at the start, not just as the outcome.

In our customs of giving ambassadors special protection against arrest, and home invasion, we do grant those foreigner ambassadors invited into our capitals some special rights, a bit like Spanish hosts. Notoriously such privileges can be abused, so embassies can become the sanctuary of spies. The open invitation to foreign visitors, temporary residents, and immigrants to offer comments on the way life is conducted might also be occasionally abused, but as with ambassadorial privilege, more benefit than injury would come from it. A sort of visitors' book should always be open to suggestions on how matters strike the outsider, in New Zealand an ongoing "Erewhon," or additions to Anthony Trollope's 1872 observation that "New Zealand is over-governed, over-legislated for"; in the US an ongoing "Democracy in America." What struck me most, when I first came to live and work in the US after New Zealand, Britain, and Australia, was the acceptance of gun ownership as normal. That still horrifies me, and all the explanations in the world of the Second Amendment,[13] and the birth of the nation in rebellion against a colonial power, fail to persuade me that it is anything other than an encouragement to violence. The other thing that struck me was the sexism that still made life difficult for ambitious young women. That was in the 1960s, and since then Condoleezza Rice, Hillary Clinton, and others have certainly demonstrated what American women can do. De Tocqueville was impressed with the self-confidence of young unmarried American women, but also by their acceptance of their fate to become devoted and obedient wives. Of course, as a New Zealander, I had high standards for women's rights. We were the first nation to give suffrage to women, and have had two women heads of state, one now well into her third term of office, while the US is yet to have one. And recently we had, besides a woman prime minister, also at the same time a woman governor general, a woman chief justice, and a woman heading the largest corporation, Telecom.

I return to the question of what kind of welcome legacy we should leave behind us. We should leave complete records, both documentary and photographic. Shaming photos of the treatment of prisoners are better than attempts at cover-up. Abu Ghraib and Guantanamo Bay are names and images not likely to be quickly forgotten, nor should they be. Thucydides wrote a history of the war he himself had been involved in, "for posterity," and posterity has a right to full records of what went on in our lifetime. As Thucydides did not write to whitewash the Athenian actions, nor should the historians of our era attempt a whitewash. We have done as well as

---

[13] The Supreme Court in June, 2008 decided that the people's "right to bear arms," which the Second Amendment guarantees, should not be taken, as its introductory clause about the need for a citizen militia to guard freedom might suggest, to refer only to the right to be a member of a citizen militia, like the National Guard.

suffered grave wrongs. We need to leave black boxes of what led us to crash, when we morally crash as well as when our planes go down. Social philosophers can contribute to these. Time capsules should be left among our ruins, so later generations can learn from our mistakes. That is the least we can do. Even if we poison our air, melt our icecaps, let nuclear weapons loose to wreak their havoc (and we should not forget who first let them loose), let there be some way that any survivors of the messes we are making can work out, after we are gone, where we went wrong. That footprint at least, in the form of honest records, we should leave among our ruins. The US department of national archives should have underground storage, even if the Pentagon does not survive the next attack. For unless we do succeed in talking with those who want to attack it, there will surely be a next attack. Freud defined civilization as hurling words rather than stones at one another, but if the words are threats and insults, they will be just as deadly. They must be peaceable words, and in the language of those they are meant for. Understanding the other's language and culture are the first steps to good relations with them; refusing to do so, isolating oneself arrogantly in one's own language community, feeling superior, even if one is the greatest global poisoner, is the surest recipe for making deadly enemies.

Were David Hume among us today, I think he would want not just to enlarge his treatment of laws of nations, with more on the obligation not to poison, but rewrite his essays on suicide and on immortality. He did not, could not, foresee how the prospect of an afterlife could tempt people to patriotic martyrdom, though he did see dangers in any belief in an afterlife. "Death is in the end unavoidable: yet the human species could not be preserved, had not nature inspired us with an aversion towards it."[14] Once the natural aversion to death is overcome by promise of paradise for religious martyrs, killing themselves along with the ungodly, the preservation of the human species is threatened. Once the fear of death is outweighed by indignation at grievances, there is no way to deter would-be martyrs, except removing their grievances, giving them some prospect of a good life here and now.

Islamic suicide terrorists have included women. That women wearing the Muslim headscarf should take on this role is as bizarre as that they should

---

[14] David Hume, *Essays, Moral, Political and Literary,* ed. Eugene F. Miller (Indianapolis: Liberty Classics, 1985), 598.

take up soccer in Canada, and provoke debate about the danger their headscarves occasion to all players. In some Islamic societies wearing a headscarf is not a symbol of modesty and inferiority to men, but a badge of allegiance against Western oppressors, just as Maori facial tattoos are in New Zealand. These soccer-playing young Muslim women, who know what Western culture has to offer, and also value their own tradition, are the ones we must hope can help mediate the differences threatening us today. For they surely can speak to both sides, and there are not so many others who can be expected to be qualified enough to be the mediators of peace that we desperately need.

Richard Rorty agreed with Montaigne, Hume, and Judith Shklar that the worst vice is cruelty. Cruelty takes many forms, and exclusion is one of the worst of them. The victims of cruelty can themselves become cruel: New Zealander's knife-wielding hijacker who wounded a pilot had herself suffered humiliation and rape in refugee camps in Kenya. We must include all our possible attackers in our conversations, not exclude any. This is the recipe not for utopia, which neither the US nor New Zealand can expect to offer, but for mere survival. Congratulating ourselves on moral progress is almost obscene, when we have only just begun to recognize some grave dangers. The dangers of ignoring the grievances of those outside our own schemes of cooperation is not new, but we have never really risen to confront it. The danger of environmental destruction is new, and calls for new forms of cooperation.

I have considered two unconnected grave dangers facing us, threatening our very survival: climate change and terrorism. To respond to them we need to put aside blinkered thinking, and exercise some moral imagination. We cannot wait for novelists to help us with these urgent challenges, but philosophers could help. Irony is a luxury we may no longer be able to afford—it is hard to achieve it as one is overwhelmed by rising flood waters. Philosophers of many kinds could help: Kantians can ask if they can will everyone to leave a carbon footprint as large as their own, Humeans can ask what new international artifice might give us the security we now lack, and pragmatists have urgent practical issues to think about. Applied ethics of many kinds have come to flourish since Rorty left Princeton, and catastrophe ethics could be added to their variety. Liberal hope is difficult to sustain, in today's world. Perpetual peace seems a pipe dream, yet, with nuclear weapons in the picture, also necessary for survival. Lifeboat ethics may soon be the only kind there is any scope for, unless somehow we avert the dangers, physical and social, now facing us. Rorty called himself a liberal ironist and an optimist. I am a socialist and a pessimist. Both of us are patriots, both also cosmopolitans, trying "to create a more expansive sense of solidarity than we presently have."[15]

[15] Richard Rorty, "Solidarity," in *Contingency, Irony, and Solidarity*, 196.

5

Why Honesty Is a Hard Virtue

Hume prefaces book 3 of *A Treatise of Human Nature* with a quotation from Lucan exhorting the lover of severe (*durus*) virtue to search for an exemplar of honesty in order to discover what virtue is. Does he himself do much in what follows to tell us what this harsh virtue consists in, or does what follows at most exemplify rather than analyze honesty? The conclusion of the book shows that Hume did think that he had shown brutal honesty rather than engaging guile in his general portrayal of morality: he had presented the bare anatomy of virtue, not draped her agreeably to make us love her. Does he give us a candid discussion or at least an honest sketch of honesty? Honesty includes truthfulness, and meta-truthfulness is particularly hard. "Perhaps nobody yet has been truthful enough about what 'truthfulness' is."[1] How truthful is truthful enough?

The Latin *honestas*, perhaps best translated as "probity," is a broad-ranging virtue, but then so is English honesty. Honesty comprises both veracity, a virtue of speakers, and also uprightness in matters of property. Dishonesty is shown by the liar, by the cheat, by the thief. In the *Treatise* Hume has tried to give us the straight story about theft and fraud. Virtually nothing, however, is said about what is wrong with deceit or lying. In *An Enquiry Concerning the Principles of Morals* both "veracity" and "truth" get included in lists of virtues, truth being singled out as one of the virtues that have complicated sources. The *Treatise* is indeed striking for its failure to analyze the vices of either the

I am very much indebted to Rob Shaver and to Ben Zipursky for ideas explored in this essay—so indebted that I have lost track of exactly which ideas these are. Claudia Card made very helpful comments on the first version, comments that led me to modify many of my original claims and to realize that the concept of one's "true" feelings is much more difficult than I had blithely assumed. I have not fully faced up to these complications even in this revised version. Its baroque complexities, as much as its oversimplifications and repetitions, may be a defense against rethinking that central point. (Am I not truthful enough with myself in this essay?)

[1] Friedrich Nietzsche, *Beyond Good and Evil*, trans. Walter Kaufmann (New York: Vintage Books, 1966), sect. 177.

liar or the murderer, two of the traditional paradigms of moral vice. Hume glances at the liar (T 461[2]) and the parricide (T 446–68) in the negative preliminaries to his theory to show the poverty of the traditional accounts of vice, but in parts 2 and 3, when he is supposedly giving us the true story about the virtues, he ignores the two most familiar exemplars of vice.

In this Hume follows Hobbes, whose laws of nature forbid neither violence nor any form of false speech except covenanting without the intention to keep the covenant, and bearing false witness. The Ten Commandments too limit the prohibition on lying to a prohibition on bearing false witness. Hobbes's only variants of the Sixth Commandment, not to kill, are his first and second laws, requiring us to seek peace and to be willing to disarm ourselves when others are also willing (*Leviathan*, chapters 14 and 15). Hume mentions danger to life and limb from the assault of other persons in his discussion of the circumstances that give rise to the need for government (T 540), but the only threats to life that he mentions when he describes the circumstances of justice are weather and natural accidents (T 485). Nor does he discuss any general obligation or duty to refrain from violence against others. Presumably, magistrates will make some forms of such violence crimes, and respect for the authority of magistrates is an artificial virtue. But for all Hume says about the matter, violence is not vicious until forbidden by magistrates. Charity, clemency (T 578), and humanity (T 603) are, of course, natural virtues, and gentleness is a virtue in masters (T 606). Magistrates will put some limits on the sort and degree of danger to life and limb we can properly impose on others, but in Hume's versions of morality we find no real equivalent of the Sixth Commandment and very little about lying.

The omission of a discussion of moral restraints on violent or murderous human desires is a real weakness in Hume's theory, and one not so easy to patch up for him. Gentleness may be in a sense an easier virtue than honesty, but it is not so easy to know exactly where it ends and the vice of undue non-assertiveness begins, any more than it is to know where honesty in speech ends and brutal frankness begins. Hume's own disposition, which combined gentleness with due self-assertion, may have led him to underestimate the threat of normal human aggression and its need for some redirection or "moral equivalent."

---

[2] References to Hume's texts will be to page numbers in *A Treatise of Human Nature*, ed. L. A. Selby-Bigge, rev. P. H. Nidditch (Oxford: Clarendon Press, 1978) (henceforth T).

What of mendacity? Even if Hume was overoptimistic about the natural-ness of gentleness to human persons, surely he was not unaware of our natural proclivity to deceive. Even if, both as a child and an adult, he found himself subject to no temptations to assault and murder, and so gave too little attention to the social control of aggressive and murderous impulses, it is implausible to suppose that he found no childhood occasions to fib, nor any adult temptations to deceive. So what would a Humean moral theory say about control of the inclination to resort to lying and deceit? Is it harm-less? Hume cheerfully tells us that poets are "liars by profession" (*T* 121), but surely he is not proposing to transfer mendacity to the column of the virtues. There presumably is a vice of mendacity, even if poets' "lies" do not display it. What sort of vice is it? I shall argue that mendacity is an artificial vice not so very different from the other sort of dishonesty that Hume did analyze, the dishonesty that consists in a disposition to take or to keep the property of others. After a Kantian detour I shall eventually propose a unified Humean account of honesty as an artificial virtue. But I shall also argue that there is a virtue (one that Hume calls "truth") whose sources are more complicated, that crosses the natural–artificial boundary and may give us good reason to blur that distinction. In brief, I shall argue that there is a natural tendency to candor in expression of current emotion, a tendency we have every reason to welcome and encourage, but I shall also argue that once we have language, then cover-up and deceit become second-nature abilities. Speech gives us the means for concealment and deceit about what we really think, believe, feel, and want. "Truth," as a virtue of those who have acquired language, is best construed as a regulation of our understandable tendency to use our acquired abilities to conceal and deceive, a tendency and an ability that are themselves superimposed on pre-speech involuntary candor. Candor in an appropriate degree and form will indeed be a virtue with complicated sources, but honesty as veracity will be a bit less complicated to analyze, both because its scope is narrower and because it is more wholly artificial.

Veracity is a virtue of talkers, and to understand it, we need to understand talk and its relation to our other, more primitive means of expression. With non-lying speech we make our fellows aware of states of mind, such as our opinions, which would be well nigh impossible to convey non-verbally even if we suppose that we could acquire them without relying in some way on our linguistic competences. Talk is used to tell others what we tend to think and what we believe, as well as what we want, plan, and intend.

For the latter purposes, non-linguistic indicators sometimes suffice, but if we are to know what our fellows believe about, say the strengths and weaknesses of the government, as distinct from whether they are for or against it, talk or its written equivalent is essential.

Kant, famous for his refusal to condone any lies, also taught that "no man in his true senses is candid." Our own good sense, backed by the will of Providence, directs us, Kant finds, to cultivate "reserve and concealment . . . that the defects of which we are full should not be too obvious."[3] Only Momus, the god of mockery and censure, would want all the contents of human hearts to become open to view. Reserve and reticence are our protection against mockery and censure. Mockery and censure, however, are not the only ills we dread; isolation is also an evil.

Man is a being meant for society (though he is also an unsociable one) and in cultivating social intercourse he feels strongly the need to reveal himself to others (even with no ulterior purpose). But on the other hand, hemmed in and cautioned by fear of the misuse others may make of this disclosure of his thoughts, he finds himself constrained to lock up in himself a good part of his opinions (especially those about other people). He would like to discuss with someone his opinions about his associates, the government, religion, and so forth, but he cannot risk it—partly because the other person, while prudently keeping back his own opinions, might use this to harm him, and partly because, if he revealed his failings while the other person concealed his own, he would lose something of the other's respect by presenting himself quite candidly to him.[4]

Kant thinks that some "exchange of sentiments" with others is required by the duty of humanity, but not at the cost of mutual respect, which apparently would be put at risk by total mutual candor. As he says in the *Lectures on Ethics*, "Fellowship is only the second condition of society."[5] Better, if need be, that we keep our hearts' shutters permanently closed than that we open them so wide in the hopes of fellowship that we sacrifice mutual respect. Mutual respect, it seems, not only is threatened by too much candor but can subsist without any. We are to respect other human persons simply because of their presumed rational personhood, not because we have gotten to know them, talked with them, and *found* them to be rational and worthy

---

[3]   Immanuel Kant, *Lectures on Ethics*, trans. L. Infield (New York: Harper & Row, 1963), 224.

[4]   Immanuel Kant, *Metaphysics of Morals*, trans. M. J. Gregor (New York: Harper & Row), 143 (repr. Cambridge: Cambridge University Press, 1991).   [5]   *Lectures on Ethics*, 224.

of respect. So selective "disclosure" in an occasional "exchange of sentiments" is the most that is required of us to satisfy the duty of humanity. Intimate friendship, with its fuller mutual disclosure, is permissible but risky, and its moral gains are not so great. "Friendship develops the minor virtues of life."[6] Better, it seems, for a man to risk regrettable isolation and be "*alone* with his thoughts, as in a prison" than for us to "place ourselves in a friend's hands completely, to tell him all the secrets that might detract from our welfare if he became our enemy and spread them abroad."[7]

In all of these homiletic pronouncements, Kant assumes that it is within our power to keep our thoughts and sentiments "locked up" in the secrecy of our own hearts. There may be both a natural impulse and a duty to some "disclosure," but disclosure is what it will be, a making public of what is inherently private. Yet Kant's metaphors of shutters, prison rooms, and locks invite the question of who or what made the shutters, the locks, and the fortress prisons that shut each man up within himself, alone with his own sentiments. If indeed, as Kant says in the *Metaphysics of Morals*, when we occasionally get out of our solitary confinement with our own sentiments, we "enjoy a freedom" rather than suffer from agoraphobia, then the solitary confinement itself must be contrived, not altogether natural to us. Shame, fear of mockery and hurt, and a wish to retain respect are what make us *want* to shut ourselves away from others, on his story, but what is it that enables us to do this when we wish to? Kant seems to assume that reserve, restraint in expressing one's mind, is the easiest thing in the world. We need merely keep quiet and then no one will get to know our possibly shameful thoughts. And we need do nothing in order to keep quiet.

But Kant knows that this is not so, at least for half of us. He remarks in the *Lectures on Ethics* that

the person who is silent as a mute goes to one extreme; the person who is loquacious goes to the opposite. . . . Men are liable to the first, women are talkative because the training of infants is their special charge, and their talkativeness soon teaches children to speak, because they can chatter to it all day long. If men had the care of children, they would take much longer to learn to talk.[8]

Women, as Kant understands them, do not shut themselves up in themselves but open their minds at least to the children in their care, and presumably

---

[6] Ibid. 209.   [7] *Metaphysics of Morals*, 144; *Lectures on Ethics*, 208.   [8] *Lectures on Ethics*, 226.

both male and female children may come to "chatter to it all day long," like their mothers and nursemaids, until shame, caution, and male dignity teach the boys to censor their utterances. "Loquaciousness in men is contemptible, and contrary to the strength of the male."[9]

So should the "shutters," "locks," and "prison walls" that enclose a person, shut him in with his own thoughts, be seen as the result of a sort of enclosure of what was in childhood more open, more automatically expressed to those around him? Those who follow Plato and Ryle in seeing thought as silent speech, so that speech proper becomes the natural expression of thought, thought liberated back into its own home range, postulate a time in childhood when all our thought was "thinking out loud," when "candid avowal" of our state of mind came naturally. We might combine this view with Kant's and suppose that it is mainly the boys who somehow learn silent thought. (They might first think aloud something like this: "Maybe I'd get into less trouble if my thoughts were less noisy. Let me see if I can have the next one under my breath." Or they might imitate their strong, silent fathers, who will be models of *sub voce* thought.) The girls will not be encouraged to lose the habit of constant chatter, for that habit will prove functional once they become childminders. By this graft onto Kant's theory we could accommodate both Kant's conviction that reticence is second nature to sensible (and well brought up) men and his realization that this sensible reticence is also a "prison," occasional escape from which counts as freedom.

But *is* it plausible to suppose that mothers and the children learning to talk from their chatter are all engaged in candid verbal communication of states of mind? A lot of mothers' "chatter" to the children will usually consist in songs, nonsense rhymes, nursery rhymes, fairy stories, white lies about birth, sex, and death, whitewashed versions of family and national history, attempted cover-ups of parental quarrels, utopian ideals of sibling love, and so on. If a child does engage for a time in candid talk, that will not be because the child has learned candid talk by example, if to speak candidly is to tell the truth and the whole truth as one sees it, to ask all and only what one wants to know, to try to utter all one's real and full wishes, all one's true and uncensored feelings. Talk, as we teach and learn it, has many uses. It is not unrelievedly serious—it is often an extension of play and fun, of games of hide and seek, of peekaboo, where deceit is expected and enjoyed, of games of Simon says,

---

[9] *Lectures on Ethics*, 226.

where orders are given to be disobeyed, of games of tag, where words have magic power, of skipping games, where words are an incantation. Speech, as we teach and learn it, is not just the vehicle of cool rational thought and practical reason but also of fun and games and of anger, mutual attack, domination, coercion, and bullying. It gives us a voice for our many moods, for deceit and sly strategy, as well as for love and tenderness, humor, play and frolic, mystery and magic. The child is initiated into all of this and gradually learns all the arts and moods of speech. Among these are the arts of misleading others, either briefly and with the intent soon to put them straight again ("I fooled you, didn't I!") or more lastingly to keep deceit going for more questionably acceptable purposes. If loquacious women are the ones who transmit the arts of speech, and their verbal arts are the arts that are transmitted, then in all honesty we should add guile to loquaciousness as the imitable attributes of those entrusted with transmitting them. Nietzsche said, "From the very first nothing is more foreign, more repugnant, or more hostile to woman than truth—her great art is falsehood."[10] If there is some truth in this, then the arts of speech that are transmitted to children are guileful arts: they empower the natural will to the guile that is an integral part of many infantile games and extend the power to demand, to coerce, and to protect and defend oneself. The constant chatter in the nursery need not always be candid chatter, unless shameless guile can count as a form of candor (as perhaps it can, but it also counts as a form of harmless and temporary deceit).

Speech enormously increases our ability to mislead others, at least for a while. Our ability to mislead is coextensive with our ability to pretend, to put on a convincing show. Pretense becomes false pretense when guided by the intent to seriously mislead rather than the intent simply to participate in a game of "let's pretend," where all concerned are led into imaginary states of affairs, so no one is misled (or if one is carried away by the game, one is as much misled by oneself as misled by others). We all have pretty good ability at pretense of intentions and feelings that we do not really have, an ability honed by all the playing we did in childhood. By the time we learn to talk, we are already actors, and speech merely increases the means we have for pretending to be in those situations and states we choose to enact, or to try on for size.

What speech adds is the ability to pretend to *beliefs*. Intentions, feelings, and some desires can be acted out without speech, but beliefs can only be

---

[10] *Beyond Good and Evil*, sect. 232.

indirectly faked before we have speech as the vehicle of pretense. What speech does is enable us to directly communicate, truly or falsely, what it is that we take to be the case, to say straight out what without speech we could only indirectly indicate. Speech enables us to tell the truth and to lie, to make public and to cover up what, without speech, had to remain only inferred from the version of our intentions and our feelings that was made public. For these latter naturally do tend to get expressed and do not depend upon speech for their communication.

Darwin's classic *Expression of Emotions in Man and Animals* (1872) explores the means by which our emotions and associated desires get expressed and recognized by our fellows. Both the expression and its recognition are universal and unlearned. What we learn, and learn variously, is when and how to inhibit natural expression, to try to fake it, or to replace or supplement it with culturally variant gestures and with speech. This universal body language, the language of eyes, face muscles, shoulders, and hands, of cries and voice quality, expresses primarily emotions along with associated desires and intentions. Candor about our emotions comes naturally to us, since reticence and faking take effort and training. But there is no such thing as natural candor in respect of the beliefs that inform our expressed emotions, desires, and intentions. Until we learn to speak, we cannot express our beliefs, and even after we have learned to speak, we may still not yet have learned candid avowal of what we believe. For our "true beliefs" do not automatically distinguish themselves from our self-deceptions and our fantasies in the way in which our true emotions make or made themselves evident. (For those, like women, whose duty it was to smile and be pleased by their masters, true spontaneous emotions may be a distant memory and acquired factitious ones the norm.) Our true emotions are the ones that express themselves without our trying to express them, without control. But there are no such "true" beliefs, since the only vehicle for the expression of belief is a learned language and self-controlled sentences. Everything we say is what we choose to say, but very little that we show in our eyes is what we choose to show. Even when we blurt out words and give away secrets, what we blurt and let out are will-mediated forms of expression, sentences we form, and learned to form, in a way we never form or learned to form a lighting up of the eyes in welcome, or the glazed look of boredom. Our natural non-verbal expression of emotion often gives us away, but what our blurted-out sentences give away are only our artifacts, sentences we accept as adequate representations of what we believe. Our control over speech is unlike our control over body language in that the latter is primarily the acquired ability to inhibit and to fake, the former the acquired ability to produce the real thing. Once we are speakers, of course, speech becomes second nature to us, and the chatterers may have to learn to inhibit their second-nature loquaciousness. But beliefs, requiring speech for their most direct expression, will still get controlled expression even in what Ryle called the most "unbuttoned" talk. Normally, we select which beliefs to express and how to express them. And unless we select them, they stay unexpressed. This is not the case with our emotions. They may remain without *verbal* expression unless we select them for attempted articulation, but they do not stay unexpressed. Expression is the norm for emotions, the exception for beliefs. Even with the greatest possible will to candor, we would be hard put to express our version of "the whole truth" on any matter, let alone to express "everything we believe" at any one time. Our beliefs must outrun their expression, but our emotions, desires, and intentions need not. They usually *do* outrun their expression, especially if we have long-term intentions and desires for goods in the distant future, but they do not outrun expression as inevitably as our thoughts do.

Both reticence and deceit concerning our beliefs, then, are quite different from reticence and attempted deceit about our emotions, intentions, and desires. For one thing, the chances of success are much greater, since what we say we believe does not, to be credible, have to square with what we otherwise directly show we believe in the way that what we say or refuse to say we feel has to square with what we more reliably show we feel. Even lie detection by polygraphs depends not on a perceived misfit between what is said and what is shown to be believed but only on revealed discomfort during the saying of it or a misfit between *actual intention* (to deceive) and *apparent intention* (to speak the truth). Bare-faced lying about one's beliefs can be carried off much more easily than bare-faced lying about one's emotions, since the face is naturally bare when it comes to beliefs. A bare face *is* the face for cool fact reporting. It is bare of the expressions faces have evolved to have: shock, delight, disgust, horror, amazement, fear, tenderness, anger. Faces can, of course, also show disbelief of what others are saying, and there are pious believing faces put on while reciting some credo, but ordinary facts are parlayed without expression. When we try to conceal or feign any expressive face, we not only have to *produce* some suitable expression, verbal or non-verbal, we also have to inhibit the spontaneous expression of what we really feel. Since there is no spontaneous expression of ordinary belief states, there is at least nothing to suppress, only something to produce, when we try to conceal or deceive others about our matter-of-fact beliefs. The only suppression needed will be of guilt or anxiety, if we feel it. Glib liars and those practiced at cover-ups will not feel it and so will have nothing to suppress. Since all talk is second- and not first-nature and since reporting talk has no natural belief expression constraining it, lies and silent closure can come as naturally to human lips as, truths, as far as factual beliefs go. Factual truth is no more the telos of speech than fairy tales are.

I have been arguing that there is neither a natural urge to accurate reporting of what we take to be the case, nor any natural prelinguistic constraint on our powers to use words to deceive and conceal our belief states, but that our natural, spontaneous non-linguistic expression of emotion does put constraints on our ability to deceive about what we feel. Our thoughts and beliefs are "shut up" within us, unless we choose to let them out, in a way our emotions and sentiments are not. So Kant was half right: right about thoughts, wrong about emotions. What is more, our experience of natural candor in our emotional life, along with the involvement of thought in emotions, explains why it may feel like liberation to share our thoughts as well as our feelings. Candor becomes an understandable ideal for us, since we are in a position to feel nostalgia for the candor we had before we learned the concealing and complicating arts of speech, and we might hope for conditions in which we can extend to belief states the candor that is present, unless we inhibit it, for emotional states. Candor is natural for feelings, but Kant is right in seeing controlled expression or silence as quite natural for thoughts.

Darwin emphasized the mutual advantage there is in the mutual awareness we have of each other's changing emotions, through their natural expression. We need to keep up to date with what our neighbors feel and intend, to adapt our activities to theirs, both to take advantage of their good will and to protect ourselves against any ill will. Do we not need for the same reasons to keep up to date with what they are thinking and what they take to be the case? Often we can infer that from communicated emotion, but much that they currently think and believe will not inform any currently expressed emotion. However, if we share the same environment and have the same sense organs, we can usually assume that our fellows' belief states will largely duplicate our own, so we will not need any "readout" of their belief states in the way we do need a readout on their individual emotion and intention states. We can often fairly safely assume that most knowledge is common knowledge. (It is significant that we have no parallel concept of "common emotion," nor of "common intention.") So we can often assume that our fellows believe what we believe: their opportunities for special knowledge will not be so frequent. But occasionally we will want to find out what they have done in our absence or have found out that we could not find out, and so truth-telling will then be welcome. For there will be no other way that we can tell what our fellows know or believe except by their telling us and our accepting what they tell us. The twin virtues of veracity and due credulity are the virtues needed when it matters to our fellows what we personally know or believe on a given question and where our fellows have some sort of need and right to find that out. These virtues, I want to suggest, are highly "artificial," in Hume's sense. They presuppose agreement on what rights we have to a kind of knowledge that is not automatic, to mutual knowledge of one another's cognitive states. The honesty of virtuous truth-telling, and with it due trust in what others say, is at least as convention-dependent as the honesty of respect for others' property, along with proper trust in others' honesty. Honest speech is a special case of respect for rights; namely, respect for another person's right to occasional access to one's own naturally private states of mind. This is as complex a right as the right to have a debt paid. It is the right to get from another what is currently in their secure possession.

Among the circumstances of justice that Hume lists are limited generosity with scarce goods, and prior experience of the benefits of conformity to agreed rules regulating the distribution of scarce goods. Hume thought that our childhood experience of family life gives us this knowledge that recognition of rights (or protorights) can improve life for all. The recognition that occurs in the family is spontaneous and needs no conventions. Are rights to know, to share knowledge, also spontaneously recognized in the natural family? Hume himself emphasized that between friends and between loving parent and trusting child there can be total openness, complete candor, when a "being like ourselves . . . communicates to us all the actions of his mind, makes us privy to his inmost sentiments and affections, and lets us see in the very instant of their production, all the emotions that are caused by any object" (*T* 353). This is candor about sentiments, affections, and emotions, and so about such thoughts and beliefs as are implied by these. It is not candor about beliefs as such. Nor is there any implication that it is specifically verbal candor. Presumably, the acquisition of language does usually occur in such an intimate circle, so verbal candor may be included in the mutual mind-sharing of intimates that Hume describes. But if what I have argued is correct, it cannot be so total. "All the emotions" one feels one may well express to an intimate, but what would it be to communicate all one's thoughts? The "actions of the mind" involved in belief, as Hume himself had analyzed them in book 1, include all its past actions as remembered and as influencing current associations. Even if one wanted to, one could not put all of that into words; one would have to be constantly condensing and expressing and updating one's intellectual autobiography. Even on a specific "limited" topic, say what one now believes about the character of a mutual acquaintance, one's beliefs outrun one's ability to confide them. Time constraints alone ensure that. One *cannot* make others privy to all one has learned and all that feeds into one's belief on any one topic. The only way others would be privy to that is by sharing one's life path, along with one's interests, and so by having had the same experience. So candor about belief is always limited. It is not so much that we *dare* not, as Kant suggested, as that we *cannot* tell the whole truth about our thoughts and beliefs even on any one topic. We can try to give truthful answers to specific questions when cross-examined. We can relax watchful internal censorship when talking to friends, but even then we cannot "let it all hang out"; there just is far too much of it. If I accept the offer of "a penny for your thoughts," I still must select which ones to give you and may deceive myself as much as you as to which were in the foreground of my attention. If I try to deceive others about my current feelings, I may or may not be caught out. If I deceive myself about my current feelings, others will soon put me straight: they may well recognize my irritation for what it is more readily than I do. But if I deceive myself about the focus of my mental attention, it will not be easy for others to correct me. For others have no access to my current thoughts except what I choose to give them, and if I am deceived, then even when I speak frankly, I may speak falsely. The truth about one's beliefs is not so accessible to oneself or to others as one's current feelings. (Even if they are to some extent artificial, cultivated by cultural pressure, they may still be truly felt on a given occasion.)

So what is it that we expect of the person with the virtue of veracity? How is the virtue of truth-telling possible? Our best way to understand it, I suggest, is as a form of the artificial virtue of being true to an understanding, often to one's word. Just as one has to *give* one's word, to renounce a natural liberty to adapt one's intentions to changing desires or circumstances, in order to be in a position to be true or false to one's word, so there must be a certain understood renunciation of one's normal liberty to use speech for any of its normal purposes, including harmless or strategic deceit and concealment, for veracity or the lack of it to be a possibility. When we are under oath or oath equivalent, the truth is expected of us. It takes a certain solemnity of occasion for anything to count as a lie. If you ask me, "How are you?" and I reply, "Fine thanks, and you?" although in fact I take myself to be far from fine, I have not lied. Even a white lie requires a more seriously fact-finding context than that. To respond to the casual greeting "How are you?" with a detailed accurate account of one's troubles is not to be veracious but to tell what one might call "black truths," unwanted, inappropriate revelations. It is to fail to have proper reticence. Whereas Kant sees reticence as primarily a self-protective necessity, a protection against public shame and mockery, on the Humean alternative I am suggesting, it should rather be seen as a form of consideration for others, a protection of them from undue embarrassment, boredom, or occasion for pity. Truth, let alone "the whole truth," is something we very rarely want told to us. We prefer to see it or ignore it for ourselves, to select for ourselves which truths to attend to. Children have a quite natural and proper resistance to the sort of schooling that consists in being sat down and *told* things purveyed as truths. Teachers in that sort of school system are professional truth-tellers, but that does not make veracity their professional virtue. For veracity is knowing *when* one is bound to speak one's mind and then speaking it as best one can. Even then, fallible judgment will be involved, snap decisions concerning how most helpfully to speak it, what sentences to produce.

As it takes special circumstances for promise-breaking to be a theoretical option for us, so it takes special circumstances for us to have an occasion when a lie is possible. One such circumstance is when we are "put on the mat," or in the witness box, under oath. Lying is then always tantamount to a form of perjury. Other circumstances of veracity are the cases where there is a clear but informal mutual understanding that truth is expected. Unless we understand what it is to have such an understanding or to have made a solemn undertaking, then whatever counter-to-fact things we say will count merely as polite conversation, "just kidding," fictional narrative, reconstruction of the past, or imaginative play. Children with vivid imaginations often have difficulty recognizing where play ends and "real life" begins. They learn the truth-telling game usually through being accused of lying. The solemn or angry faces of their accusers teach them the limits of the freedom to protect and to pretend, limits that they need not have realized from any exemplary behavior on the part of the adults who now accuse them. (Children are not expected to call adults liars, even when they come to disbelieve the stories those adults tell them about Santa Claus, storks, heavenly homes where grandparents have gone to, and so on.) Learning what counts as a lie is like learning what counts as a debt or a broken promise. Complex rules are involved, and fairly subtle contextual clues have to be picked up. It is not just a matter of telling a serious or solemn face from a merry one, for serious and solemn faces are often assumed in games. It is a matter of telling real solemnity from pretend solemnity, the rules of real life from the rules of the games that partially fill it. This is a matter of coming to recognize what authority can overrule other more limited authorities, what concerns can preempt other concerns. It is not that real life in adult society is structured by an overarching will to have only the truth spoken; it is rather that for our multiple uses of speech to go well, we need to be fairly confident of at least some of one another's intentions, and this may lead to an occasional check on beliefs, and so to inquisitions, cross-examinations aimed at verbal revelation of states of mind. We assume that if any statement of intent can be relied on, that made in a vow can, in part because it incorporates acceptance of a conditional threat. So we take it that if a person has vowed to tell the truth, she is more likely to do so than if she had not so vowed. Of course, if the vow is made without any conviction, as with "so help me God" spoken by the atheist, then it will be ineffective: a lying promise not to lie will scarcely ward off lies. But we do the best we can and use what verbal and other magic we hope works best.

If it is harder to deceive about intentions and feelings than about beliefs, because the former are expressed in non-linguistic as well as linguistic ways, then it is understandable that we bootstrap our way to reliable communication to belief via the more reliable communication of feeling and intent. We bully others into swearing to tell the truth, trusting their solemn oath in part because they trust our threat to punish oath-breakers. They must tell the truth to carry out their expressed agreement and must keep their agreement if they are to avoid the threats we convincingly make. Or we lure others into truthful confidences with expressions of assurance of love and reciprocal candor. We use the more secure reliability of expressed feelings and immediate intentions to secure the reliability of expressions of belief when it matters enough to us that they not be false. The truth of what we say and tell piggybacks on the truth of what we show in other ways.

The obligation not to lie, as I have construed it, is conditional on a clear understanding that the truth is then to be spoken. A lie is false pretenses, an untruth where truth was offered, perhaps even promised. But we are under no permanent duty to deliver the truth about our states of mind to others, and it would be an intolerably inquisition-prone society that would force us to take on such a duty, say by a promise. It would bring the artifice of promise into disrepute for it to be so employed, and truth-telling would share in the degradation. If revelation of our states of mind on request were a duty, voluntarily offering them to selected intimates would lose value, we would come to offer our best deceits, rather than our "confidences," as free gifts for our friends. We would then perhaps dare to conceal our states of mind from them in ways too risky with others, engage in a sort of intimate mental game of hide and seek. In our actual society, which does tend to find implicit vows all over the place and to deceive itself about its will to truthful disclosure, our special relations with our intimates are probably a mix of these two extremes: some candid confidences are reserved just for them, and some special cover-ups are also kept for them alone, covers that are not expected really to conceal but rather to drape agreeably or to tantalize a little, to create some pretend mystery. It is not, after all, just anyone that we would bother deceiving or bother going through the motions of deceiving.

Information about some of others' states of mind is something we get used to having, because when those states are emotional states, they are spontaneously expressed to us. It is understandable that we want more than we easily get: we sometimes want to know our fellows' cognitive states as well as their emotional and conative states. So we sometimes try to get that information, by quizzing and cross-examining them. We meet with proper resistance, and language, the medium of the asking and the answering, is a wonderful screen and camouflage. It enables us to mislead nosy people, to mislead them about our cognitive states and sometimes about some of our emotional states too. Outwitting becomes the name of the game, but success in it is hard to recognize, especially if we take ourselves in. "Lively natures lie only for a moment: immediately afterwards they lie to themselves and are convinced and honest."[11] Is this success or failure at the outwitting game?

Kant in his ethics links the wrong of lying very closely with that of promise-breaking. To lie is to break an implicit agreement to speak only the truth, an agreement that he takes to be made in the very act of speaking at all. To make an explicit promise, then, will be to make a lying promise if the will to keep it is not firm. On this theory, we make ourselves retrospectively into liars whenever we break a promise, and we make ourselves into prom-ise-breakers whenever we lie. I have accepted the close Kantian link between speaking the truth and being true to a mutual understanding, perhaps to one's word, but have resisted the suggestion that this understanding is in permanent effect, that the telos of speech is disclosure. On the contrary, its special contributions are to make storytelling possible and to give us the means of superior camouflage of what *is* naturally disclosed, namely our current emotions. Still, there are occasions when that special speech artifact, the oath, is used to commit a speaker to truth-telling. On those solemn occasions the point of speech becomes disclosure, and truth-telling becomes a solemn duty. But these occasions are rare, and rightly kept rare. At the other extreme from the cases where lying amounts to perjury are the cases where it amounts to treachery, where what one's false words make one false to is not some formal or quasi-formal vow to tell the truth but rather to a personal loyalty, an understanding with friends or comrades. In such close associations there is an expectation not just of truthful responses in serious talk but also of some freely offered disclosure of known facts and of thoughts. We expect more candor of our friends than of strangers, not just in the form of less inhibited expression of feeling but also in the form of shared thoughts, shared knowledge, shared opinions. If in the guise of offering voluntary disclosure, making the gift of greater candor, one in fact offers deceitful words, then one is not merely a liar but a false friend. One's false words in this context make one false not so much to one's word (unless one has taken a vow of friendship) as to something more fundamental than one's word—to one's trusted gestures of friendship. It is one's open arms and open face, the show of friendship, that is false. False confidences are like gifts of poisoned

[11] Friedrich Nietzsche, *Daybreak*, trans. R. J. Hollingdale (Cambridge: Cambridge University Press, 1982), sect. 391.

chocolates: the lie, that which harms or violates the other's right, is masked as a special treat to a special person, and one that is trustingly accepted only because of the special relationship. Between these two extremes of answering under oath and free offerings to friends lie all the cases where misinforming is disappointing a reasonable expectation and so, unless one has a good excuse, malicious and wrong. It may be a breach of a special professional responsibility voluntarily entered into. Scientists publishing faked data, reporters making up the news, bureaucrats falsifying official records, all clearly fail to deliver the goods it is their job to deliver—the facts as they know them. But it is a bit harder to say what we demand in the way of truth in medical care of the dying, in advertising, in sermons, in editorials, in politicians' speeches, in bargaining, in high school (or for that matter, in college) teaching, or in philosophy essays. (Could I be lying in this essay?) Saying what one does not oneself believe is sometimes a breach of one's professional responsibilities, but it can also become a professional responsibility (in a defense lawyer, in an official spokesperson, maybe in a national leader in times of national danger—"We shall never surrender").

Knowingly false or misleading statements made in contexts where those statements are tantamount to neither perjury, treachery, malice, nor breach of professional responsibility are not lies but normal purposeful talk, verbal ploys made to others who understand the games we speakers play and realize that inquisition, informing, reportage, mutual revelation are only a few of our many forms of talk, all structured by rough mutual understandings and mutual acceptance of multiple purposes of talk. It takes rather special contexts for veracity to be a possibility, more special ones for it to be obligatory, and even more special contexts for verbal *candor* to be welcome. The *Oxford English Dictionary* tells us that candor in its oldest sense is "dazzling whiteness," and we tend to shield ourselves from what dazzles. To have candor is for one's mind to show itself with a pure white light, to kindle or candle in others an awareness of one's own total mental state. As Kant recognized, it is less discriminating than veracity. It is more than sincerity, since sincerity can coexist with reticence. The *OED* cites Johnson's 1751 use: "He was sincere, but without candour." Johnson, in his dictionary, notes the Latin etymology (which links candor with candy), then gives this entry: "sweetness of temper, purity of mind, openness, ingenuity, kindliness." The sweetness seems an accidental addition to the whiteness. It may, however, take a certain sweetness, trust, and innocence of temper to be willing to open one's mind freely to others, so that the person with aggressive intentions will sensibly avoid candor. In principle, but rarely in practice, could we be as candid about schemes to harm others as about our good intentions. The Darwinian story, which makes non-verbal candor come naturally to us, makes the evolutionary point of natural expression lie as much in "fair warning" of evil intentions as in reassurance of sweetness and light. Were candor a virtue, its circumstances would be a need to adapt to others' intentions, along with the unlikelihood of successful deceit. Once we have language, we are not in these circumstances. Our deceiving tongues combine with our grabbing hands to create the circumstances of the virtue we *do* recognize, namely honesty, a willingness to let others have some of what we might have seized from them, and some knowledge of what we might have concealed from them. In both cases complex conventions tell us exactly what others have a right to in what specific conditions. Honesty in both its main forms is an artificial virtue. As a virtue of speakers, it is indeed an artificial virtue needed to regulate the workings of what is itself an artifice, natural language. Honesty regulates the mutual deceit that language makes possible by allowing language occasionally to work with, not against, natural expression, to reveal rather than conceal states of mind.

The honesty of veracity is more like the second artificial virtue that Hume discusses in the *Treatise* than it is like the first. The first was willingness to accept and respect rules fixing individual possession, to put a stop to the insecurity and instability of possession of scarce goods. Hume construes this agreement as one that created property rights that were not yet rights to voluntary transfer but rights only to entailed property, as it were. Each gets something and can keep it to himself, but as what each gets depends very much on chance, "persons and possessions must often be very ill-adjusted. . . . The rules of justice seek some medium between a rigid stability and this changeable and uncertain adjustment" (*T* 514). In the state of nature there was uncertain adjustment when each simply tried to grab what he thought he needed. Transfer by consent is the medium that restores to possessions some of their previous mobility, but without the violence and insecurity that property rights were invented to cure. Orderly voluntary exchange of property is the civilized replacement of the state of nature, a state where everyone tried "to seize by violence what he judges fit for him." The second artifice restores the human condition to something closer to the state of nature than the hypothetical condition of "rigid stability" existing after the first artifice. If we adapt this highly artificial story of a sequence of agreed artifices, the later correcting the excesses of the earlier, from property rules to language rules (encouraged by Hume's own analogy at *T* 490, between conventions "fixing" private possession and conventions "fixing" word meanings), then we can see the acquisition of language as bringing as great a change to human life as the acquisition of the first property rights and as bringing as dubious an advantage, the advantage of denying others access to what earlier they might have had access to. Now each can fence off and enclose something as all her own, her own property, her own thoughts, posting No Admittance signs and setting traps for would-be trespassers. There will still be some unenclosed "commons": we may still be free to grab what fresh air we can, what rainwater we can. Similarly, we may still have some access to the states of mind of others. The arts of language, while giving us thoughts we can keep to ourselves, may not give us the ability fully to camouflage the natural expression of our emotions, so we will not be able to stop sometimes giving ourselves away. Just as unprevented trans- fers of air and water from one owner's place to another will still occur, which reminds the right-holders of the old natural instability, so unpre- vented expression will still occur, which reminds the wily speakers of the lost candor of pre-speech communication. And as the disadvantages of the new ways become evident to all, some medium will be sought between old and new ways, some reform that will enable us to keep what was advanta- geous in the old ways without losing the powers that the new ways have given us. Hume presents "transfer by consent" as such an additional artifice, one enabling property owners to make gifts and exchanges, to transfer and trade their rights. We have no special word for the honesty that shows itself in completing agreed transfers, as distinct from refraining from trying to transfer what there has been no agreement to transfer, and Hume simply uses "justice" to cover both. He has a special word, "fidelity," for completing those agreements to transfer that take the special form of promises or contracts, and we might extend this to cover respect for any agreement, whether or not secured and solemnized in the way promises are. If we did this, then we could say that veracity is parallel to fidelity in that each consists in conformity to an artifice that counteracts the effects of a previous artifice and does this by a social agreement giving force to individual agreements, to acts of consent and of vow, enabling them to create new obligations and new rights. Whereas the effect of the new virtue of fidelity is to restore some beneficial *instability* to private possession of "external" goods, the effect of the invention of the virtue of veracity will be to restore not so much mobility as some publicity to what language had enabled us to make into private possessions, namely our states of mind.

At the start of his account of the artificial virtues, when Hume describes the circumstances that give their invention some point, he lists

three species of goods we are possess'd of; the internal satisfactions of our mind, the external advantages of our body, and the enjoyment of such possessions as we have acquired by our industry and good fortune. We are perfectly secure of the first. The second may be ravish'd from us, but can be of no advantage to him who deprives us of them. The last only are both expos'd to the violence of others, and may be transferr'd without suffering any loss or alteration; while at the same time there is not a sufficient supply of them to supply everyone's desires and necessities. (*T* 487–8)

Are our states of mind goods (or ills) of the first sort, perfectly secure? Some of them, our cognitive states, may be possessions like the third sort, "acquired by our industry and good fortune," and they can in a sense be transferred to others without alteration and be of advantage to them. The alteration they will undergo if "transferred" will be from private to public, from secret to shared knowledge, and that may be an alteration significant to their value to the original possessor. That is why it may take a "ravishing" to get that knowledge. But once the knowledge is "transferred," it is not *lost*, even if it is devalued, to the one from whom it was taken. In Ben Zipursky's term, it is "replicated" and strictly not transferred at all.[12] It comes to be in a "place" it was not before, but not by leaving the place it was in. It becomes less scarce by becoming fertile. Knowledge can be and come to be in many places at once and does not always have to be exclusively possessed to be valuable. Hume's division of goods ignores those privately possessed goods that can replicate without thereby devaluing themselves, and it altogether ignores public goods, ones available as easily to many as to one. We can either regard knowledge of an individual's state of mind as a fertile private good, one that can be "spread" to others without being lost to its original possessor, or as a possible public good. Naturally expressed emotions provide public and common knowledge, and awareness of this sort of state of mind is best

---

[12] Ben Zipursky, "Objectivity and Linguistic Practice," Ph.D. diss. (University of Pittsburgh, 1987). Zipursky is a legal scholar, specializing in the law of tort, but he began as a philosopher of language.

treated as a (perhaps impure) public good. An individual's conscious knowledge is a replicable private good. It is fairly "secure" in any possessor of it in that it would take memory-destroying interference to take it from a knower, but it is not perfectly securely kept from others. Hume divides the private goods he considers by cross-cutting criteria: degree of security from loss by seizure, degree of "externality" from the possessor, degree of scarcity (demand in excess of supply). He assumes that mental states are all internal and that only the most external of goods can be transferred "without suffering loss or alteration." Both assumptions are false. Emotional states are as external as they are internal, as much a matter of the eyes as of the brain. Awareness of them is internal, but both it and awareness of an individual's cognitive states can be transferred (in the weak sense that does not imply their ceasing to be where they were) without suffering any loss or alteration except loss of secrecy, an alteration from being private to becoming more public. Whether that alteration is of consequence will depend upon other factors.

In conditions where the dominant game is mutual deceit and outwitting, secrecy and non-replication of many cognitive states will be valued. We will *want* others to share with us at least knowledge of the language we speak, since we can outwit them better with a common language than we could without one, but much other information that we have we will prefer to keep to ourselves, since keeping it from others may give us competitive advantage. Veracity as an artificial virtue requires us sometimes to replicate what we might have kept infertile, to make public what could have been private and exclusive. It creates a duty to increase supply, to tackle scarcity not just by a distributive scheme but by a distribution of duties to allow the scarce goods to replicate themselves.

Hume's initial account of the advantage of social cooperation in adoption of agreed rights and duties was that thereby three "inconveniences" of the hypothetical state of nature would be remedied: insufficiency of power, insufficiency of ability, and lack of security against "fortune and accident." "By the conjunction of forces our power is augmented: By the partition of employments, our ability encreases: And by mutual succour we are less exposed to fortune and accidents" (*T* 481). The odd thing about the first artifice he describes, recognition of individual rights to fixed possession, is that the only "conjunction" of forces it involves is the conjunction of all right-holders in recognition of the distribution of property rights, the only "partition of employments" whatever might accidentally follow from the fact that different employments might be needed to make the best of different initial lots. Until there is the right to exchange, there will be no impetus to the partition of employments. Clearly Hume does think that when rights to trade and to have contracts kept are added to property rights, increase of goods will in fact occur. The need for the artifice of government is said to arise "long after the first generation" of property owners and only when the first three artifices (property, transfer by consent, promise) have led to "an encrease of riches and possessions" (*T* 541). No particular artifice is directed at facilitating this increase: the artifices Hume describes are all concerned with allocation of what is already somehow there. However, point of social coordination is not just security of possession but decrease of scarcity through conjunction of forces and partition of employment. If we are to adapt Hume's account to cover the immaterial goods of information and intelligence, it seems pretty clear that the role of "conjunction of forces" will not be restricted to conjoining to protect rights to private exclusive possession or to transfer by consent (let increase take care of itself) but will include conjoining forces and perhaps partitioning employment to *increase* available information, to pool and replicate individual knowledge states. (Hume's later interests in the cultural impact of the printing press and in freedom of the press of course acknowledge this.) Although it takes no cultural contrivance for there to be some sharing and replication of awareness of emotional and intention states, knowledge and belief states are directly replicable only through the cultural contrivance of language, which is as good at preventing as at facilitating replication. It will take normative rules to introduce a sharing of knowledge states, to allow them to replicate. Veracity is respect for those rules, giving others a right of access to what we are in a position to block access to. As rules of property regulate without completely immobilizing our grabbing hands, so rules of truthfulness regulate our wily, secretive, deceitful tongues without outlawing all deceit. Veracity is the just or adjusted medium between the natural candor and easy access of pre-speech states of mind and the natural secrecy and deceit of human speakers.

Kant is by no means the only philosopher who takes there to be the opposite presumption, the presumption that if we speak at all, we naturally speak the truth. Those who link thought itself very closely to language as its vehicle take the first thinking to be thinking aloud and "candid avowal" of thoughts to be an ever present possibility, a simple lifting of the acquired inhibition of the vocal chords. On such a view, the only artifice that truth-telling requires will be that of language itself. Speaking deceitfully will be "unnatural" in a way that speaking truthfully is not. David Gauthier postulates, in those who are to bargain their way into a morality, a natural "translucency" to one another, an incapacity for sustained deceit.[13] If what I have said in this essay has any truth in it, then all these philosophers are deceiving themselves about our capacity for deceit. "Translucency," for those who have acquired language, takes some social and moral contrivance and will be only intermittent. Only if we can *already* keep agreements are we likely to speak the truth (as we see it) about what we know. Veracity cannot be supposed to be already in place before we can expect to have fidelity to mutual understandings. Veracity is part of the artificial virtue of honesty, not part of its "natural" foundation. The foundation, I have suggested, is an inevitable degree of non-verbal candor about current emotion and immediate intention states, combined with a natural reticence about belief states and a tempting verbal capacity for both benign and less benign deceit. The circumstances of veracity include the ability and the temptation to deceive along with prior experience of the advantages to be gained from some reliable mutual expression (of immediate intentions and emotions) and of our proven capacity for some mutual trust and mutual coordination.

Veracity is a form of the artificial virtue of honesty, a virtue consisting in conformity to conventions allocating rights, in this case rights to get straight answers to questions one has a right in certain circumstances to pose. Hume lists truth as a virtue, as well as veracity, and seems to mean it to include a *natural* virtue shown by friends and lovers who are true to one another in more than verbal or verbally mediated ways. "Truth: see also troth," says the *Oxford English Dictionary*. There is even an obsolete verb "to truth," which was to trust. The first senses of "truth" and "true" that the *OED* gives are "truth" and "true" as applied to persons, "truth" as faithfulness, fidelity. Clearly, we do not need troths and truth for candor, except where spontaneous candor has already been interfered with by the new means of deceit that language brings. But veracity may indeed involve reliance on the natural virtue of *truth to* fellow cooperators, a virtue of which both it and fidelity to promises are artificial extensions. Truth-telling or veracity is fidelity to an intermittently operative linguistic troth, consent to share on some occasions what we might have tried to keep secret. It is a social linguistic remedy for

---

[13] David Gautier, *Morals by Agreement* (Oxford: Clarendon Press, 1986), 173–8, 266.

a linguistic condition, an excess of mental camouflage, of bluff or double bluff. The hard thing is to recognize which times are the times to which this consent applies. That makes honesty as veracity a hard virtue.

There is one last question that needs to be addressed to complete my Humean account of veracity as an artificial virtue. That is the question of what passion it is, if indeed it is only *one* passion, that is in the long run better satisfied by the discipline or regulation that veracity imposes than it would have been if left unregulated. Hume cites avidity, the desire to accumulate material goods, as the desire that the kind of honesty that he analyzes satisfies in a superior, non-violent, and civilized way. Is it avidity that both tempts us to deceive and also motivates us to accept restraints on our proclivities to deceive? Avidity for what? The power to protect ourselves from others who pose a danger can be what motivates deceit as well as the reticence that Kant sees it to motivate. This can be danger to the relatively powerless from those who would dominate and control them or danger to the dominators from those who would be less docile if not systematically deceived. So there can indeed be an interested passion that motivates deceit, the passion for defensive and aggressive power. It might in some conditions control itself the better to further its ends. Could honesty in speech serve our self-protective and self-assertive ends better than lying and deceit? In what conditions? Those are hard questions to answer. Nietzsche wrote, "The demand for truthfulness presupposes the knowability and stability of the person. In fact it is the object of education to create in the herd member a definite faith concerning human nature. It first invents the faith and then it demands truthfulness."[14] Must we make ourselves into herd members to get any general benefits from truthfulness? It may be as hard to invent the "right" detailed version of veracity as it is to invent the "right" property rules.

Deceit is sometimes motivated by a less interested passion, namely the wish not to hurt those we love. Some white lies are loving and tender lies, not bullied or bullying lies, and so some self-regulation of the impulse to deceive could be motivated by the hope of avoiding inflicting the worst hurt, the realization that our loved ones have not trusted us to be able to share hard truths with them. Love and friendship themselves can be the values invoked both to excuse deceit and to justify the self-regulation of the impetus to resort to it. But again, it will be only in some conditions that we

---

[14] Friedrich Nietzsche, *The Will to Power*, trans. W. Kaufmann and R. J. Hollingdale (New York: Random House, 1967), 227.

really hurt our loved ones less by frankness than by judicious deceit, by a few secrets and silences. In what conditions? The hard questions remain. Honesty in friendship, as much as honesty in politics and in public life, remains a hard virtue and a matter of fallible judgment.

Hume assumed much too blithely that *any* version of private property rights was better than none, that honesty is always worth its social and individual costs. Honesty, in both its main manifestations, is not just a hard virtue to exhibit but also a hard one to design. Because of its fluid and changing design in our culture, every display of honesty will also be an exercise of good (but contestable) judgment, perhaps of creative redesign. It will not be easy to recognize honesty when we encounter it, to distinguish it from false or brutal frankness. Even with Diogenes' lamp to help our search, we may well not agree in selection of any exemplar of this hard virtue.

Postscript

It strikes me now, at some temporal distance from the thoughts expressed in this 1990 essay, that I do there exaggerate the importance of the role of language to deceive. I still think it true that involuntary body language is more automatically candid than what we say, but I think that speech gives us not merely the means to cover up the truth about our feelings, but also, to give, when we choose, a more detailed version of the truth than mere body language possibly could, to give the truth about what *exactly* we feel, and why we feel it, as well as about other matters. Great poets and tragedians tell us more about grief, and about other emotions, than our faces and posture ever could. It is true, I think, that language is used as much to tell entertaining and instructive stories as to tell the truth about our own experiences, but of course it can do the latter too, and much more accurately than can our frowns, smiles, or shrugs. Telling the detailed truth, as much as covering up the bare bones of the truth, is what it takes language to do. As Bernard Williams points out in the endnote to his splendid swan song *Truth and Truthfulness*,[15] the Greek word for truth, *aletheia*, is a privative, meaning what is not overlooked or forgotten. (Heidegger too had made much of this etymology.)

In fact language may have had as its most primitive function not to exchange confidences about how we feel, nor to communicate any matter

---

[15] Bernard Williams, *Truth and Truthfulness* (Princeton: Princeton University Press, 2002).

of fact, but to give orders, as in Wittgenstein's "slab" game. For cooperative activity, the commands of the one in charge must be taken as sincerely meant, else the activity will be undermined. If we take the imperative mood as the basic linguistic mood, then meaning what we say must be the norm. The indicative mood is the one which provides opportunity for deceit, but since deceit about how we feel is difficult, given body language, deceit about other matters, including what we believe, is the more natural area to allocate to language's power to deceive. I still think this power is not to be under-estimated, but I would now retreat from the claim that it is speech's main advantage. There are many things we could not do without speech: refer to past and future, refer to what is not present, make conditional claims, compose and enjoy poems, write and read history, give and obey instructions. Of course, most of these can take the form of lies, as well as candid speech. Few lies have been poems, and it may be hard to see just how a poem *can* lie, but a love poem to a particular person could be insincere. Would Shakespeare's sonnets be any the worse, as sonnets, if their sometimes brutal apparent honesty was false pretense? Truth, while it matters much, is not always what matters most. Nevertheless, telling the truth may not be quite as unnatural as this essay of mine made it out. It was a little over-clever to make candor the preserve of what our bodies show, deceit what our powers of speech make possible, except when we deliberately inhibit those powers, and swear to tell the truth. Sometimes the truth is naturally blurted out, just as at other times we naturally spin tales. To tell the whole truth about truth-telling is quite a challenging task.[16] And to give a full account of what only language can do would take more than a postscript. I have attempted to say something about that in other places, such as "Mind and Change of Mind."[17] What this honesty essay of mine does is remind us of how language, among the many things it does, enables us to tell tales, either to entertain, or to cover up such truths as our more automatically candid body language has not given away. Lie detector tests are not needed for body language; indeed such tests use the body and its involuntary reactions as a check on what is said. Both truth-telling and tale-spinning are quite natural activities.

February 2009   A.B.

---

[16] Bernard Williams has made a fine start on this, but even he does not claim to have told us the whole truth about truthfulness.

[17] In Baier, *Postures of the Mind* (Minneapolis: University of Minnesota Press, 1985).

6

Getting in Touch With Our Own Feelings

According to René Descartes, the passions or passive states of the soul that are emotions, evaluative reactions to what we take our state to be, cannot, as sense perceptions can, mislead us, since they are "so close and so internal to the soul that it cannot possibly feel them unless they are truly as it feels them to be ("elles sont si proches et si intérieures à notre âme qu'il est impossible qu'elle les sente, sans qu'elles soient véritablement telles qu'elle les sent").[1] But according to Sigmund Freud, "Like the physical, the psychical is not necessarily in reality what it appears to be,"[2] and our consciousness of mental processes is likened by him to our fallible sense perception of the external world. Where Descartes draws a contrast between consciousness of external objects and consciousness of our own thoughts and emotions, Freud draws an analogy.

Do we know what we feel? Do we know something, but not everything, about our feelings, just in virtue of their being ours? What do we automatically know, what may we have to find out about our own feelings with or without the aid of Freudian analysis? Are feelings known in the same way thoughts are, or are there interesting differences? Are there differences between how we get in touch with the feelings of other persons and how we get in touch with their "cognitive processes"? I shall turn to Descartes, Freud, and then Darwin to get some answers about our understanding of our own and others' feelings, as compared with our understanding of thoughts. In the course of this investigation the very contrast between emotional and cognitive processes will, however, come under suspicion. As we realize the pervasiveness of "hot cognition" and "frozen affect," we may

---

[1] René Descartes, *The Passions of the Soul*, sect. 26.
[2] Sigmund Freud, *The Unconscious*, trans. James Strachey, sect. 1.

come to doubt that these categories of cognition and affect are the most helpful ones for understanding ourselves. I shall, however, begin by trying to work within Descartes's conceptual system, in which some "ideas" or "perceptions" are *tanquam rerum imagines*," and their acceptance or rejection is part of our search for truth, while other "passions of the soul," passive modes of the conscious thing, have as their function to suggest to us where our *good* lies, and to prompt us to voluntary actions other than simply affirmation, denial, or postponing judgment about truth claims. Descartes's own example, in *Passions of the Soul*, sects. 36–9, is the distinction between the sense-prompted intellectual belief that some dangerous thing or animal is close to one, and the emotional reaction—the fear which may lead one to flee, or the boldness that may enable one to try to attack or defend oneself against this danger. Freud too takes the vicissitudes of "ideas," would-be representations, to be distinguishable from the vicissitudes both of instinct, and of the "affect" in which instinct may discharge itself. He reserves the term "idea" for what Descartes in the fifth paragraph of the Third Medita-tion calls ideas in the "strict" sense, ideas as would-be representations. I will try to work with this contrast between cognitive processes, aimed at accu-rate representation, and affective and motivational processes, aimed at some-thing else, until it collapses on us.

The apparently contrasting claims of Descartes and Freud concerning the "transparency" of emotions which I quoted at the start soon yield, when one looks at their wider context, to a fair measure of agreement in answer to the question of what exactly we adults are automatically in touch with, in our emotional lives, and what we may have to be got in touch with, as we come to notice and learn what earlier we had missed. For many of the things that Descartes tells us about our emotions, if they are true at all, will come as a surprise, if not a complete surprise, to many of his readers. Not merely may we have failed to notice that love speeds the digestion and provides steady heat in the chest, while hatred slows the digestive processes and makes the blood heat in the chest erratic (sects. 97 and 98), but we may also have needed Descartes's help to become aware that when we experience "*horreur*" at the touch of an earthworm, the rustling of a leaf, or our own shadow, these things represent to us sudden and unexpected death (sect. 89). (As far as the shadow goes, Freud seems to agree: in *Reflections on War and Death* he tells us that we naturally invent ghosts when we think of death, and invent a ghostly spectator of our own death when we think of it.[3]) What we shy away from in horror, if Descartes is right, is any intimation of mortality. He may well be right, but it took more than the closeness and interiority to his soul of the revulsion he analyzes for him to realize this truth about it. Descartes's *Passions of the Soul* devotes more space to middle-depth psychology than to speculative physiology, and the psychological claims are by no means all truisms. The definitions themselves can inform and mildly surprise the naive reader, even when Descartes expects them to seem obvious. Is it, as he claims, "obvious" (*évident*) that desire always concerns the future (sect. 57)? Is it obvious that love is willing union? (sect. 79). Other philosophers, such as Hobbes and Hume, did not define love that way. (Hobbes's definitions too can shock and enlighten, as when he defines anger as sudden courage, amusement as sudden glory.) There clearly is much we can come to be led to see about our own passions, even before Descartes begins his physiology lesson. So it is implausible to suppose that he thought all of his non-physiological claims were self-evident ones to anyone who had experienced the array of human passions which are his subject matter. However much becomes evident to us about love, laughter, and disgust, as we consider the suggestions Descartes makes, these things need not have always been evident to us simply by our having experienced those emotions. Descartes gives us a fair bit of "depth psychology." He is fully aware of the formative impact of infant experience:

the strange aversions of some people that make them unable to bear the smell of roses, the presence of a cat, or the like, can readily be recognized as resulting simply from their having been greatly upset by some object in the early years of their life. Or it may even result from their having been affected by the feelings their mother had when she was upset by such an object while pregnant...(sect. 136)

Descartes tries to "deepen" our knowledge of our own revulsion or fear in two ways: by generalizing to find the common factor in our varied revulsions, and by delving back in time to locate some primitive occasion of revulsion which the subsequent ones can be seen as repeating. In this enterprise, he obviously is a precursor of Freud.

The statement from Freud that I quoted at the start concerns mental processes which may be unconscious, and inadequately represented by what we have become conscious of. But do such processes include emotions? Are

---

[3] Sigmund Freud, *Reflections on War and Death*, trans. A. A. Brill and Alfred B. Kuttner (New York: Moffat, Yard, 1918).

there unconscious emotions? Freud and his followers speak mainly of "affect," and this is close enough to Descartes's "passion" in its connotations for the comparison to be a fair one. Freud sometimes does want to speak of unconscious affect, but with qualification. What will be unconscious will strictly be the postulated instinctual drive whose "discharge" a given affect is taken by Freud to be (such instinctual drives are never conscious), and possibly also the ideas representing the nature and object of this drive. For Freud, ideas can be conscious or unconscious, instinct can only be unconscious, and "strictly speaking... there are no unconscious affects as there are unconscious ideas."[4] So Freud is in a sense in agreement with Descartes, that, as Freud himself says, "It is surely of the essence of an emotion that we should be aware of it, i.e., that it should become known to consciousness."[5] This consciously presented feeling is "a final manifestation of a process of discharge," according to Freud. Hence it is a bit like the lava expelled by the psychical volcano: *it* is obvious enough, but the fires in the depths (the instincts) and the full idea of what inflamed the fires to discharge on this occasion (the "true" object of the felt emotion) are usually hidden. Something essential to disgust, its feel and its apparent object, is evident when one is disgusted, but much that is equally essential need be far from evident. Freud and Descartes seem thus far to be in agreement. They differ, fairly obviously, in their beliefs about how the hidden is to be uncovered or inferred, and they may disagree as to whether there are both conscious and unconscious desires, as well as not yet conscious objects of emotion and desire behind any felt emotion. Descartes apparently takes it that no special techniques like hypnosis or free association, no expensive methods like long-term psychoanalysis, are needed for us to come to learn what we are fundamentally disgusted by, drawn to, afraid of, and so on. But they are in agreement that we must be in touch with some aspects of our feelings, and that we are often not in touch with other dimensions or aspects of them.

Can we get from Descartes or from Freud a plausible thesis about what if anything is distinctive about emotions, among our mental states? Descartes clearly believes that thoughts are like emotions in being "interior to the soul," in being conscious states, so automatically known to the person whose thoughts they are. He gives us no physiology of thought to parallel his physiology of the passions (although there is a physiology of the

---

[4] Freud, *The Unconscious*, sect. III.   [5] Ibid.

imagination). He tells us nothing about whether the blood in the chest is more steadily warm when we affirm than when we doubt, nor how long chains of inference affect the digestion. There is, it seems, no "hidden" physiological side to Cartesian intellect. It is all "software," without even the relatively soft "hardware" of "animal spirits." Does Descartes give us any "depth" cognitive psychology to tell us what we are *really* thinking of, when we think of circles, light, vortices, or God? If, when we react with "*horreur*" at our shadow, or the touch of an earthworm, it is really our own future ghost or cold corpse we are repelled by, must we not be *really* alluding to death and corpses when we think we are attending only to shadows and earthworms? It is hard to see how Descartes can consistently hold one thesis about the content or intentional objects of emotions, that they need not be only what they seem, and a different thesis about the content and objects of thoughts and attention, namely that these must be only what they seem to be. And indeed a lot of his own philosophy does a sort of intellectual depth psychology on our cognitive life. He "clarifies" our ideas. He shows us that, contrary to the way things seemed to us, our idea of the sun is of a separately movable roundish part of a plenum, a part which like the rest has only geometrical properties, not heat or force, and whose motion or rest is simply its position or change of position relative to other parts of this full but colorless and forceless world, itself perhaps a kind of dead shadow of its lively Creator, who keeps all the force for Himself, giving his creation only less "eminent" simulacra of that power, namely immensity, conservation of quantity of movement, some causal powers, etc. The naive reader is as surprised by what Descartes teaches her about what her ideas of the world *must* be, when clarified, as about what it is that must be repellent to her. (It becomes in the end a bit of a mystery why the slight alteration in the jointly movable parts of the world's not so solid geometry, that counts as one person's death, should be anticipated not merely in passionless intellectual predictions but in shudders at the touch of "cold" earthworms, themselves just similar temporarily jointly movable but smaller parts, but this, I suppose, is no more of a mystery than why the soul should attend at all to any part of the non-psychical world, be it the living body it is temporarily conjoined to, or the more extensive subject matter of astrophysics.) There is, however, a significant difference between Descartes's clarification of our truth-aspiring ideas and his interpretation of our emotions: with ideas the clear version is to displace the confused version, but with emotions we *keep* the apparent object of the horror, namely the worm or the shadow, merely adding to it what stands behind it, that which it "signifies." We augment the content of our emotions to understand them, but it seems that, as far as increased intellectual understanding goes, less is more: we are to reject all those confused ideas of color, heat, solidity, space, replacing them with combinations of clear and distinct mathematical ideas. We do not keep our confused idea of yellow, and enrich it with a grasp of the geometrical properties of pineal glands, brains, eyes, light, lit objects, etc., which together perhaps contain yellowness in a more "eminent" form so it can produce ideas of yellow in us; rather we dismiss the idea of yellow as "proceeding from nothing," from the limitations of the perceiver, or at least as containing so little objective reality that it is not worth tracing it to any material source.

In the Sixth Meditation, Descartes does take seriously that minuscule reality of the yellowness, what there is of it that is other than is contained in the primary properties of the minute parts of what causes us to see yellow, properties which we can in principle also perceive, and perceive to be non-identical with our idea of yellow. He takes yellowness to be there to guide us towards our good in this life, to serve as a sort of lure to make us go towards sunflowers, honey, and other attractive yellow things that by and large are good things for us to "join ourselves" to. The very intellectual confusion of the secondary qualities, and perhaps also of the sensed version of the primary qualities, makes them "in their own way distinct" as guides to the good. So sensed qualities serve two different functions for Descartes, first as evidence of what really exists outside of us, and of what that reality is like, and second as guides to our good. In the former capacity ideas of warmth, coldness, red, yellow, are hopelessly confused, but in the latter capacity they are far clearer and more distinct than any intellectually distinct mathematical equation. So the sort of "clarification" of ideas which replaces the ideas of sense with different mathematical ideas is not intended to replace them in their practical role, in our search for "the good," but only to banish them from our search for "the true."

For Descartes, then, the sense perception of the cold earthworm is not, as a stimulus to "*horreur*," to be replaced by an idea of the primary properties of its multiple causes, but left as it appears. But we are encouraged to see, behind it, the remembered, fantasized, or anticipated cold contact with a corpse, or even with a worm-inhabited corpse. When we see the earthworm's representative role, we see why we shrink back. Both the representative and the represented are to be conceived *sub specie boni*, not *sub specie veri*, if we may so speak. The problem for Descartes's philosophy as a whole is this value dualism. Can we seriously believe that our pursuit of truth and our pursuit of our good are as separate as he makes them? Either Descartes's version of the true, or his version of our good (or both), must be a false pretender, if it is good for us to seek truth, and if it is true that in shuddering at the worm we have intimations of mortality. (The very phrase "false pretender" alerts us to the fact that truth is a moral and evaluative matter, and that epistemology is a branch of value theory.)

To get in touch with our feelings, in a Cartesian manner, one thing we must do is to try to see behind the apparent object of our feelings to their more fundamental and usually more obviously appropriate object. But in what sense is it "appropriate" to shudder at the touch of a corpse, or at the thought that some corpse will be our own? What is appropriate about that ur-shudder? What sort of "fit" or misfit is there ever between our emotions and their objects? In the case of the cat phobia, Descartes's own explanation of why we have it takes us back to a cause which is not really a reason for the fear. If behind the cat which one now is averse to stands the cat who startled one's mother when she was pregnant, then the aversion is not made comprehensible by being linked to some "appropriate" aversion. Averse as we all properly are to being unpleasantly startled, we do not think it appropriate to continue the aversion against the "innocent" startlers. Is horror at corpses any less brutely contingent than being startled by a cat when it makes an unexpected fast entry through one's window?

Descartes has no worked-out theory of appropriateness in objects of human emotions, although he does give us some helpful hints. He tells us not just that horror is essentially of death, but also that love is for one who will complete one's own incompleteness, for one with whom one can make a "whole," in which one may not oneself be "the better part" (sects. 79–82). This is still a bit abstract, and Descartes wants it to be general enough to cover cases ranging from religious devotion through parental love to "the affection a man has for his mistress" and even to "what drives the drunkard to wine, or the attraction of a brutish man for a woman he wants to violate," but the common element he sees is a sense of incompleteness, and a recognition in another, or in some external thing, of what would complete that assumed incompleteness. What is the original, the paradigm case of such incompleteness, as horror at corpses is supposed to be the quintessential horror? Descartes does not tell us, but his willingness to go back to prenatal experience to explain adult emotions makes it not implausible to say that he would have given a sympathetic hearing to Freud's suggestion that separation from the mother, at birth, is the quintessential breaking up of what had been to the infant a satisfactory "whole." The other natural candidate for quintessential wholeness, and appropriate love, namely sexual union, is treated rather sardonically by Descartes, and treated as a contingent and primarily adolescent phase of our emotional life. Nature, he says, has implanted certain impressions in the brain that "bring it about that at a certain age and time we regard ourselves as deficient, as forming only one half of a whole, whose other half must be a person of the other sex" (sect. 90). He gives this as a case of "attraction," a passion which is closely associated with love, but which lacks that essential element of "willing," or endorsement, which he makes essential to love. So sexual attraction is treated by him as a bit like the attraction to us of flowers (to look at) or fruit (to eat). It is *one* but only one of the modes of union with other things which nature suggests to us, for our will's acceptance or refusal.

Freud (wittingly or not) develops Descartes's hints about the quintessential or original objects of our emotions. We love our mothers, we are anxious at separation from them, we feel guilty at displeasing stern fathers, and all our subsequent objects of love, anxiety, guilt are substitutes for these perfectly appropriate objects, all of our subsequent loves, anxieties, guilts are repetitions of these primal loves, anxieties, guilts. These later ones are to be understood by tracing their ancestry. A given adult emotion with its apparent object will be a more or less appropriate emotion depending on how little repression or other "pathological" diversions of instinctual energy and its discharge figure in the causal ancestry of that emotion. Phenomena like transference and identification are inevitable, not abnormal, and even some repression may be inevitable. A Freudian-cum-Cartesian test for the appropriateness of one's present emotions to their current apparent objects could be put this way: Would this emotion survive awareness of its own ancestry? Does it *disturb* or change the character of the emotion for awareness of what de Sousa calls its "paradigm scenario"[6] to occur? If behind my current loved one I see all the previous loved ones, back to my loved mother, does that or

⁶ Ronald de Sousa, "The Rationality of Emotions" and "Self Deceptive Emotions," in A. Rorty (ed.), *Explaining Emotions* (Berkeley: University of California Press, 1980).

does it not devalue or destabilize the present love? If I see my horror at the earthworm as horror at corpses, will that increase or decrease my horror? Here, perhaps, we need to amend the test to "Will that make us see our emotion as misplaced?" For we may be in the grips of an emotion that we see to be inappropriate. One odd feature of Descartes's definition of love is that, since to love is to *will* to be joined to what we find attractive, to love is to *endorse* the attraction, so that to love what we see to be an inappropriate object of love seems a conceptual impossibility. Descartes has to redescribe all those frequent cases where we take ourselves to be in love inappropri- ately as cases of inappropriate attraction which, if the inappropriateness is acknowledged, are for that reason not love. To love, one can gloss Descartes, is to endorse one's own attraction towards another. Cartesian love is an intrinsically reflective emotion. It then becomes problematic if an infant's love of its mother *can* be the paradigm of love. Only if something else can be found that is the paradigm of will, reflection, and endorsement—if behind these adult phenomena we can find childhood precursors. We will need a depth psychology of adult mental acts to supplement our depth psychology of adult emotions and our "clarification" of our intellectual beliefs. (This perhaps we can and should get.)

My question was whether the dimensions of emotion unearthed by Descartes and Freud give us any plausible way of completing the sentence "Emotions are those states of mind which…" One completion which suggests itself is "…which have 'deep' intentional objects," where "depth" is a matter of either the historical autobiographical layering of successive substitutes for the original object of that emotion-type, or some other less autobiographically generated series of substitutes for the primary object of the emotion, the object that is "most appropriate" for it. Even if horror *is* of death-associated things, it is implausible to suppose that the infant first experienced horror for a corpse, then let earthworms or shadows serve as substitute objects. In this case the primary object is not "primal" in the sense of first in the child's experience. It is, on the contrary, dimly antici- pated, or fantasized, thanks to what has to be regarded either as inherited race-memory, or unconscious wish, or both. Freud in *Totem and Taboo* invokes a sort of trans-individual memory to explain how the primary object of guilt could be parricide, but in *Civilization and Its Discontents* he puts more stress on the unconscious wish to kill the simultaneously loved and hated frustrating father. "Whether one has killed the father or refrained from so doing is not the really decisive thing. One is bound to feel guilty in either case, for the sense of guilt is an expression of the conflict due to ambivalence."[7] What is essential to the depth of the object of emotions is not an actual history of substitution for the primary and appropriate object, but some basis for such substitution. Thus, the child's first love or fear also has a "deep" object—for the primary object is deepened by all its possible substitutes or representatives.

Is this "depth" peculiar to the objects of emotions, or is it found also in desires and beliefs? It seems to be as readily attributed to conscious desire as to emotion, and indeed for Descartes felt desire is just one emotion among others. For Freud the matter is more complicated, due to his postulation of necessarily unconscious instinctual drives lying behind all conscious desires, as well as behind all emotions. These basic instincts do not have "deep" objects, but rather have constant ones (self-preservation, pleasure, death). Still, some exchange or substitution between them is postulated by Freud when in the 25th and 26th Lectures of his *General Introduction to Psychoanalysis* he supposes that the sexual instinct and the self-preservatory instinct can each be freed from its object and attached to the object of the other, unsatisfied libido taking the form of neurotic fear and anxiety, egoism taking the form of narcissism. So there is some "depth" even in unconscious instincts, some potential for substitution of objects. But it is limited to two layers: behind the object of narcissistic libido stands the self-preserving ego, behind the object of fear stands the absent object of libido. Ordinary desires, that is desires accessible to consciousness, admit of greater depth, since whether libidinous or self-preservatory they can have more primary objects behind their apparent objects. Thus, it seems as if the characteristic depth does not distinguish affect from motivation.

What of beliefs, or cognitive states? Do they differ from desires and emotions in lacking depth? Well, they have a different sort of depth, or at least dimension, namely what they imply. Each belief or belief combination comes vaguely trailing all its implications, as emotions come trailing the emotional situations they repeat or anticipate. Depth in cognitive states lies in their only partially acknowledged logical implications. These, however, do

---

[7] Sigmund Freud, *Civilisation and Its Discontents* (1930), trans. Joan Riviere, rev. James Strachey (London: Norton, 1961), 89.

not seem to lead back to *primary* belief objects, except for foundationalists, and for Fregeans, who can treat any accepted belief as a representative of "The True." If one is a coherentist about truth, or holds a redundancy or prosentential theory of truth, then following the implications of a person's beliefs will lead us not back to some primary beliefs, some ur-truths, but round and round the mulberry bushes and mazes. So cognitive depth, if seen as logically implied beliefs, is more like the "depth" of instincts, namely a matter of mutual reciprocity, than like the depth of affects, leading us back to some termini.

Do beliefs have no other depth dimension? Can they be "closed" under other ties than logical implication? Earlier I suggested that Descartes does seem in the *Meditations* not merely to trace logical implications, but to *replace* objects of thought with more ultimate objects of thought: the sun as indistinctly sense-perceived is replaced by the sun as object of the astronomer's calculations, where this really is, at least at first, a replacement.

Certainly, the two ideas which I have of the sun (from sense perception, from theoretical astronomy) cannot both represent the same sun, and reason leads me to believe that the idea which seems to come more immediately from the sun's appearance or presence to me (sense perception) is the one that is most misleading.[8] Similarly, I think there is a switch of ideas of God, from the God of theological tradition to the "true God," the one known by Descartes's proofs. The *Meditations* are full of substitutions of "true ideas" of something for their more specious forerunners. True suns, true gods, true circles, true matter, replace apparent suns, apparent gods, and specious preliminary versions of circles and of matter. These replacements of the apparent by the less apparent but "true" version do not come about just by tracing the logical implications of the apparent versions—such moves lead only to negative results, to *reductios* that show up those first versions as *not* the true versions. To get the "true" idea of God or of a circle, one must turn one's back on the theological tradition, and on non-analytic diagram-using geometry, and "turn to the things themselves," to one's own self-generated idea of God, and (if one is a mathematical genius of Descartes's stature) to one's own intellectual idea of continuous magnitude. Once these "true" ideas are obtained, one can go back and try to see why one ever had the less true ones, why the things themselves took on such less than true appearance

---

[8] René Descartes, Third Meditation, eleventh paragraph; my parenthetical additions.

to one, and so in a way save or redeem the appearances by linking them with the truth, but one cannot first get to the truth through the appearances. Where "experts" are needed to find the true objects of mental states, for Descartes, is in cognition, more than in affect.

Freud agrees, once again, with Descartes. *Ideas* in his narrow sense, which is also Descartes's narrow sense, *tanquam rerum imagines*, are the least self-illuminating of our mental states. *What* they are images of cannot be read off from them. "Objective reality" is hard to recognize, is *not* borne by an idea on its sleeve. What Descartes called "material falsity" is the rule, not the exception, and material truth is hard-won. Rarely is the idea in the unconscious mind "the same" in content as its representative or surrogate in consciousness. I shall not rehearse Freud's well-known doctrines of the discrepancy between what we *think* we are thinking of, and what we are really thinking of, but merely note that it is the idea-component of an emotion whose "vicissitudes" provide the depth of emotions, so cognition as an ingredient in emotion must have "depth." It is unlikely that cognition as a component of affect has depth, while cognition as such does not, unless we reconceptualize "cognition as such" as dissociated cognition, a "hot cognition" which has been pathologically "cooled." There may be contexts in which thoughts lack "deep content," but these will be the exception not the norm.

So far, then, this dip into depth psychology, old and more recent, has not given us a feature whereby we can distinguish emotion from thought or from instinct and motivation. Depth is typically found in the intentional objects of all three. Maybe we should look at the social or "horizontal" as well as at the temporal or "vertical" dimension of emotion, at a given emotion episode's relation to the emotions of other emotion-havers at roughly that time. Darwin helps us to do that. Emotional states for Darwin are those mental states which communicate themselves to our fellows, the states we involuntarily *express* in ways understood by our fellows. They do not, of course, always read our faces and tone of voice aright (women are better "readers" and vocal and facial "writers" than men, it seems[9]) and sometimes we successfully try to inhibit at least some of the "body language" that would display our mental state to others. But, as Wittgenstein pointed

[9] See R. Rosenthal, J. A. Hall, M. R. DiMatteo, P. L. Rogers, and D. Archer, *Sensitivity to Nonverbal Communication: The PONS Test* (Baltimore: Johns Hopkins University Press, 1979).

out, "The best picture of the human soul is the human body."[10] Emotions are what show so readily in the eyes and face, as well as the voice tone and body language, so Wittgenstein's judgment may imply that the core of the human soul is its "heart," its emotion repertoire and the music it makes from that. Crucial constraints on an adequate account of emotions are provided by two uncontestable data: that emotions show in face and voice, and that music as well as the other arts arouse emotions. "Cognitivists" about emotion come to grief over those two facts, since beliefs do not show on the face nor does most music serve as food for *thought* as readily as it serves as food for love, joy, sadness, amusement, sexual arousal, or the sustaining of martial aggressiveness.

Our faces, voices, gestures do present our emotional state to others. As Caroll Izard writes, this expressive presentation does several important things: "(a) signalling something of the expressor's feelings *and intent*; (b) providing a basis for *certain inferences about the environment*; (c) fostering *social* interactions..."[11] Darwin had earlier made the same points: that the spontaneous expression of emotion, along with its automatic understanding by one's fellows, serves to forewarn others of what we are likely to do, to indirectly inform them of the environmental conditions, and to coordinate social interaction. These transparently expressive movements, he says, "are in themselves of much importance for our welfare. They serve as the first means of communication between the mother and her infant..."[12] According to some developmental psychologists, the *social* function of our expression-bent emotions is not just an extra bonus, in a well-adapted species, but is of the essence of our emotions. Colwyn Trevarthen writes, "emotions are inseparable from contacts or relationships between persons... Emotions are not part of the mental processes of isolated subjects as such."[13] If we are to accept what these Darwinian emotion theorists say, then emotions are essentially and not just contingently interpersonally accessible. What of

[10] Ludwig Wittgenstein, *Philosophical Investigations*, trans. G. E. M. Anscombe (Oxford: Blackwell, 1997), pt. II, sect. iv.

[11] "Emotion–Cognition Relationships and Human Development," in C. E. Izard, J. Kagan, and R. B. Zajonc (eds.), *Emotion, Cognition and Behavior* (New York: Cambridge University Press, 1984), 18; my emphasis.

[12] Charles Darwin, *The Expression of the Emotions in Man and Animals* (Chicago: University of Chicago Press, 1965), 364.

[13] Colwyn Trevarthen, "Emotions in Infancy," in K. Scherer and P. Ekman (eds.), *Approaches to Emotion* (Hillsdale, NJ: Lawrence Erlbaum, 1984), 137.

beliefs? Can we distinguish the "cognitive" from the "emotional" by the systematic elusiveness of beliefs, the systematic inescapability of emotions, at the interpersonal level?

One access to the beliefs of others is by inference from their "hot cognitions" and what we take to be their "information-sensitive" emotions, since both of these will get expressed unless there is an unusual degree of control over body language. What of real language? Suppose someone tells us what they believe. Is that not the *best* access we can have to their cognitive state? Well, as Darwin points out, non-verbal expressions "reveal the thoughts and intentions of others more truly than do words, which may be falsified."[14] It is far easier to deceive with words than to deceive with face, tone of voice, or hands. Language may be reasonably regarded (*pace* Kant[15]), as the tool our species fashioned for mutual deceit. It is the means of indoctrination, propaganda, cover-up, and only rarely the means of candid communication. In the philosophical literature we get a great reliance on the possibility of "candid avowal," appeals to what sentences a person *would* utter to express her beliefs and intentions were she to be "candid." But the conditions of candor are insufficiently investigated, and are as crucial to a sentential theory of belief as the conditions of cooperation are to a theory of justice. Candor with others is not so easy, and may be hardest of all with oneself.

The great thing about body language is that what is hard there is not candor but deceit. So if I want to know what I felt, the best way is to be audio- and videotaped and then to hear and "read" my own expressions as I would hear and read others'. Hume wrote that we learn about the emotional reactions of others not only from experience but also "by a kind of *presentation* which tells us what will operate on others by what we feel immediately in ourselves."[16] It is just as true that if we would know more about our emotions than what we feel immediately in ourselves, then that will come via the "presentation" of those feelings to others, and so to ourselves if we can share their angle on us. To avoid self-deceit, to be candid with ourselves, we must utilize the medium in which we are most candid to others: the spontaneous expression of feeling in voice, eye, face, neck, shoulders, hands, feet, perhaps even hair. ("She went grey within two years of marrying him.")

[14] Darwin, *The Expression of the Emotions in Man and Animals*, 364.
[15] Immanuel Kant, *The Metaphysical Elements of Virtue*, pt. I, ch. 2, sect. 9.
[16] David Hume, *A Treatise of Human Nature*, ed. L. A. Selby-Bigge, rev. P. H. Nidditch (Oxford: Clarendon Press, 1978), 332.

Does this hard-to-avoid candor give our thoughts away as it gives our feelings away? J. L. Austin said that we would be in a pretty predicament if each could "introspect" the other's states of mind.[17] Keeping our thoughts to ourselves does seem, not merely an easier achievement than keeping our feelings to ourselves, but a less pathological objective. Emotions have to be "bottled up" if they are not expressed, but silent thoughts stay quietly enough within the "black box," giving the thinker no trouble, and usually not missed by her fellows. We are not significantly hindered by not knowing most of our fellows' streams of thought, and might be in some pretty predicaments if we did know them. When we *are* helped by knowing another's thought is where the private cognition is part of intention formation, and the intentional action is one with which we need to coordinate our own action, and also where we have divided the cognitive tasks, and so are counting on having at least the conclusions of some stretches of thought, the products of some mental work, made available to us. Then we do need to know what our fellows think. How do we find out? If, as I have argued, their verbal reports should not be just assumed to be trustworthy expressions of their beliefs, how do we get at their beliefs when we need to?

The answer, surely, is that we need the more trustworthy evidence of what they are feeling to supplement the less trustworthy evidence of what they are saying. The shifty-eyed person is not believed. We believe what another tells us of what they believe and intend, unless there is "dissonance" between that and what they are apparently doing and feeling. We need the verbal evidence, but we also need to make inferences from their expressive and purposive behavior. We can infer belief (and desire) from expressed emotion, especially over time, and we need these data as a check on the evidence we get from verbal behavior and other purposive behavior, both of which are more easily faked than is body language.

---

[17] J. L. Austin, "Other Minds," in Austin, *Philosophical Papers*, ed. J. O. Urmson and G. J. Warnock (Oxford: Oxford University Press, 1961), 83. Austin earlier in this paper (pp. 76–7) gives a good account of the close link between an emotion like anger and its natural expression, which he says it would be "nonsensical" to treat simply as an "effect" of an inner state, and at p. 83 gives a suggestive account of the different link between the anger and the angry person's verbal self-report: "Believing in other persons, in authority and testimony, is an essential part of the act of communicating, an act which we all constantly perform. It is as much an irreducible part of our experience as, say, giving promises, or playing competitive games, or even sensing colored patches." I would myself add to that that disbelieving people, like refusing to give promises, and abstaining from competitive games, is an equally familiar part of our experience, one of its essential possibilities.

I seem to have painted a grim picture of us as a bunch of liars, self-deceivers, and false pretenders, whose tone of voice, or discrepancy between tone of voice and hand or jaw twitches, sometimes gives us away. Of course, that is a gross "idealization" of the actual. We do often take what people say on trust, and would be in a pretty predicament if we could not. But that is because often there *is* no dissonance between what people say, between their tongue, mouth, and epiglottal "language," and the rest of their body language. As long as their total "speech" is coherent or harmonious, we trust it. But if it is not coherent, if there is "dissonance," we do and rightly do trust body language more than we trust verbal reports. Body language gives us "non-inferential access" to people's emotions, only inferential access to their thoughts. This, I think, is as true in the first person case as in the second and third, although we rarely use these more reliable data to get at our own beliefs. We tend to systematically ignore the evidence that might lead us to lose trust in our own verbal self-reports, and that is why self-deceit is so prevalent. Were we to "verify" our own belief reports, as we do tend to verify those of others, we might get into as good a position to know our own beliefs as we are to know those of others. That is never very good, since beliefs do elude us in a way emotions do not, and our only access to them is inferential. They, along with desires, are theoretical postulates to explain the "hard" data—what we intentionally do and say, and what we unintentionally express.

If that is at all right, then "artificial intelligence" is the worst possible route to understanding each other. For we have sensibly made our computers so that they cannot help but be candid belief reporters. Only when we give them the capacity to lie will we have made them adequate models of ourselves. But to give them the capacity to lie we would have to give them some reason to lie, and that would mean giving them fears, uneasiness, guilt, compassion, and all the usual reasons we have to lie. One of the reasons we sometimes have to lie is to throw up a verbal smokescreen to hide or distract attention from truths which we are revealing in other ways. If computational devices were to have this reason to lie, they would need to have some body language "readout"[18] as well as their usual printouts. If, as has been

---

[18] I take the term from Ross Buck, who treats emotion itself *as* a readout of the "prime motivational/emotional" state of the person. This readout takes three equally essential forms: physiological changes (read most easily by one's physician), bodily expression (read by one's fellows), and subjective experience. From this last subjective "reading" may come a verbal self-report, but it will be mediated by cognitive

suggested, interpersonal or inter-animal expression is essential to emotion, then we could not duplicate our emotional capacities except in a spontaneous self-expressor. If, as Freud and Descartes plausibly maintain, our emotions have "deep" objects, the depth being dependent on our history as a species and our individual histories as intelligent mammals, then we would have to make artificial life to make any artificial intelligence that is at all like our own.

The model that helps us get in better touch with both our emotions and our beliefs and desires is the obvious model: a fellow person. We then can have a clearer view both of the developmental history which gives depth to the objects of attention, and of the expression that reveals true feelings and beliefs, than we are apt to have if we try turning our gaze directly on ourselves. We must see others in historical and social dimensions to understand them, and we must use others to understand ourselves. These are the lessons Descartes, Darwin, and Freud together can teach us.

and verbal processing, as well as affected by the person's conscious goals. So it is not "readout" in the way body language is. It gives us indirect and fallible indicators of the emotion, whereas the spontaneous expression is constitutive of the emotion itself, which Buck treats as itself an indicator of the state of satisfaction of primary motives. Like Freud, Buck takes "affect" to manifest something of the motivational state of the person. Like Darwin, he takes it to be of the essence of emotion to be "readable," to communicate. See Ross Buck, *The Communication of Emotion* (New York: Guilford, 1984).

7

How to Get to Know One's Own Mind

Some Simple Ways

One's own mind should be contrasted, one would think, with others' minds, just as one's own body contrasts with other people's bodies. But in our philosophical tradition we have this odd phrase "other minds," which recurs in discussions of our access to facts about minds. In John Stuart Mill's presentation[1] of the infamous argument from analogy (although he does not characterize the argument as one employing analogy), we find "other sentient creatures," and "other human beings," not "other minds." F. H. Bradley has "other selves" and "foreign selves," and Bertrand Russell has "other people's minds." "Other minds" is found in A. J. Ayer, C. I. Lewis, C. D. Broad, John Wisdom, J. L. Austin, Alvin Plantinga, and a host of others.[2] My guess is that "other minds," like Bradley's "other selves," is a secularization of George Berkeley's phrase "other spirits," used when he presents what, as far as I know, is the first version of the infamous argument. He is mainly concerned to present a vindication of that really other super-spirit, the Berkeleian God, but along the way grants that we know not just ourselves as active spirits, making and unmaking ideas at our pleasure, but, less immediately, "other spirits" who are "human agents." We know of them, Berkeley

A version of this essay was given as the Irving Thalberg Memorial Lecture, at the University of Illinois, Chicago Circle, in Sept. 1992; another version as the Keynote Address at the Northern New England Philosophical Society, University of New Hampshire, Oct. 1992. I am grateful to the many people who have helped me better to know what I think about this topic.

[1] J. S. Mill, *Examination of Sir William Hamilton's Philosophy*, ch. XII.

[2] James Conant, spurred into action by my offensive suggestion that "the problem of other minds" may have been a straw problem invented by Wittgenstein, as material for dissolution, drew my attention to the discussions of "the problem of other minds" to be found in Mach, Carnap, Schlick, and C. I. Lewis. I restricted my list to those who wrote in English, and used "other," rather than "others."

says, "by their operations, or the ideas of them, excited in us. I perceive several motions, changes, and combinations of ideas that inform me there are certain particular agents, like myself, which accompany them and concur in their production."[3] Presumably for Berkeley, as before him for Descartes,[4] speech is a very important case of such a recognizably spirit-expressing operation, but he would have problems distinguishing the easily intelligible speech of his fellow Britishers from the less easily decoded language of the "author of nature," seen or heard as much in ideas which get interpreted as human speech or other expressive human behavior as those which get interpreted as animal, vegetable, or mineral changes.

Thomas Reid, to whom Mill is responding when he presents the infamous argument, wrote that he found no principle in Berkeley's system "which affords me even probable ground to conclude that there are other intelligent beings, like myself, in the relations of brother, friend, or fellow citizen. I am left alone, as the only creature of God in the universe ...'[5] Reid either did not read the passage of Berkeley which I have quoted, or was unimpressed by its claims. He finds these "egoistic" implications an "uncomfortable consequence of the theory of Berkeley," but Berkeley, despite his "egoism," is treated gently by Reid compared with the treatment given to Hume. This doubtless was because Reid was at one with Beattie in judging Berkeley to have been a man of conspicuous virtue, who had striven valiantly to overturn what Reid terms the "fortress of atheism" which sheltered more materialist and less virtuous philosophers.

It is quite understandable that Berkeley should identify human agents with "spirits," and so contrast himself as a spirit with "other spirits." But later thinkers who shared neither his theology nor his idealism speak very oddly when they contrast their own minds with "other minds," rather than with

---

[3] George Berkeley, *Principles of Human Knowledge*, A145; see also A148. I discussed Berkeley's problematic account of the "concurrence" between divine and human agents in "The Intentionality of Intentions," *Review of Metaphysics*, 33/3 (Mar. 1977), 389–414.

[4] In Descartes's *Discourse on the Method*, pt. 5, the criteria given for distinguishing real thinkers from automata include versatile verbal response to what is said to the thinker. Descartes does not offer these criteria to answer any skeptical worry about "other minds," but rather to emphasize the non-mechanical nature of thought. His passing reference in the Second Meditation to the possibility that what he takes to be men passing outside his window may for all he knows be automata in hats and coats makes a point about seeing, and interpreting what we see, following on his discussion of the wax. It is not intended to present grounds for doubt on new matters, to add to the First Meditation doubts. (Descartes's meditator seems to care very little whether or not he is the only finite mind.)

[5] Thomas Reid, *Essays on the Intellectual Powers of Man*, II. x. 13. I am grateful to Myles Burnyeat for drawing my attention to this passage.

others' minds. Austin (whose "How to Talk, Some Simple Ways" my title imitates), rightly remarks, "misnaming is not a trivial or a laughing matter."[6] This is not exactly a misnaming, and may be a matter best laughed at, but whatever sort of mis-speaking it is, it is no trivial mismove. Did all these writers, like Berkeley, assume that they *were* their minds? Surely Broad, Ayer, and company took living bodies more seriously than that would suggest. Wisdom and Austin use the phrase in implicit shudder quotes, which is what it deserves. In "Other Minds," Austin demotes Mill's and Russell's supposedly "deep" problem of our epistemological warrant for attributing any mental life at all to any others and of attributing particular states of mind to particular others at particular times to an addendum to a discussion of the folk epistemology of bird-watching, making it seem just as silly to keep asking "How do you know" of the person who claims to know that another feels angry as it would be to try to create a skeptical problem for the bird-watchers who are identifying bitterns, goldfinches, and goldcrests in the agreed ways for making such identifications. He also dismisses the basis of the solipsist's worry in one brief final note: "*Of course* I don't intro-spect Tom's feelings (we should be in a pretty predicament if I did)."[7] This witty paper really did, I think, subvert a whole, if admittedly reassuring, short[8] tradition in the philosophy of mind, and did so several years before the publication of Wittgenstein's *Philosophical Investigations*. ("Other Minds" dates from 1946—it may show the indirect influence of Wittgenstein through the acknowledged influence of John Wisdom's *Other Minds*—but its method, namely that of laughing a silly pompous philosophical position out of court, is quite different from Wittgenstein's, or indeed from Straw-son's later exploration of such issues in *Individuals*. By then, the high serious-ness of the Wittgensteinian manner, the turning of philosophy into a species of religious devotions, had come to hold sway, whereas Austin came very close to actually doing what Wittgenstein himself allowed as a possibility, albeit one he certainly did not realize, of writing a philosophy book which took the form of a series of jokes.) Witty moral psychology is taking quite

---

[6] J. L. Austin, *Philosophical Papers*, ed. J. O. Urmson and G. J. Warnock (Oxford: Oxford University Press, 1961), 51 n. 2.   [7] Ibid. 83.

[8] Myles Burnyeat has drawn my attention to the report of Diogenes Laertius (9.69–70) that Theodo-sius said that Skeptics should not call themselves Pyrrhonians, since they did not know Pyrrho's mind's movements. But as Theodosius is reported as using the first person plural as confidently as Hume did, he clearly did not doubt that Pyrrho and others had minds, and ones that did move and have dispositions.

a while to make any sort of comeback, after its partial eclipse under the somber Wittgensteinian mantle of quasi-religious solemnity. John Passmore once complained of the tediousness of the aesthetics of the time, and I think there is ground for some current complaint about the humorlessness of that part of the philosophy of mind that is seen as having any link with ethics. Dan Dennett has certainly brought humor to his treatment of the philosophy of mind, but even he turns very solemn in papers like "Conditions of Personhood"[9] where his philosophy of mind is brought into relation to matters of moral importance. Hume's plea for a morality that has room for gaiety and frolic has, in the subsequent tradition in ethics and moral psychology, fallen on pretty deaf ears.

C. D. Broad should be given credit for introducing at least an occasional note of salutary ridicule into the philosophical discussion of our cognitive access to the minds of our fellow persons, in his Tanner Lectures of 1923, long before Wisdom and Austin. Before giving his fairly solemn and very complicated revised versions of Mill's argument (one version takes a page and a half to state, the other two and a bit pages), as a way of answering any skeptical doubts that might arise about minds other than one's own, Broad distinguishes the proper role he takes this argument to have, to vindicate the natural convictions we all have that we are not the sole exemplars of human nature and human mentality, from its improper use to give an account of how we came by our solipsism-banishing belief in human company. He writes:

the notion that, as a baby, I began by looking in a mirror when I felt cross, noting my facial expression at the time, observing a similar expression from time to time on the face of my mother or nurse, and then arguing by analogy that these external bodies are probably animated by minds like my own, is too silly to need refutation.[10]

This sort of use of ridicule as a philosophical tool, one might add, was condoned even by Reid, that relatively solemn critic of the wittier Hume. Reid ridiculed Hume's views throughout his *Essays on the Intellectual and Active Powers of Man* and at one point defended his own methods by claiming,

⁹ Daniel Dennett, "Conditions of Personhood," in A. O. Rorty (ed.), *Identities of Persons* (Berkeley and Los Angeles: University of California Press, 1976).

¹⁰ C. D. Broad, *The Mind and Its Place in Nature* (London: Kegan Paul, Trench, Trubner, 1937), 324.

"Nature has furnished us with...[ridicule] to *expose absurdity*, as with...[argument] to *refute error*. Both are well fitted to their respective offices, and are equally friendly to truth when properly used."[11] Since ridicule "cuts with as keen an edge as argument," and Reid aimed to cut the Humean view to shreds, he supplemented his argument if not with wit, at least with plenty of ridicule. I do not know if Broad read Reid as well as Mill's reply to Reid, which he surely had read, but he certainly takes himself to be warranted to supplement lengthy argument with passing ridicule of absurdities. Another nice example of his humor is found at the beginning of his chapter "Mind's Knowledge of Other Minds" (an extraordinary title, where "mind" is either a sort of abstract particular, getting to know from what it is abstracted, and sorting its concrete base into one introspected mind plus other "extraspected" ones, or an abstract particular getting to know other related abstract particulars, a sort of "Life meets Extra-terrestrial Life"). Broad's ironic explanation of why the supposed "problem" of knowledge of an "external world" had received more philosophical attention than that of "other minds" runs like this:

We should be doing too much credit to human consistency if we ascribed this to the fact that all convinced Solipsists have kept silence and refused to waste their words on the empty air...I think that the real explanation is that certain strong emotions are bound up with the belief in matter. The position of a philosopher with no one to lecture to, and no hope of an audience, would be so tragic that the human mind naturally shrinks from contemplating such a possibility.[12]

Broad's sense of the tragic predicament of the solipsist philosopher is an ironic intellectualized variant of Reid's sense of the emotional discomfort of those of Berkeley's followers who found their relatives and friends converted into "parcels of ideas," and of the moral predicament of Fichte, finding himself saddled with a moral law demanding that he show respect for the rights of others to whose real personhood he had no access from theoretical reason. He was driven to make the reality of other right-holders a sort of extra postulate of practical reason, by a transcendental argument from the reality of his duties to the reality of those mentioned in them. For sheer comic value, Fichte's argument for other minds may take the prize.[13]

---

[11] Reid, *Essays on the Intellectual Powers of Man*, VI. iv. 18.

[12] Broad, *The Mind and Its Place in Nature*, 317–18.

[13] See Fichte, *Sämmtliche Werke* (Berlin, 1845), iii. 39. I am grateful to Jerry Schneewind for pointing me towards this philosophical treasure trove.

Reid noted that ridicule is not well tolerated on religious topics. "If the notion of sanctity is annexed to an object, it is no longer a laughable matter."[14] Since morality was so long allied with religion, some remnants of protective sanctity still cling to it. And self-knowledge is one of those topics where the dead seriousness thought appropriate to ethics has infected the treatment of the topic in epistemology and philosophy of mind. Since "γνωθι σεατον" ("Know thyself") is a hallowed commandment, the modes of self-knowledge have been taken to have the character of serious moral exercises—if not the severe self-examination of conscience, at least the serious inward gaze of introspection. Descartes deliberately uses the religious genre of "meditations" as the vehicle for his attempt to "understand this 'I' that necessarily exists," and until Wisdom and Austin took their fresh approach, most other philosophers also took the topic of self-knowledge to be one to be treated with some solemnity, even when, like Broad, they let knowledge of others' minds occasionally be laughing matters. Hume,[15] of course, had introduced a definitely light-hearted tone when he asked religiously inclined self-seekers, in particular Samuel Clarke, just how they conceived of the conjoining of an indivisible spiritual thinking self with one of its own impressions or imagistic representations of spatially extended body: "Is the indivisible subject . . . on the left or on the right hand of the perception?" (*T* 40), here echoing the very challenge that he had earlier put into such "theologians" mouths, when he made them ask if the indivisible thought were on the right or the left of the thinker's divisible body, "on the surface or in the middle? On the back or the foreside of it?" (*T* 234). He himself claimed that when he tried to use their preferred method of "intimate entry" by introspection, he failed to find anything whatever answering to the rationalists' conception of a spiritual perceiver, distinct from its own perceptions. This famous finding or non-finding of Hume's led Reid at least to exempt him from the charge of "egoism," which he had leveled at Berkeley. But he has other charges.[16]

The same supposedly skeptical Hume, whose system, Reid charged, "does not even leave him a *self*," in book 2 of the *Treatise* cheerfully announces

---

[14] Reid, *Essays on the Intellectual Powers of Man*, XI. iv. 19.

[15] David Hume, *A Treatise of Human Nature*, ed. L. A. Selby-Bigge, rev. P. H. Nidditch (Oxford: Clarendon Press, 1978) (henceforth *T*).

[16] One of Reid's loaded "Questions for Examination," placed at the end of his presentation of Hume's views in Essay II, reads: "Hume exceeds the Egoists in disbelief and extravagance?"

that "our consciousness gives us so lively a conception of our own person that 'tis not possible that any thing can in this particular go beyond it" (*T* 317). So vivacious does Hume take this "idea or rather impression of ourselves" to be that he explains our ability to transform mere ideas of other people's joys and sorrows into sympathetic fellow feelings by supposing that the surplus liveliness of our self-perception spills over into our ideas of others' experiences, thereby enlivening them from mere ideas of feelings into fellow feelings. For us to have an *impression* of ourselves, not just impressions of pride enlivening our mental life, we must have become considerably more bodily than we seemed to be in "Of Personal Identity," so that sense and kinesthetic impressions of ourselves now play a role in our self-perception. Our perceived relations to others, relations of resemblance, contiguity, and causal blood ties, are taken by Hume to "convey the impression or consciousness of our own person to the idea of the sentiments or passions of others, and [make] us conceive of them in the strongest and most lively manner" (*T* 318).

This extraordinary thesis of Hume's neither repeats nor implies Berkeley's infamous argument by analogy for knowledge of other people (which some think they find elsewhere in Hume—in particular in the *Treatise*, book 3, at *T* 576). Hume here in book 2 simply seems to assume that we reasonably believe, for example, that another person really is suffering when we hear them moaning. "'Tis obvious," he says, "that nature has preserv'd a great resemblance among human creatures, and that we never remark any passion or principle in others, of which, in some degree, we may not find a parallel in ourselves" (*T* 318). He finds it obvious not only that he is not the only intelligent being, but that he resembles the others so closely that nothing human is alien to him—nor much that is animal either. The sequence he gives here is that we "remark" others' passions and then look for parallel ones in ourselves. It is almost as if, for getting to know minds, *we* become the "other," they the main case. What he is explaining in this passage is not our firm belief in the reality of others' feelings, which he takes as unproblematic, but rather our natural sympathy, our tendency to come to "catch" another's joy or suffering, as if by infection. As to how and with what warrant we come to be so sure that others are indeed suffering when they moan, or are delighted when they laugh and jump as if for joy, in book 2 (as indeed in book 1 also), he ignores these particular "abstruse" questions, and simply says that we do take ourselves to be members of a species who have the same range of feelings and express them in the same ways. "The minds of men are mirrors to one another" (*T* 365). The "rays of passions" that are mirrored are, of course, not in any way mysterious, since they are rays of *expressed* passions. As Darwin was later to emphasize, we depend vitally on natural expression for communication and coordination of emotions. And even when we do not need to know how others feel, we often do know, and fairly often come to share their feelings. "A chearful countenance," Hume writes, "infuses a sensible complacency and serenity into my mind; as an angry or sorrowful one throws a sudden damp upon me" (*T* 317). This sympathetic spread of feelings is said to depend upon our sense of similarity to those with whom we sympathize. This sense shows both in the fact that we expect to have feelings parallel to those that we "remark" in others, and also in our being naturally guided by "a kind of *presensation*; which tells us what will operate on others, by what we feel immediately in ourselves" (*T* 332). There is symmetry between oneself and others as far as cognitive access to minds is concerned. Only later, in book 3, does he do anything at all to transform our natural convictions about what others are feeling at particular times into the conclusions of "inferences" that proceed from sense perception of the typical causes or effects of some passion, in another's case, to a belief in the other's feeling that passion.

But even there Hume does not make such an inference an inductive generalization from one's own case to that of others, nor into an argument from analogy. Hume had discussed inductive arguments from analogy in the book 1 section "Of the Probability of Causes." In such reasoning, he wrote, we do have a fully constant conjunction for some class of cases, which is then extended to a case or cases which to some degree resemble the first set, but only imperfectly. "An experiment loses its force when it is transferred to instances, which are not exactly resembling" (*T* 142). By this account, our taking peacocks to feel pride when they strut would be such an argument from analogy, but scarcely our taking fellow human persons to feel pride when they strut, since Hume never suggests that we each see ourself as something only a bit like our fellows as far as our nature goes. It is *human* nature, not his own nature, that he treats in his famous work, even if his first reviewers did think he fell into "egotisms." Only very briefly, in the Conclusion of book 1, did he contemplate the possibility that he might be unrepresentative of humanity, and even there it was not skepticism about other minds that he entertained, but fear that he might himself be "some strange uncouth monster." Even at the height of his despairing doubt he still can ask, "Whose anger must I dread?" No suspicion that he might be the only one capable of real anger ever seems to have entered his mind, even at the depth of his doubting mood. The inference at T 576 is presented by Hume as a standard inference, a "proof," not a probability, and not as that imperfect sort of inference that he calls argument from analogy. (Mill follows him here, claiming that the argument conforms to "the legitimate rules of experimental enquiry. The process is exactly parallel to that by which Newton proved that the force which keeps the planets in their orbits is identical to that by which an apple falls to the ground."[17])

In Mill's version of the inductive generalization in question, we generalize from our own case to that of others, taken to be closely similar in anatomy, powers of speech, etc. Similarity of mind is inferred from similarity of body and behavior. In the book 3 passage, Hume *begins* rather than ends with the assertion that "the minds of all men are similar in their feelings and operations." The inference to belief in another's particular state of mind is taken as an instance of the already granted truth that no one can "be actuated by any affection of which all others are not, in some degree, susceptible" (T 576). This shared susceptibility facilitates the sympathetic sharing of particular emotions. "As in strings equally wound up, the motion of one communicates itself to the rest; so all the affections readily pass from one person to another and beget correspondent movements in every human creature" (ibid.). Hume treats the perceived causes or effects of another's passion as the cue that activates in us the general certainty that others feel as we do, for the same sorts of reasons, and a specific belief as to what someone is now feeling, leading naturally to the sharing of that passion. The "signs" of others' feelings are not treated as giving us premises for some inference needed to establish that others ever feel as we do. He does say that we "infer" others' specific passions, but he also says that the inference is "immediate." "When I see the effects of passion in the voice and gesture of any person, my mind immediately passes from these effects to their causes" (ibid.). We immediately anticipate the pain of the patient undergoing "any of the more terrible operations of surgery," even if we ourselves have been so far spared the surgeon's knife. The causal inferences

---

[17] Mill, *Examination of Sir William Hamilton's Philosophy*.

involved here do not seem to depend on constant conjunctions that the inferrer need herself have verified in her own case: we are taken by Hume to have a predisposition to believe that we are not unique in our reactions, and that our conspecifics' reactions to, say, surgery without anesthetic are the best possible indication of what our own reactions would be. As he presents the matter, the signs of anxiety in the surgery patient as the instruments are prepared and the irons heated have a great effect on the sympathetic spectator's mind, exciting pity and terror. The generalization is as much from the way the patient reacts to the way one expects one would oneself react, as vice versa.

We might in theory try to take Hume's remarks about the inferential nature of our "discovery" of what another feels on a given occasion, from the "effects" that feeling has in how the person looks, sounds, and behaves, to mean that the spectator's inference runs like this: "I would feel terror if those instruments and irons were being prepared for me. The patient is pale, and shuddering, which is how I would be if dreading the surgery, so I suppose that he really feels terror." From the causes—sight of the preparations—and the effects—anxious behavior—one infers the passion of terror. But if one asks how one knows that one would oneself pale if in terror, one soon realizes that the inference is not from purely first-personal "discovery" of the typical terror causal chain, all the way from terror-causing expectations through feeling to paling and gibbering, for one's knowledge that one would pale, or does pale, seems as extrapolation-dependent as the certainty that others do really feel. For, to repeat Broad's point, how many of us have been offered a mirror when we pale with fright? Yet we have no reasonable doubt that we do, like everyone else, pale when frightened, flush when angry, and so on. Even Descartes, supposed believer in our privileged access to our own mental states, had no skeptical doubts on that score; indeed, he thought he knew all sorts of interesting facts about the natural expression and physiology of human emotions, such as that love speeds the digestion (*Passions of the Soul*, arts. 97 and 107). To verify that one does oneself exhibit the typical face, voice, and gestures of the sad person when one is sad, or of the frightened person when one is frightened, or of the angry person when one is angry, one depends upon what others, or what mirrors or cameras or tape recorders, tell one about the expression of such emotions. (To realize the effects of love on one's digestion, one depends on others a little less.) One surely knows from one's own case that feelings tend towards their own expression, but just how that expression appears to others one learns only with others' help.

It is indeed from such other people who do take one's expressive face to express what such a face normally does that one learns the words and concepts we have for discriminating different emotions, moods, and attitudes, even the difference between being awake and being asleep and dreaming.[18] So one very simple way to get to know one's own mind, at least as far as its emotional states go, is to return to this original source of knowledge about such matters, and to ask others to share their knowledge of one's state with one. I think that it is pretty obvious to all of us that we are not especially good at recognizing our own emotional states for what they are, whereas our friends, or even our enemies, have a much more reliable access to this dimension of our minds, or should I here say "hearts," than we do ourselves. Of course, they, especially our enemies, may refuse to share their knowledge with us, since knowledge is power, and their ability to manipulate us for their own ends will be greater the less self-knowledge we have.

It might be conceded that one simple way to know what emotions are eating one up is to ask a well-disposed but frank companion to read one's face for one. But, it might be said, emotions are not everything, and my title spoke of "knowing one's own mind," which refers more properly to one's intentions than to one's passions. Against this objection I would argue first that intentions are not so separate from ruling passions, and that even those aspects of them that are not passion-determined may be as clear or clearer to a well-placed observer as to the agent herself. So the simple ways already mentioned, namely asking a friend what we appear to be up to, or having one's behavior audio- and videotaped so that one can get an approximation to a privileged outsider's viewpoint on it, still hold good. We do, surely, pretty confidently predict our close acquaintances' future decisions, whereas our own seem to be veiled from us.

What we do often know better than others about our own intentions is the answer we will give when asked how we came to be doing what we are doing, and what it is that appeals to us in the goal we are aiming at—though even this is something that an old and perceptive friend can often anticipate, both when our answers are self-deceptive and when they

---

[18] I discuss this in "Cartesian Persons," in Baier, *Postures of the Mind* (London: Methuen, 1985).

are sincere. The passing thoughts and images that deck out our decision-making and our intention formation, that are strewn along our paths to the carrying out of our intentions and adorn our subsequent satisfaction or regret, are what are safest from public scrutiny, at least by current techniques. But who would say that our automatic access to our own stream of consciousness is enough to enable us to know our own mind? The command "Know thyself" is not obeyed simply by avoiding deep anesthetics and blows on the head.[19] Locke, talking about reflection, took it at least to require some special attention.[20] Reid, commenting on Locke, emphasized that reflection was difficult, and took training and practice.[21] One reason why it was difficult, he thought, was what Hume had called the "inconceivable rapidity" (*T* 252) of our changes of perception. But even if we could survey a stretch of our own stream of consciousness in slow motion, giving our full attention to it, we still might not find our thoughts self-characterizing. Some interpretation of the drift of our fantasies, the direction of our thoughts, needs to be offered before we can even pretend to self-knowledge. What is needed for self-knowledge is not just consciousness, but raised consciousness. And for that, most of us need a little help from our friends and enemies.

Knowledge is contrasted both with error and with ignorance. It is easy to be in error about one's own resentments, motives, and character traits, and ignorance about one's deepest wishes is presumably what many people pay their psychiatrists large sums to have remedied. Why do we grant others, as we surely do often grant them, the right to correct us in our self-descriptions, and to teach us how to read our own motives? Not just because we cannot see our own giveaway faces, nor even hear our own expressive voices, in quite the way others do, but because one thing that most of us do know about our own motives is that we frequently have motives for deceiving

---

[19] Elizabeth Anscombe, "The First Person," in Anscombe, *Metaphysics and the Philosophy of Mind: Collected Philosophical Papers*, ii (Minneapolis: University of Minnesota Press, 1981), 36, cites William James's account of poor Baldy, who, when he came to after a blow on the head received when he fell out of a carriage, asked "Did anyone fall out?" When told "Yes, Baldy did," he replied, "Poor Baldy" (William James, *Principles of Psychology* (London, 1901), 273 n.). Anscombe takes this story to show that one can be conscious without being self-conscious, and so it does. So my point needs to be put by saying that neither consciousness nor self-consciousness ensure self-knowledge.

[20] I am indebted to David Finkelstein for drawing my attention to Locke's words in *An Essay Concerning Human Understanding*, II. i. A7, that unless one turns one's thoughts towards the operation of one's mind, and considers them attentively, one will not have clear and distinct ideas of reflection.

[21] Reid, *Essays on the Intellectual Powers of Man*, I. vi. I.

ourselves about ourselves, and that self-deception is not easily unmasked by the self-deceiver, all on her own. Donald Davidson calls self-deceit "an anomalous and borderline phenomenon."[22] Either he must be a lot freer of it than most of us, or he is subject, as we all tend to be, to meta-self-deception. Of course, we do often have motive for avoiding the truth not just about our own but also about our friends' motives and characters, so that there can be conspiracies of mutually aided self-deception. Still, for most people their self-conception is more jealously guarded from threat than their conceptions of even their best friends. Hume, discussing the relations between pride and love, wrote, "The passage is smooth and open from the consideration of any person related to us, to that of ourself, of whom we are every moment conscious. But when the affections are once directed to ourself, the fancy passes not with the same facility from that object to any other person, how closely soever connected to us" (T 340). Hume is not here denying the force of love, nor of sympathy, but simply noting the special importance to us of our self-assessment, of the centrality of self-directed passions among the full array of human passions. There is an important asymmetry not so much in our knowledge of ourselves and our fellows as in our concern about what is known about ourselves and others.

To be capable of the sort of pride, humility, and resentment of insult that Hume attributes to us, it is not enough that we tend like peacocks to strut, like beaten dogs to skulk and whimper, and like offended cats to spit and strike; we also need to have a self-description, a sort of self-written testimonial to ourselves secretly stored away, ever sensitive to challenge and on the watch for endorsement. In discussing the pride of animals, Hume emphasizes both the fact that the higher animals do seem to seek and take pride in our approbation of them, and also the fact that their pride is taken solely "in the body, and can never be plac'd in the mind" (T 326). This, he writes, is because they have "little or no sense of virtue or vice," so no conception of their own character traits. We do have a conception of our own Humean virtues and vices, that is to say our dispositions and abilities or disabilities, and it is this which we guard so jealously, which motivates most of our self-deceit, and so throws us back on frank talk from friends or enemies for any hope of becoming less deceived about ourselves.

---

[22] Donald Davidson, "Knowing One's Own Mind," *Proceedings and Addresses of the American Philosophical Association*, 61 (1987), 441–58.

Hume, a little cynically, lists another's willingness to flatter our vanity among the chief causes of love (*T* 347–9). Since "nothing more readily produces kindness or affection to any person than his approbation of our conduct and character" (*T* 346), those we love as friends will have to be very careful about the "service" they render us in the way of disabusing us of our more optimistic self-interpretations. If "a good office is agreeable chiefly because it flatters our vanity" (*T* 349), then the office of frank critic is not likely to be perceived as a good one. Hume notes both our tendency to make friends with those who will not perform this thankless task too often, and also our tendency to discount the assessments of those whom we do not ourselves respect. Since we do not easily admit that we respect flatterers, then we often have some difficulty finding people who can fulfill one of the friend's main roles, that of "seconding" our evaluations (including our self-evaluations), while at the same time avoiding appearing too openly to be willing to "flatter our vanity." "Tho fame in general be agreeable, yet we receive a much greater satisfaction from the approbation of those whom we ourselves esteem and approve of, than those, whom we hate and despise. In like manner, we are principally mortified with the contempt of persons, upon whose judgment we set some value ..." (*T* 321). This sets the scene for self-deception about oneself to need to be allied with some self-deception about the friends who nourish and support one's self-delusions. Maybe the best solution is to look to one's enemies, not one's friends, to keep one honest, while making some allowance for their special bias. Strangers, although free of bias, will not do, since they tend to be polite, and in any case they have no reason to give particular notice to the way we are, but enemies do tend to keep track of us, and to be more willing to violate norms of politeness. Nor is their bias likely to be any greater than our own, so it can serve nicely to correct it.

There is a wonderful example of the plight of the person who is left to his own devices for knowing his own mind in the novel *The Margin*, by André Pieyre de Mandiargues,[23] interestingly discussed by Adrian Piper in her paper "Pseudorationality."[24] The 42-year-old hero or

---

[23] André Pieyre de Mandiargues, *The Margin* (winner in 1967 of the Prix Goncourt), trans. R. Howard (New York: Grove, 1969).

[24] A. Piper, "Pseudorationality," in B. P. McLaughlin and A. O. Rorty (eds.), *Perspectives on Self Deception* (Berkeley: University of California Press, 1988).

antihero, Sigismond, is during the time of the novel's narrative artificially isolated from his normal companions, since he is on a brief visit to Barcelona, where he has never been before, and knows no one. In his three days there, the only person he gets at all to know is a pretty young Castilian prostitute, Juanita. She speaks no French, he little Spanish, so he does not disclose much of himself or his preoccupations to her. He is virtually on his own, as far as knowing his own mind goes. His is a good case, for our purposes, for what he clearly needs some help with includes knowing what he believes, knowing what he feels, and knowing what he intends. He has travelled from his home in France, leaving his wife and little son there, to do some business in Barcelona for his cousin. On the way he bought some condoms, so that he could try the pleasures of the city, of which his cousin had given him graphic accounts. He is portrayed as a fairly self-deprecating man, happy in his marriage to the younger and more vivacious Sergine, whose frequent mockery of his more stolid ways he treats as loving mockery. Then on his arrival he receives a letter from home, from his old servant. He opens it and reads enough to know that it reports some woman's suicide by throwing herself from a tower on his property. He reseals the letter, puts it on a table in his hotel room, builds a little shrine around it and engages in a sort of ritual at this shrine, regularly caressing both it and the phallic bottle, in the shape of the Colon tower, with which he has weighted it down. (After receiving the letter, he had made for the Colon tower, ascended to the top of it, and considered how it would feel to throw oneself from it.) He adds a black tie to the outfit he is wearing and for nearly three days lives in what he terms "a bubble," explores the city's red light district, sleeping each evening with Juanita. He thinks repeatedly of his wife, remembering times together, imagining what her reactions would have been to the sights he is seeing and the Catalan food he is eating, even imagining how she would look as one of the "sea of prostitutes" his cousin promised him he would move in, in Barcelona, and that he does move in. He thinks of Sergine's body as he looks at Juanita's body, and he thinks of her in what is ambiguous between the present and the past tense. But when he sees just the gift to take (to have taken?) back to her, he does not buy it. He does not bother to use the condoms he has prepared himself with, nor to wash after making love to Juanita. He does not bother to change his clothing. Eventually he reads the letter properly, learns that it is indeed his wife who has killed herself, after their little son's accidental death by drowning in a pond in their garden, while she was reading nearby. He then drives out of the city, pulls over into a quarry, and shoots himself through the heart.

Sigismond's state of mind is described by the author, near the end, thus. "He feels no surprise, upon reflection, for he knows that without having exact knowledge, he had apprehended the disaster in its irredeemable totality, and he prides himself on having been capable of sidetracking it for two days before it burst upon his consciousness at a moment of his own choosing."[25] Sidetracking apprehension of disaster and choosing the time to bring it onto the main track is a very interesting thing to be proud of. The novel makes it quite clear that Sigismond has, since the letter arrived, been bent on suicide, that his final fling is a desperate one. He was not really self-deceived, just unnaturally self-controlled. He delayed full "exact" knowledge, full acknowledgment, for three days. Why? That is the more difficult question, and it raises the question of his motives. Is his suicide occasioned, as Piper believes,[26] by the destruction of his idea of himself as centre of his wife's life? Or simply by despair at the prospect of life without wife and son? Or did it take disgust at his own chosen style of mourning—namely, going ahead with his eagerly awaited binge in Barcelona—to firm up his suicidal intentions? These questions are not answered by the novel, and human motives can remain enigmas even to omniscient observing or creating novelists. But any roommate or companion could have corrected Sigismond's impression that he had really sidetracked his apprehension of disaster. To make a fetish of a letter is not to sidetrack it—on the contrary, it is to put it in a central place. A simple question to Sigismond as to why he was wearing a black tie, and not bothering with normal hygiene, could have ended any pretence that he was having his planned good time, as distinct from revving up to shooting himself. (Indeed Juanita's question on their last meeting, when she notes his disregard for hygiene, and asks, "Are you ill?" may be taken to be what breaks Sigismond's bubble.) He knew his own belief, despair, and suicidal intentions well enough to act intelligently in the

[25] De Mandiargues, *The Margin*, 206.
[26] I discuss Piper's interpretation more thoroughly in "The Vital but Dangerous Art of Ignoring. Selective Attention and Self Deception," presented at the conference "The Self and Deception," East–West Center, Honolulu, Aug. 1992; in Roger T. Ames and Wimal Dissanayake (eds.), *Self and Deception: A Cross-Cultural Philosophical Enquiry* (Albany: State University of New York Press, 1996).

light of them, and yet he was not wrong in thinking that he did choose the moment to let this knowledge, this despair, this intention, "burst on his consciousness." He performed an elaborate act of postponing, out of somewhat murky motives. Determination not to be cheated out of his fun weekend? Uncertainty as to what his response to his wife's suicide should or would be? Need for time for the news to sink in? We can understand St Augustine's prayer "Lord, let me be pure, but not yet," but the prayer "Let my empty life end, but not while I am having such a good time," is a little harder to make sense of. And was it because he could, or because he could not, drown his grief in dissipation that his suicidal drift turned into purposeful action? The novel is to be recommended for the disturbing doubts it leaves us with, as much as for its fine writing and its less ambiguous psychological insights.

Sigismond does, through the letter, get insight into how others, in particular his wife, must have seen, overlooked, or ignored him. But his ability to delay full acknowledgment of the impact of the news of her suicide, to keep his bubble unbroken, was a function of his virtual isolation in a foreign city, moving among strangers. Another case of delayed self-knowledge through isolation, and one closer to the philosophical nerve, is that of Descartes in his *Meditations*, and it is a bit like Sigismond's in that pride is taken in the very act of putting aside what is granted to have a legitimate demand on his attention. In Descartes's case, the isolation is broken once copies of what he wrote are circulated by Mersenne to those who wrote the Objections, and they were quick to challenge Descartes's version, in the text, of what he had done there, intentionally and according to plan. Descartes, in his Replies, of course makes a very good self-defense, but the Replies are as interesting as they are to us as much for the *new* information they give us about how the Cartesian story goes as for their mere repetition and clarification of the narrative or argument line of the original text.

The expressed intentions of Descartes's meditator, at the end of the First Meditation, include this:

I think it will be a good plan to turn my will in completely the opposite direction, and deceive myself, by pretending for a time that these former opinions are utterly false and imaginary. I shall do this until the weight of preconceived opinion is counterbalanced, and the distorting force of habit no longer prevents me from perceiving things correctly. In the meantime, I know that no danger or error will result from my plan, and that I cannot possibly go too far in my distrustful attitude.

This is because the task in hand does not involve action, but merely the acquisition of knowledge.[27]

Descartes's announced plan is to treat the uncertain as if it were the false for a limited time, namely until his earlier prejudices are counteracted. But how long exactly is this? He does not tell us when he judges himself cured of prejudice,[28] so can revert to treating the uncertain as uncertain, the probable as probable, instead of treating, or pretending to treat, all such claims as false. Did he forget to? Did he think that we the readers should see when was the time for him to end the controlled self-deception? Or did he deliberately confuse the shift from pseudo-negative claims to seriously meant negative claims?

Mersenne, in the Second Set of Objections, wrote that the

vigorous rejection of the images of all bodies as delusive was not something you actually and really carried through but merely a fiction of the mind enabling you to draw the conclusion that you were exclusively a thinking thing. We point this out in case you should perhaps suppose that it is possible to go on to draw the conclusion that you are in fact nothing more than a mind, or a thinking thing.[29]

Descartes in reply points out that it was not until the essence of body had been shown to be intellectually comprehensible spatial extension, in the Fifth Meditation, and the essences or natures of body and of mind compared, in the Sixth, that the real distinction of himself as a thinker from any body was inferred. But Mersenne's implicit gentle charge, that what began as a "fiction" had not been clearly concluded as a fiction, still stands unanswered.[30]

Arnauld in the Fourth Set of Objections, Gassendi in the Fifth Set of Objections, and Bourdin in the Seventh, all join Mersenne in querying the move from "I can know I am a thinking thing without yet knowing whether I am an extended thing, that is, while pretend-denying that I have a body," to

---

[27] *The Philosophical Writings of Descartes*, ii, trans. John Cottingham, Robert Stoothoff, and Dugald Murdoch (Cambridge: Cambridge University Press, 1984), 15 (henceforth CSM); *Œuvres de Descartes*, ed. Charles Adam and Paul Tannery, 11 vols (Paris: Librairie Philosophique J.Vrin, 1983), vii. 22 (henceforth AT).

[28] He does, at the beginning of the Fourth Meditation, claim now to have no trouble attending to intelligible as distinct from sensory things, but not all the old beliefs made doubtful in the First were sense-based, so it is not clear that all his former prejudices are yet counterbalanced. His earlier assumptions about the scope and freedom of his will are yet to be corrected.   [29] CSM 87; AT 122.

[30] I discuss what trouble this makes for Descartes's argument in the Fourth Meditation, and for his various claims in the *Meditations* about deceit and self-deceit, in "The Vital But Dangerous Art of Ignoring."

"I know I am a thinking and unextended thing," which is what is asserted in the Sixth Meditation proof of the real distinctness of mind and body. Gassendi and Bourdin are less gentle than Mersenne. Gassendi suggests that Descartes's policy amounts to adopting a new prejudice, rather than relinquishing old prejudices, and says that critics will accuse Descartes of artifice and sleight of hand. Now, if Descartes in fact makes the move from "I could be and was certain I was a thinker while still uncertain that I had a body, that is while I was pretend-denying that I had a body (as a counter-ploy to any powerful beings who might be trying to deceive me into uncritical belief that I did have a body)" to "I am certain that I am a thinker who does not need (even if he in fact has) a body in order to be a thinker," then he has indeed either taken himself in, has done what he said he intended to do but deceived himself more thoroughly than he intended, or else there is intentional "sleight of hand." For he will be guilty of confusing his pretend denials, those of the Second Meditation, with serious denials, those needed for the reasoning of at least the Fifth and Sixth to succeed, and to have done this by blurring the transition from fake to real denials. He has forgotten or covered up the fact that his denials are untrustworthy, or rather that some of them need decoding.

It took the watchful eye of Descartes's friendly and less friendly critics to raise the question of when the pretence, or controlled temporary self-deception, came to an end, and whether the cogency of the Sixth Meditation demonstration of the real distinction of soul and body depended on forgetting to put an end to it. Descartes, of course, indignantly rejected such a suggestion, and gave a restatement of the notorious demonstration that is supposed to save it. But even if his defense works, it took Mersenne and the others to get him to attend explicitly to the question of how consistently he had carried out his announced plans, of how many changes of mind he had undergone along the way in the supposed six days of mental labor. Our friends and enemies often play this indispensable role of reminding us not merely of our earlier promises to them, but of our earlier expressed intentions, which appear from our behavior to have been either dropped or conveniently forgotten. And just as often we throw a retrospective appearance of coherence over our doings, reconstructing certain past moves to make them look as if we did not swerve too wildly nor lose control of our benign self-deceptions, as if we *did* know our own mind throughout. But we usually convince our friendly and less friendly critics of this no more successfully than Descartes has convinced his critics of the lucidity of his intentional thought moves throughout the *Meditations*. Taking heed that we may be mistaken about what we intended and intend, what we believed and believe, what we wanted and want, is a vital step in the improvement of our knowledge of our own minds. We will have taken it only when charges of self-misunderstanding are, if not welcomed, at least respectfully entertained. This is as true of our intentions in our philosophical writing as of any others. I am pretty sure what Descartes was up to, but what am I up to?

8

The Moral Perils of Intimacy

Richard Rorty has said that "the problem is that love (and therefore courage and cowardice, sacrifice and selfishness) looks different after one has read Freud. It is not that we have learned that there is no such thing, but rather that it has been described in ways which make it difficult to use the notion in moral reasoning."[1] But this will be a problem only for those who have tried to use the notion of love in their moral reasoning, or have relied on it in their moral sentiments. A striking feature of modern moral *philosophy* is the avoidance of the concept of love. It is as if our great moral theorists, since Hobbes, have tried to formulate a morality acceptable to unloving and unloved persons, an impersonal morality that is to govern relationships between persons seen as essentially strangers to one another, ones having no natural interest in each other's interests. Should there be closer ties between any particular moral agents, these are then thought to superimpose extra rights or duties on the rights and duties of strangers among strangers.

The so-called core morality governs relations between aloof adult strangers, and this core may be supplemented but not supplanted by special duties to children, friends, or loved ones. In the dominant Western liberal moral tradition, a person is, morally speaking, first of all an autonomous individual (or a potential one, or an ex-one), whose privacy and freedom are to be respected, and only after that and compatibly with that a lover, friend, parent, child, or co-worker. For such moral reasoning as Hobbes and Kant have taught us to engage in, the transformation of the concept of love will have no consequences whatever, since it figures there only incidentally and peripherally. Such sacrifice and selfishness as our modern moral philosophers have been led to consider are linked not to love, but only to self-love and its overcoming. And as David Hume emphasized, self-love is not love

---

[1] Richard Rorty, "Freud, Morality and Hermeneutics," *New Literary History*, 12 (1980), 180.

"in a proper sense."[2] Nor is that love of humanity, or of truth, or of intellectual freedom that Rorty thinks supplanted love of God as the driving force in liberal secular morality. To find any accounts of morality in which love in a proper sense figures centrally, one must turn to Christian moralists, and among philosophers to Christian moral theorists such as St Augustine, St Thomas Aquinas, and Bishop Butler. (But Butler's discussion of love of one's neighbor, like Nietzsche's words on love of one's non-neighbor, do not really make love in a proper sense central to anything they thought of much importance for morality, or for what lies beyond it.)

Rorty says, just before the previously quoted passage, that "neither the religious nor the secular and liberal morality seem possible, and no third alternative has emerged."[3] That, I think, is to ignore not merely Hegelian and Marxist moral theories but also to overlook the distinctive contribution of Hume's moral philosophy. For Hume offers us a basis for a secular morality that is free of the false psychology and bad faith of liberalism, and it is a moral theory that both gives love in a proper sense a very important moral role and treats love quite "anatomically" and realistically. Humean heroes and heroines not only can but must be both ironists and lovers (as Hume himself was). And Humean love needs no unmasking, since whatever masks it may wear are appreciated by Humeans for what they are.

Hume discusses love at great length, and, unlike many other moral theorists, does not see it as merely a *psychological* possibility, to be contrasted with moral necessities. But his subtle account of love is no *more* essential a preliminary to his account of the moral sentiment and morality than is his account of pride, of avidity, and of a "sympathetic" communication of passions that presupposes no love, so it would be an exaggeration to see his moral theory as love-based. To the extent that his moral philosophy relies on the actuality of love between parents and children, between friends, and between lovers, more than do most modern moral theories, the transformation of our understanding of love that Freud wrought seems to me to strengthen rather than weaken Hume's moral philosophy. This is because Hume's own version of psychic energy, of love, and of the dependencies and interdependencies love produces and is produced by, itself in some ways anticipates Freud. Hume has no starry-eyed romantic conception of love, vulnerable to more

[2] David Hume, *A Treatise of Human Nature*, ed. L. A. Selby-Bigge, rev. P. H. Nidditch (New York: Oxford University Press, 1978), 329.   [3] Rorty, "Freud, Morality and Hermeneutics," 180.

realistic revisions. He is both a clear-headed moral "anatomist," seeing human love and its variants as special cases of animal or more specifically mammalian love, grounded in physical needs and dependencies, and also a subtle discerner of all the delicate refinements, variations, and vulnerabilities peculiar to love between those who have human understanding as well as human needs and human feelings.

Hume is a tireless reporter of the oddities of human affection—that a son's tie to his mother is weakened by the mother's remarriage, but his tie to his father weakened "in a much less degree" by the father's remarriage; that "a mother thinks not her tie to her son weaken'd, because 'tis shared with her husband: Nor a son with his parent, because 'tis shared with a brother," whereas having to share it with a stepbrother and a stepfather is another matter.[4] These "pretty curious phenomena" attending our "love of relations" are noted by Hume, and explained by him in terms of his associationist theory, itself a theory of "relations" between ideas and impressions that he himself has just associated with "one *relation* of a different kind," namely, "the relation of blood."[5] Although some of his associationist explanations of the vagaries of our affections may seem strained and overintellectualized, they assume a rather different complexion when one bears in mind the close relation Hume forges between relations of ideas and impressions and that "relation of blood" which forges "the strongest tie the mind is capable of, in the love of parents for their children."[6]

My purpose here, however, is not just to present Hume as a moralist who offers an alternative both to liberalism and to a religion-based morality, and who does not need to be sheltered from the insights Freud gave us, but more particularly to direct attention to the fact that Hume is atypical among moral philosophers in the modern period in seeing any need to discuss love in order to understand our specifically moral beliefs and attitudes. I also want to raise the question of why it is that most of our great modern moral theorists do *not* find love to be of any particular moral importance, and so do not, presumably, need to revise their conclusions in the light of anything Freud has taught us about love.

One explanation of the "lovelessness" of modern moral theory in the dominant Western tradition is suggested by the recent findings of Carol

[4] Hume, *Treatise*, 355–7.   [5] Ibid. 352.   [6] Ibid.

Gilligan regarding differences between typically male and typically female moral development, or rather of the development of the conceptions of morality in men and women. For our great classical moral theorists not only are all men but are mostly men who had minimal adult contact with women. Hume, Hegel, and Sidgwick are the exceptions among a group of gays, misogynists, clerics, and puritan bachelors (the status of J. S. Mill and of Bradley is unclear). If Gilligan is right about male understanding of morality, in its usual mature form it takes morality to be more or less what Kant takes it to be: a matter of respect for the more or less equal rights of free autonomous persons who have learned to discipline their natural self-assertiveness and self-aggrandizing tendencies in order to make it possible for many such natural self-seekers to coexist without mutual destruction or unnecessary mutual frustration. The male "genius" in moral matters, according to the story Gilligan gives, is the capacity to arrive at, institute, and obey rules regulating competition among selfish individualists. Girls, by contrast, seem initially both less self-assertive and competitive, and less willing or able to institute rules to control or arbitrate such interpersonal conflicts as naturally develop. They see themselves as born into ties to others, as having responsibilities for the preservation of these "natural" ties, not as inventors or even very good respecters of humanly forged, formal rule-dependent relations between persons.

The conflicts that Gilligan's women want a satisfactory morality to avoid or resolve are not so much conflicts between self-interested persons as conflicts that present themselves to a single other-centered person finding herself with incompatible responsibilities to a variety of persons. The situation of a woman who tries to care both for her aged mother and for her husband whose psychosomatic health troubles are aggravated by the aged mother's presence (or by his wife's attention to her mother) is *not* like that of someone who has to arbitrate a head-on conflict of wills between a demanding old woman and a demanding middle-aged man, both competing for one woman's attention and care. If the woman loves both her mother and her husband, she cannot take up the position of an impartial arbitrator, and no Solomonic wisdom can settle the matter for her. For even if she knows that her husband's intolerance of her mother's company and need is unreasonable, she will, if she loves him, prefer to tear herself in two rather than refuse to try to partially satisfy his needs and wishes, however unreasonable.

The women in Gilligan's abortion study,[7] who unwillingly and with lasting ill effects in their own lives decided for abortion to try to please their men and to prolong their relations with them, are melancholy testimony to the typical female unwillingness to resolve a conflict of emotional demands by cutting ties with the less "innocent" of the two demanders. The usually futile effort is somehow to have it both ways, to share oneself between those making competing calls upon one. No list of rights, and no techniques of arbitration, will settle such emotional and moral conflicts. It is noteworthy here that men writing on abortion tend to address the issue in terms of the right (or lack of right) of the fetus to life and of the woman to control of her body, while women often find all such talk beside the point. The point, for them, is not what they or others have a right to, but whom, among those they *want* to care for, they should reluctantly abandon or neglect in these conflict situations, where none of these persons need be seen as having any *right* to their care. The morality that solves or avoids such dilemmas will need different concepts and will encourage a different sort of moral reflection from those liberal ones that have evolved to resolve disputes between egoists.

It is sometimes claimed that the altruists' dilemmas are of essentially the same sort as the egoists' (so-called prisoner's dilemma),[8] namely, a matter of conflict between the best interest of one person and the parallel and incompatible best interest of another. But the altruist, torn between continuing to support her mother and her husband, or between keeping her mate and keeping her unborn child, is *not* in the position of a judge asked to arbitrate between the conflicting interests of different parties, for her own interest and her own wishes are also part both of the problem and of most possible solutions. She must choose not just who is to be hurt or harmed by her action but what sort of person she herself is to become: a child-abandoner or a mate-abandoner, a mother-neglecter or a husband-neglecter. Her own future, as well as that of those she wishes to care for, is at stake. The sort of wisdom needed to avoid, or to best make and live with, such choices is different from that needed by the judge, peacemaker, or referee. But since none of our moral theories have come from women, nor been articulated

---

[7] Carol Gilligan, *In a Different Voice* (Cambridge, Mass.: Harvard University Press, 1982), chs. 3 and 4.

[8] After writing this I was pleased to read Ian Hacking's negative assessment of the popular big boys' game of prisoner's or prisoners' dilemma in his review in the *New York Review of Books* (June 28, 1984) of Robert Axelrod's *The Evolution of Cooperation*.

to "rationalize" such womanly moral wisdom as may exist on such matters, all we have, as yet, are old wives' tales, not alternative moral *theories* giving intellectualized voice to women's insights into what seem to be typically female moral issues.

It is possible, of course, that women's moral insight is intrinsically resistant to theoretical reconstruction—that we old wives are essentially antitheorists. If men can detach intellect from passion more readily than women, and put more value on such passionless intellect, and if theories are purely intellectual products, then it is to be expected that moral theory will continue to be a typically male product, independent of the degree of liberation, wisdom, power, or self-consciousness of women. (I myself have in the past given voice to some antitheoretical sentiments,[9] but I am uncertain whether the impetus was antitheoretical, or merely antagonism to the style and content of the currently dominant theories.)

There are, as already acknowledged, some male moral philosophers who do not see the main moral problems and solutions in the dominant modern way as arising out of clashes of perceived self-interest. Both some Marxists, who look forward to a realm of freedom where communal pursuits fulfilling to all parties replace competitive individualism, and some Hegel-influenced non-Marxists, such as Alasdair MacIntyre,[10] see the central problem not as what to do to achieve fair settlement of interpersonal clashes of interest, but rather as what form of life to institute so that interpersonal conflicts are avoided, and so that the propensity to those narrowly self-interested and self-indulgent pursuits that usually lead to such conflicts is overcome. Such a theory is, like Hume's, an important alternative to liberalism. It does not take relationships between mutually disinterested strangers as morally central, but directs attention to relationships between persons of unequal authority and expertise who are united in a common but non-universal practice, in pursuit of a shared substantive and to some extent esoteric good.[11] MacIntyre's voice in moral theory can, as much as Hume's, be more easily tuned to harmonize with the "other voice" Gilligan has heard than can the liberal male voice. But MacIntyre shares, with liberalism, a conception

[9] See my "Doing Without Moral Theory?" and "Theory and Reflective Practices," in Baier, *Postures of the Mind* (Minneapolis: University of Minnesota Press, 1985).

[10] Alasdair MacIntyre, *After Virtue* (Notre Dame, Ind.: University of Notre Dame Press, 1981).

[11] See MacIntyre, "Rights, Practices, and Marxism: A Reply to Six Critics," *Analyse and Kritik*, 1 (1985), 234–48, for a clear statement of his position on this point.

of morality as discipliner of desire, including desires attendant upon love, rather than as any sort of development or fuller expression of naturally arising love, so his theory, as much as that of liberals, seems untouched by anything Freud has taught us about love. At most Freud will have informed all such male moral theorists of some interesting details about the genesis and ancestry of the passions a rational morality has to control.

Of more consequence to all such "disciplinary" conceptions of morality will be Freud's account of the origins and nature of the superego, the impetus to self-discipline, and self-denial. Had Rorty said that the *disciplining* of desire, along with the associated concepts of conscience and duty, look different after Freud, and are now less easily invoked in moral reasoning, his remarks would have applied more tellingly to the moral reasoning of most modern philosophers, liberal and anti-liberal. The courage and sacrifice needed to obey conscience and deny desire are at least as transfigured by what Freud taught us as are the courage and sacrifice that love sometimes entails. A version of morality, like MacIntyre's, that demands of us a willingness to let our tastes be reformed and our desires disciplined by some authoritative tradition will be received with some suspicion by those who have learned from Freud that self-proclaimed authoritative voices tend to be those of jealous fathers or their envious imitators and epigones.

The idea of a practice into which novices get initiated, receiving at each point what is due to them in virtue of their position and their performance there, and such that conflicts of interest (or at least of what comes eventually to be accepted as true interest) are avoided—thus needing no or minimal machinery for settlement—would be an appealing one, did not the shadow of the tyrannical patriarch darken its promise. The assurance that we are being disciplined for our own real good, forced to be truly free, denied so that we can be better satisfied, has been too often the drug used on the victims of patriarchs, oppressors, and brainwashers.

It is not, of course, impossible that there should be a form of life that really did offer self-transformation without exploitation, guidance by authoritative experts without dictatorship, dominion without domination. But given the record of such promises, it will not be surprising if we are suspicious of those who, like MacIntyre, tell us that we cannot expect to see the justice or the good of what we are to undergo until we have undergone it. The same thing has been said to those burnt at the stake for their souls' and their creator's sake, by slave-owners to slaves, and by males to the females trained to serve them (and trained to train other females to continue that service).

If the debit side of the liberal morality is, as MacIntyre has vividly portrayed it, the danger of anomie and non-communication, the debit side of MacIntyre's alternative is the danger of patriarchal (or patriarch-supplanters') oppression. Obedience and self-denial are dangerous virtues, both for those who possess them and for their fellows. They invite, on the part of others, tyranny and self-aggrandizement, and they poison both communication and communion. "Lo, here is fellowship; one cup to sip; and to dip in one dish faithfully, as lambkins of one fold. Either for others to suffer all things; one song to sing in sweet accord, and maken melodie. Lo, here is fellowship." A fine ideal, except that sheep come with shepherds, choirs with music directors and conductors, who tend to sip first and dip more deeply in the common dish than their followers.

The moral heritage of our patriarchal past includes not only the myth of the paternal omniscient authority but also that of the *loving* father. Moralities that require of us that we love, and respond to love, can be equally apt to encourage tyranny and coercion. "Whom the Lord loveth, He chastiseth." The claim "You won't like this, but I do it for your own good, and one day you will be glad I did it," is made not just by superiors to novices and teachers to pupils, but also by loving parents to children. Parental love, paternal or maternal, is as dangerous a central concept for ethics as is expert wisdom. Should some of Gilligan's females whose moral genius it is to successfully sustain, combine, and express their love of their co-revolutionaries, friends, lovers, parents, and children have the wish to produce a moral theory that does justice to their conception of morality, then *they* will be the ones who will need to heed what Freud, his followers, and his critics have taught us about the love between parents and their young children, and its relation to other loves. Rorty's claim will be tested only when we have some fully articulated love-based account of moral reasoning and moral feeling. Like MacIntyre's, such theories will face the difficult task of steering between the Scylla of empty formal rights and the Charybdis of substantive exploitation in communal activity. The challenge for any moral theorist today is to find a recipe for avoiding the loneliness and anomie for which the liberal morality of "civil society" is the breeding ground, and also the intrusive and smothering closeness of life in a tyrannical family, be it a natural, a communist, or a religious "family."

What, after all, did Freud teach us about love? That it begins in dependency, that its first object is the more powerful but loving mother who has been the loving infant's whole world, and who remains the source of nourishment, security, and pleasure. The pathologies of love all develop from this initial situation of unequal dependency. Mother love, if it is to be good of its kind, has to avoid both exploitation of the mother's immensely superior power and that total self-abnegation that turns the infant into the tyrant. Love between unequals in power is good of its kind when it prepares the less powerful one for love between equals. It fails when what it produces is either a toleration of prolonged unequal dependency or a fear of any dependency, rather than a readiness for reciprocal and equal dependency. As Nancy Chodorow's important work *The Reproduction of Mothering*[12] has shown, mother love in our society tends to prepare sons for independence rather than for reciprocal dependency, and to prepare daughters both to accept continued unequal power (with parents, and, later, husbands) and to use their eventual power over their own children to perpetuate this pattern of both crippling male adult inability to accept the dependencies of love, and crippling female adult inability to assert themselves enough to become equals to their male fellows in politics, love, war, and peace. We urgently need a new assignment of social roles, and a new morality, whether or not it is backed by a new moral theory, to enable us to stop maiming each other in the way we have long been accustomed and trained to do. Such a morality would give us guidance where no current moral theory even attempts to guide us, and where currently received moralities misguide us—on how to treat those close to us so that closeness, chosen or not chosen, can be sustained without domination or mutual suffocation, as well as on how to respect the rights of strangers, so that distance does not entail moral neglect. Only when intimacy becomes morally decent, and when moral decency braves the perils of intimacy, will we have achieved a morality worth trying to present, for those with intellectual tastes, in the form of a new, different, and better moral theory.

---

[12] Nancy Chodorow, *The Reproduction of Mothering* (Berkeley: University of California Press, 1978).

9

Feelings That Matter

Emotions and the Important

We all accept the idea that emotions are reactions to matters of apparent importance to us: fear to danger, surprise to the unexpected, outrage to insult, disgust to what will make us sick, envy of the more favored, gratitude for benefactors, hate for enemies, love for friends, and so on. And sometimes the felt emotion can precede knowledge of precisely what the danger, the insult, the nauseating substance, and so on is. Emotion then plays the role of alerting us to something important to us: a danger, or an insult. As I write this essay, a young man on trial for stabbing his mother to death in the family home (just down the road from where I live), whose defense is insanity, claims memory loss for the time of the murder but says he knows he must have done it, since, quite apart from the overwhelming physical evidence, he has "the guilty sort of feeling, like I have done something."[1] This is a rare and doubtless pathological case, but emotions can on occasion play the role of showing us that something important has occurred before we clearly understand what exactly it is.

In such cases emotions alert us to important matters, good or ill. And the emotion itself may at least help constitute the good or the ill. Descartes says all the good or ill of this life depends on the passions. Hume and many other writers about human passions have divided them into the pleasant and the unpleasant, on the one hand those that respond to, alert us to, or constitute goods; on the other hand, ills. There are some purely unpleasant

A version of this essay was prepared for the conference "Passion, Thought, and Virtue" at Uppsala University, Sweden, Oct. 2001, to mark the sixtieth birthday of my friend and critic Lilli Alanen. Changed circumstances, in my family and in the world, conspired to force me to cancel that journey. My talk about the important, along with its planned revisions after critical discussion at the conference, was overtaken by the indisputably important, the tragic and massively disruptive events of September 2001.

[1] *Otago Daily Times*, Aug. 29, 2001.

emotions, such as boredom, grief, and guilt, and some purely pleasant ones, such as relief and joy. But as Hume (and Kant) knew, gratitude, although occasioned by what is a good to us, may be itself unpleasant for a proud person to have to feel, and anger, response to a perceived injury, can be invigorating and releasing, not altogether unenjoyable. Hume would explain such cases by saying that the pleasure of receiving help is mixed with the pain of humility, of needing the help, the pain of being injured with the satisfaction of incipient aggression to the injurer. There surely can be mixed feelings evoked by one event or situation. But some individual emotions, or at any rate states for which we have a single name, while they have a distinctive phenomenological feel, seem to have an essentially mixed hedonic tone—nostalgia, for example. And some, I shall suggest, are neutral in hedonic tone, neither pleasant nor unpleasant. Surprise and interest seem of this hedonically neutral sort, unless boredom is the worst evil. I want to direct attention on an emotion very close to interest, perhaps a variant of it.

Consider this case: a person receives a long-distance phone call from a close relative. When she answers the phone, the first words her caller says, after greeting her, are "Are you sitting down?" At once she knows that the message to come is of importance, and she feels an appropriate emotional disturbance. As she finds a chair and seats herself, she may reply, "Why? Has someone died?" But she may not jump to that conclusion, and the news may be momentous but good, say that a son listed missing in action has after many years been found safe and well. She certainly feels strongly while awaiting the news that is about to be given her. She will go on, once the news is broken to her, to feel joy or sorrow, but the first feeling seems neither joy nor distress. Interest, concern, anticipation, and nervousness, yes, but more than that, some sort of shock, and intense seriousness. For what she now anticipates is no ordinary good or bad news, unlikely to cause her to need support. Nor is uncertainty alone enough to explain the emotion she feels even before the big news is given her. But what name has this emotion, felt for the important, simply as such? *Interest* seems not quite right, since one can be interested in quite trivial news, or relayed gossip, which one could with no danger receive while on one's feet. *Concern* in its older sense of "what regards one" would be close, but in its contemporary English sense it is too close to anxiety for the hedonically neutral emotion I am after.

In the case I have sketched, the opening question creates drama, and until the momentous news is given there will be uncertainty. Hume noted that uncertainty itself intensifies an emotion, as does mixture of contrary emotions from simultaneous different causes.[2] His example of mixture, the man who gets, at one time, news both of the loss of a lawsuit and of the birth of his son, resulting in an alternation of extreme joy with extreme distress, can be adapted for my purpose. Suppose this man is waiting for news of both his lawsuit and the delivery of his child. On Hume's view, the uncertainty will make both fear of losing at court and hope of a safe delivery especially violent. Suppose a messenger appears, so he at once knows that one of the uncertainties is about to be ended, but not which or how. He will feel this so far nameless emotion, no doubt along with his fear and his hope, and considerable impatience. But in this case he will likely tell from his messenger's face whether that person is the bearer of good or bad tidings, so it is unlike my telephone call case, in which no fear or hope precedes the call. My adaptation of Hume's example will not be a pure case of an emotion reserved for the important, as such, as distinct from the important threat, loss, insult, enmity, or for the important joy, victory, honor, friendship. And pure cases of a feeling reserved for the important may be quite rare.

Expression of Emotion

What made my adaptation of Hume's case impure, as an example of an emotion reserved for the important as such, was both the expectation of getting news and the inevitable bodily expression of sympathetic emotion in the messenger that indicates whether the news is good, bad, or mixed. As Hume emphasized, we do tend to sympathize with each other's emotions, and this is facilitated by the point that Darwin made that we have evolved to share information about what emotions we are feeling by our involuntary bodily expression of them. For, quite apart from sympathy, we need to know if our companions are angry with us, and whether they hate us or not. Do we need also to know what others find important? Well, we will know that, up to a point, by seeing and hearing any of their emotional displays,

---

[2] David Hume, *A Treatise of Human Nature*, ed. L. A. Selby-Bigge and P. H. Nidditch (Oxford: Clarendon Press, 1978), 441–2.

since all emotions are felt as something taken to be of some importance, something that affects us. But is there a special bodily expression that shows our feeling that we are encountering or considering something of definite importance? What would be the face and posture of the one seating herself to hear news so momentous that she should not receive it while standing unsupported?

She might go pale. Her face would be attentive, that is to say (if we accept Carroll Izard's analysis of the bodily expression of attention and interest[3]), her lower eyelids may be slightly raised as if to focus better, her lips slightly opened, her chin dropped. The plates of psychologists who, like Izard and Paul Ekman, have catalogued the bodily expressions of different emotions tend to cut their subjects off at the neck, as though the face is all that counts, but, as Darwin knew, stance and movement of arms and hands are also revealing. One thing our nervous receiver of important news will not be doing is shrugging her shoulders, expressing nonchalance. She might assume a crouched protective posture. Even should she later dismiss the news as not as important as her caller deemed it, and shrug off the honor she has received, say, or the blow, as long as she treats what is coming as important, her shoulders will, like her chin, be lowered, to take on board what she is told and its significance for her. Harry Frankfurt, who has written about the important in our lives, says that we are the beings to whom things matter,[4] and that seems undeniable. By the same token we can say that we are the mammals with shoulders we can shrug, or lower, to dismiss as unimportant or to accept as important.

It might be agreed that the shoulders have, among their many expressive uses, the particular expressive function I have claimed, namely the acknowledgment of or refusal to acknowledge importance, without agreement that any special emotion is thereby expressed. Our bodies can express our wills' determination, as well as our emotional state. And Rodin could make posture express thinking. So why have I claimed that there is an emotion that is reserved for the putatively important, as fear is for the putatively dangerous? Had there been such an emotion, surely Aristotle, the Stoics, Descartes, Spinoza, or Hume would have included it in their lists. Darwin, who does discuss the shoulder shrug (after quizzing missionaries to confirm

---

[3] Carroll Izard, *The Face of Emotion* (New York: Appleton-Century-Crofts, 1971), 242.

[4] Harry Frankfurt, "The Importance of What We Care About," in Frankfurt, *The Importance of What We Care About: Philosophical Essays* (New York: Cambridge University Press, 1988), 80.

that it was universal), takes it to express the antithesis of aggression, to express helplessness, at least when accompanied by suitably disempowering arm and hand movements—that is, elbows in, hands opened outward.[5] Darwin was, in this discussion, interested mainly in the expression of the emotions we share with other animals, and so it is not surprising that he should not have discussed an emotion such as the one I am postulating if it depends on peculiarly human capacities, and that he omitted to consider the shrug's purely general dismissive function, as distinct from the aggression-dismissing function of raised shoulders along with demobilized arms and hands.

Did any writer about emotion recognize this emotion I am discovering or inventing? Aristotle has the *spoudaios*, the person who is serious about things, but this is an ongoing attitude, for the Stoics a virtue, rather than an emotion. Descartes thinks forms of wonder and awe are of great import-ance, but does not, as far as I know, mention a feeling for the important as such, as distinct from the admirable or the despicable, the providential and the catastrophic. If the feeling I am postulating is the antithesis of noncha-lance, we could call it "chalance." (Or, if you prefer, "souciance," the antith-esis of insouciance, but that sounds too close to *souci*, worry or concern. The French *soin* may be better.) As nonchalance is temporary lightness of being, chalance, or seriousness, may be granted to be a temporary state of being bowed down with some weighty matter. (The German *wichtig*, meaning "important," is related to *gewichtig*, meaning "heavy.") But it might be deemed a mood or attitude, even a spell of thoughtfulness. Why call it an emotion?

To answer that, we need to have some general account of what emotions are, and what distinguishes them from pleasures and pains, wants, attitudes, moods, resolves, beliefs. I assume that emotions are felt occurrent mental states with intentional objects, and that, while not themselves beliefs, they involve beliefs, or sometimes merely suspicions or wishful thinkings. While not themselves wants or resolves, they tend to lead on to them. Fear, for example, involves the belief that one is in danger from what one fears, and usually the desire to escape it. Emotions are felt, and they are episodic, lasting minutes rather than days. Moods, like them in many respects, are longer lasting and have very vague and general intentional objects, or none

---

[5] Charles Darwin, *The Expression of the Emotions in Man and Animals*, introd. Paul Ekman, 3rd edn. (New York: Oxford University Press, 1998), ch. II.

at all. Attitudes, like emotions and moods, affect motivation but need not be felt by the one who has them, who may be completely unaware of her attitude. In this last respect attitudes are like beliefs. Emotions, unlike any of these other mental states (except perhaps moods and attitudes), tend to have not just typical physiological accompaniments outside the brain—ones that might, like butterflies in the stomach, be unobservable to an onlooker—but also stereotyped involuntary cross-cultural bodily expression.

Paul Ekman makes this last a necessary condition of calling anything an emotion; to be exact, he writes that nothing counts as an emotion unless there is "a distinctive universal facial expression associated with that state."[6] Ekman, with this requirement in mind, finds there to be only six emotions: surprise, anger, fear, disgust, delight, and distress. Philosophers' lists tend to be longer, to include wonder, jealousy, envy, guilt, and shame. I do not think that my thumbnail sketch of what counts as an emotion is very controversial (it is, for example, pretty much in agreement with Bennett Helm[7]), but there is some disagreement on how thought-mediated a state can be and still count as an emotion. Most agree with Hume that there must be some "idea" component in an emotion—thus, surprise, but not startle (i.e., being startled), counts as an emotion. But some theorists, such as Paul Griffiths,[8] refuse to count any beyond Ekman's basic six as emotions, deeming states like jealousy and guilt too thought-mediated, too brainy, to so count. Emotions proper, he thinks, all involve distinctive physiological changes outside the brain, in blood pressure, muscle tension, and so on, which go with their involuntary bodily expression. But jealousy or guilt or resentment we may keep to ourselves, secret, as it were, in our brains, not secreted in sweat, or other giveaway bodily signs.

In postulating an emotional state of chalance, or gravity, directed on what one takes to be of some importance, I am perhaps stretching the admittedly ragbag philosophical category of a passion or emotion, inherited from Descartes, Spinoza, and Hume, but I am keeping the requirement that there be a distinctive feel to an emotion, as well as a distinctive thought content, and some motivational potential. I also assume there will always be some

---

[6] Paul Ekman, "Expression and the Nature of Emotion," in Klaus Scherer and Paul Ekman (eds.), *Approaches to Emotion* (Hillsdale, NJ: Erlbaum, 1984); my emphasis.

[7] Bennett Helm, *Emotional Reason: Deliberation, Motivation, and the Nature of Value* (New York: Cambridge University Press, 2001).

[8] Paul Griffiths, *What Emotions Really Are: The Problem of Psychological Categories* (Chicago: University of Chicago Press, 1997).

physiological change, something like Descartes's animal spirits agitating themselves in distinctive emotion-specific ways, leading to some distinctive, involuntary, facial or postural expression that others can read. So, in discovering or inventing chalance, I am much encouraged by the fact that there does in this case seem to be a universal bodily expression, at least of the admittedly faint negative emotion of finding something of no importance, namely the eloquent "so what?" shoulder shrug. But if you ask me if chalance, gravity, is not more of an ongoing attitude to what we take to matter, or a resolve to give it due attention, or a tendency to think about it, than any sort of affect, all I can do is ask you if you have not experienced the special feeling, neither especially pleasant nor, like *souci*, unpleasant, a sort of inner settling feeling, with which we encounter, reencounter, consider, or remember something that matters much to us. (The example I began with involved important news, and so some sense of shock, but chalance is more usually felt at unchanging matters of importance to us, not reserved for changes in the landscape of the important.)

Among the things that may evoke such a feeling are moods, attitudes, beliefs, and also other emotions, whose significance may perhaps belatedly strike us. Suppose we hear from a friend with whom we have not been in touch for years. We are pleased, feel delight. Then later, when someone who hears us unaccustomedly singing asks us why we are so cheerful all of a sudden, we realize the significance of our joy, how much that friend, and our feeling for him, matters to us. We accept the importance of the friendship in our life, as we might not have done if not prompted to reflect on it, and react to it. In such a case the felt emotion of chalance will be a meta-emotion, whose object is affection for the friend with whom we have resumed communication. Emotions and friendships, enmities and angers, can be felt as important, and usually, but not always, their degree of importance to us will correlate with the importance to us of the friend, the enemy, the one we are angry at. Should, however, our anger make us ill, even when we no longer care much about the person who made us so angry, nor want any revenge, the anger may continue to matter much, while its object has come to matter less. We may have to be given drugs to quiet and subdue the crippling anger. Then we will have occasion to feel chalance at our anger, take it seriously, while no longer finding the object of the anger so important in our life. But normally, that is to say in non-pathological cases, the emotion will matter only as long as its object does.

Emotion and the Will

Of course, when something matters to us we will usually act accordingly. Our plans and goals will usually show what we find important. Recent philosophers who have written about this elusive topic, what matters, have shown rationalist and voluntarist tendencies. Harry Frankfurt speaks of what we will to will, of "volitional necessities," and of our "investing ourselves" in what we "cannot bring ourselves" not to care about. But he also cites Trollope's character Lord Fawn, in *The Eustace Diamonds*, every *feeling* in whose nature revolts against a decision he thought he had taken, preventing him going ahead with it.[9] Feeling may be what prevents us from disregarding what really matters to us. Frankfurt takes such a case, where feeling revolts against a decision, as still a case of the will, of a (perhaps feeling-prompted) change of mind. He writes, in a later essay, "To care about something is not merely to be attracted to it, or to experience certain feelings. No one can properly be said to care about something unless, at least to some degree, he guides his conduct in accordance with the implications of his interest in it."[10] For him, Luther proclaiming "Here I stand. I can no other" is a paradigm of "volitional necessity." Luther's certainly was a case of resolve and action. Is his implacable face the face of the one recognizing what matters? His stance was likely pugnacious as he spoke those famous words, and he likely did feel chalance, feel that the occasion was momentous. He certainly was not shrugging his shoulders.

But not all emotions lead to resolve and motivated action in the way outrage can lead to defiance. Hume thought pride was "compleated within itself."[11] (It leads at most to strutting.) And grief often leads only to helpless laments. There may be nothing to decide, when what is important to one is the loss of a loved one. Once any decision about a memorial is taken, the grief that matters to us may have no outlet in intentional action. When it returns with special intensity on anniversaries of the death, the most one may be able to do, and not always even that, is take fresh flowers to a grave. The importance to us of the loss, and the person lost, will show more in strength

---

[9] Harry Frankfurt, "Rationality and the Unthinkable," in Frankfurt, *The Importance of What We Care About*, 183.

[10] Harry Frankfurt, "On the Usefulness of Final Edns," in Frankfurt, *Necessity, Volition, and Love* (New York: Cambridge University Press, 1999), 87.   [11] Hume, *Treatise*, 367.

of feeling than in any acts of the will. Our will may get involved in coping with the initial grief but is powerless to change the fact of the loss. Depth of emotion, not resoluteness of will, is what will show how much we care.

Frankfurt is not alone in taking our future-directed intentions to be what best shows what we care about. Charles Taylor endorses Alastair MacIntyre's talk of "quests" as showing what we take to be worth caring about, and Michael Bratman has written that it is a "deep fact about us" that our agency is temporally extended, so that our lives can be structured by long-term plans.[12] It is an equally deep fact about us that our emotions reecho over time, that grief at loss, guilt at neglect, recur long after there is anything we can do about the lost one or the neglected one, reminding us of what mattered and matters to us, giving us, I suggest, occasion for feeling chalance.

Sometimes feeling may contradict what even acted-on will purports to reveal about what matters to a person. Suppose a person in her sixties, after a good life, decides to risk it by giving a kidney to be transplanted into a younger stranger who will die unless a suitable kidney is made available. This decision reflects, the donor thinks, the fact that her own life expectancy is of no great concern to her, that she is content with the life she has already had. But the night before the surgery she cannot sleep and realizes that her continued life does matter more to her than she thought. Her emotions show her the truth about how much she cares. Her decision had misrepresented that. She may, if especially strong-willed or noble, go ahead with the risky surgery, but that will not show that her life's continuance is of little concern to her, as she had thought and claimed earlier. Thought and decision, even acted-on decision, can lie about what matters to us, or how much it matters. The emotions the sleepless would-be kidney donor is subject to likely will include anxiety, perhaps regret, or puzzlement at herself, but as she thinks how this may be her last period of conscious thought and looks back on her life and forward to her death, she will, if I am right, also feel weighted and grave. She will feel chalance.

The person who really does not care about her life ending could spend the night sleeping soundly (as King Charles I of England supposedly did before his execution), or, if wakeful, reading an amusing book, or joking and

---

[12] Michael Bratman, "Two Problems about Agency," *Proceedings of the Aristotelian Society*, 101/3 (2001), 309–26.

clowning around with friends. Or she might calmly update her will. She need not shrug off the risk she is taking, in the sense of denying it to be real, but she might, if really content to die, shrug her shoulders when others call her act self-sacrificial. Such a nonchalant attitude to one's own end is not likely to be often found. (We might admire it if we found it. Hume, when he wrote in his *History of England* about Charles's death, clearly admired the royal calm. When his own death approached, he too was calm, almost light-hearted. I do not want, by focusing on seriousness about something, to agree with the Stoics that the serious person is morally better than the one who has cultivated nonchalance on matters most people find weighty. Nor were either Charles I or his later historian, Hume, without some due seri-ousness in preparing appropriately for their own deaths. Charles's last word was "Remember!", spoken to Bishop Juxon, whom he had instructed to implore the absent crown prince to forgive his father's killers. We admire both the serious preparations Charles made and his sound sleep. We admire both Hume's serious attention on his deathbed to the posthumous publica-tion of his dialogues, themselves not without sly satire, and his ability to joke with his visitors almost to the last.)

What Really Matters

I have said that it is our emotions, or lack of them, that will speak the truth about if and how much something matters to us. It may be objected that emotion too can surely be wrong about that. Fears can be exaggerated, even sometimes self-fulfilling, anger crippling, envy unbased, pride vain and silly. (Buddhists supposedly recognize 84,000 dysfunctional emotions, and as many antidotes.) In cases like these, the danger, the insult, the cause of envy, the honor or accomplishment in which foolish pride is taken, is not important enough to justify the person's felt emotion. Or we may later find our earlier mild reactions too muted. Thought and reflection, perhaps after discussion with others, may correct what the initial emotion got wrong. If there is a special feeling, gravity or chalance, which is directed specifically on what matters to a person, can it not also be wrong, and need correction?

This postulated feeling that something is of great importance to us, and its antithesis, will usually be among the most thought-mediated and reflective of our emotions. Indeed, it will typically come into play when other earlier emotions are self-criticized. One may later shrug off the accomplishment in which one earlier felt exaggerated pride. Or one may feel, on reflection, that a past insult should have angered one more than it did at the time. How much trust should we put in our feelings about what matters? The relative who phones to tell someone of the safe return of a lost son, or the finding of his corpse, will have no doubt that the news matters to her hearer and is surely right about that. Many beliefs, memories of earlier communicated anguish, and sympathy all feed into her request that her hearer seat herself. And the hearer infers from that request that something momentous is about to be revealed. The emotion she feels as she awaits the news is inference-based and imbued with trust concerning how well her caller can judge what will matter to her. Then when she gets the good (or bad) news, let us suppose that her son is found and safe, its impact will be mediated by all her past anxiety.

What matters to a person stays in the mind, and memory preserves what relates to that with particular tenacity, as experts on improving one's memory are well aware. What is of little concern to us we tend to forget quickly. (How many of your past shoulder shrugs can you recall?) What stays in the memory and keeps resurfacing to the forefront of attention is what mattered and matters. But it is said that memory can lie, and so, it might be suggested, can our feelings about what is and is not of importance, which affects what memory retains. Of course any emotion based on a false belief or unsound inference can be in that derivative sense false. If the caller who asks her hearer to be seated before she continues goes on to tell her a joke so funny that she might have fallen over laughing, the feeling of chalance will have been misplaced. Jokes, however good, are not occasions for that. But if there is no mistaken factual belief, nor faulty inference, can the feeling itself mislead us? Can we not attribute, on the strength of it, too much import-ance to something, exaggerate or underrate how much it matters?

Were there such a thing as objective mattering, God's-eye or, rather, God's-shoulder mattering, and were that reliably communicated to us, then our personal findings of importance could be said to be correct or incorrect in comparison with the divine standard. But for non-theists, the most we can expect is that criticism of personal findings of relative importance may come from later such feelings, and from spokespersons for cultural prior-ities. We may grant the adolescent that he does not care about tidiness but try to get him to care. In our rhetoric with him we may well say things like, "You are wrong to think tidiness does not matter—it matters to us who live with you." In my childhood there was a nasty little song that ran, "Don't care was made to care. Don't care was hung. Don't care was put in a pot and boiled till he was done." This indicates how we try to change what matters to a person, when we do. We work on what already matters to them—in this case whether or not one gets to be hanged and boiled. We do manipulate, as best we can, other people's feelings about what matters. But that does not really establish that the changed feelings are more correct, in any other sense than more politically correct, than what they superseded. We can change our minds, or, if I am right, our hearts, about how much something mattered, but that is what it will be, a change. We update our priorities, but the later ones, even when better informed, need not be any wiser than the earlier. Wisdom is a good sense of what matters more than what, but it takes it to discern it. Our criterion of relative wisdom will keep up with our changes of mind about what matters most. We will disapprove of too frequent reversals or fluctuations in our evaluations of what matters. Vanessa Bell is reported to have refused to go to social occasions at which formal dress was expected, since such grand parties "changed one's values" in unwanted ways. There is a kind of integrity in not having one's version of what matters to one change too easily with change of scene, or of company.

To appreciate the sense in which a person's feelings about what matters to him at a particular time are the final word on that, consider a person who faces a driving test on his birthday and refuses any celebration until the test is behind him. He may seem, to those close to him, to be taking the matter unduly seriously. They assure him that he is well prepared for the test, that he is a good driver, so has no need to worry. He may reply, "I admit I am a little nervous. Passing this test is very important to me." Should there be thought to be any real chance that he might fail, we might tell him that it was not the end of the world if this happened. But it might be the end of his world, the world he wants to continue in. For if the birthday he refuses yet to celebrate is his eighty-fourth, and if failure to pass this particular test would mean the end of his driving life, we might have to agree with him that the test was a serious matter. His mobility and independence would be at stake. We would still try to point out that reduced versions of these undisputed goods might still be available to him, but we would not be correcting or challenging his feeling that such goods matter very much. Aging may bring new things into a serious light—renewing one's driving license in one's eighties cannot be taken as lightheartedly as it might have been earlier, for the experienced driver. But the older person's sense that mobility and independence matter is continuous with the toddler's and the adolescent's valuing of them. It does not take the wisdom of age to discern their value, merely to realize more vividly how temporary our hold on them may be. Should our man fail the test, his life will be seriously the worse, however stoically he adapts to his reduced style of life. To say that our feelings about what matters have the final word is at the same time to say that feelings decide value. As Hume said of some passions, feelings of chalance "properly speaking, produce good and evil, and proceed not from them."[13] Values by definition matter, and how much more one thing matters than another determines what comes before what in our long-term plans, what stands out in our retrospective surveys of our lives, what images return, and what emotions resound. What matters is what we mind about, have minded about, will mind about. Charles Taylor has criticized as "naturalist illusion" any Humean account of moral or other value that takes it to be simply the projection of our own passions, however reflective the passion.[14] For Taylor, there must be "hyper-goods," discerned in "strong evaluation." The values thus discerned, he says, are "not rendered valid by our own desires, inclinations, or choices, but rather stand independent of these and offer standards by which they can be judged."[15] Now, offering standards by which desires, inclinations, and choices can be judged is one important role of emotions such as regret, remorse, shame, sorrow. A feeling can be what prevents Frankfurt's decision-taker from bringing himself to carry it out. But Taylor wants higher than human standards to validate human evaluations. He wants "ontological frameworks" within which to find "spiritual values."

There is a persistent tendency in philosophy to make a mystery out of value, and the word itself, by this point in its history, may encourage this, at any rate more than "mattering" does. Even G. E. Moore, guru of the Bloomsbury group, for whom the adjective "important" was a favorite term of appraisal (at least according to some sour critics, such as Ethel Smyth, to

[13] Hume, *Treatise*, 439.
[14] Charles Taylor, *Sources of the Self* (Cambridge, Mass.: Harvard University Press, 1989), 23.
[15] Ibid. 4.

whose musical compositions the "Bloomsbury word" was apparently not often enough applied)—even sensible Moore, who, as Woolf ironically says, "made us all wise and good," finds something non-natural about goodness. He took value to be discerned by "intuition," whatever that is. (Woolf, persuaded by her male Cambridge friends in 1908 to read *Principia Ethica*, reported in a letter to Clive Bell that it caused in her brain "a feeble disturbance, hardly to be called thought."[16] The moral epistemology of Moore's book, I have to confess, had a similarly faint effect on me, and certainly did not make me wise and good.)

I am offering the feeling of chalance as a naturalist alternative to Moorean intuition, Frankfurtian meta-willings, and Taylorian strong evaluation. But I find myself in belated agreement with Taylor in thinking that it may take upright posture to communicate the sort of evaluations of what does and does not matter, that we are familiar with, in ourselves. Having earlier scoffed at Taylor's stress on the way we walk, I am now finding the shoulders of us relatively broad- and mobile-shouldered mammals the means by which we communicate our findings of what does and does not matter—and communication matters, if anything does. (I do not, of course, want to make the implausible claim that only to us who can shoulder things can anything matter. For all expressed emotions show something about what matters to us, and to other animals. My cat's tiny shoulders are too incipient for shrugging or lowering without lowering her whole front body with them, but she leaves one in little doubt what does and does not matter to her. She may not feel chalance, but her walk can seem to be nonchalant, she can turn a cold shoulder, and she can dismiss things by turning her back on them.)

Thomas Nagel writes that "if there is reason to believe that nothing matters, then that does not matter either."[17] Is he shrugging his shoulders as he communicates this very logical conclusion? He says that the one who thinks there is reason to think that nothing matters will live his life with irony, rather than despair. But irony is not the same as the dismissal of importance that I have taken the shrug to signify. The ironist will wear a faint, world-weary smile. What we smile and laugh at is usually of some importance

---

[16] See Woolf's letter dated Aug. 13, 1936, in Woolf, *Leave the Letters Till We're Dead: Collected Letters*, vi: 1936–41, ed. Nigel Nicholson (London: Hogarth, 1980). The reference to Ethel Smyth and "important" as "the great Bloomsbury word" is in letter 3160, to Ethel Smyth (p. 63); the reference to Moore's *Principia Ethica*, "the book that made us all so wise and good," is in letter 3610 (there's a coincidence!), to Judith Stephen (p. 400).

[17] Thomas Nagel, *Mortal Questions* (New York: Cambridge University Press, 1979), 23.

to us. Laughter can be used to mock others' priorities and solemnities, but as Freud knew, the objects of our amusement are of some importance to us. We may laugh when a pompous man slips on a banana skin, but we would mind if we were the ones who slipped, and it is because we know what people mind that we find the spectacle funny. Our jokes can reveal our deepest concerns. In any case, few could honestly say that nothing matters to them, that they take nothing seriously.

A slightly different variant on Nagel's nihilist's question is whether mattering itself much matters. Should one trust any of one's feelings or judgments about what does or does not matter? One seems doomed to trust at least one of them, even if it is the judgment that mattering does not matter, only fun does. If on reflection one finds all one's previous findings of importance exaggerated, perhaps shrugging off one's old concerns, or even swearing off any use of the Bloomsbury word, this is usually because some new concern, say the danger of a world war, makes the old fade into insignificance, or the applicability of some new term of appraisal, such as "cool," comes to matter more. Mattering is the ontology of minding, and what we mind does often change over time, even when fickle fluctuations are not evident. What we mind may shrink in scope as we age, but total apathy will be a rare, and usually a pathological, condition. What is more likely is that, over time, while some things cease any longer to matter, new, but not altogether new, things come to matter. (It has taken me seventy-two years to find the shoulder shrug important.) But changed values and priorities will usually show their genealogical links with earlier concerns, as well as show their cultural inheritance. I inherit an interest in the expression of emotion from the authors I have read, from Descartes, through Hume, to Darwin, Izard, Ekman, and Eibl Eibesveldt. And my interest in arms and shoulders could be traced back to my mockery in my 1990 APA presidential address of Charles Taylor's emphasis on our two-leggedness, our upright, armed, dignity-affording walk. However spiritual, or ironic, our transvalued values, they will pick up on our earlier values, either by refining them, or by vehement denial of them, or by humor at their expense. Birth, death, birthdays, anniversaries of deaths, usually continue to matter, even to revolutionaries, terrorists, and subversives. Black humor, defacing gravestones and disinterring graves, is a backhanded agreement with the conventional majority that graveyards are places of importance, that death and the rituals of death matter. Even those who cheered when they heard about, or saw on television, the fiery collapse of the Manhattan World Trade Center Towers into a monster graveyard showed that they knew the significance of those thousands of deaths.

In an earlier essay about emotion,[18] I made the Freud-influenced claim that emotions typically have "depth" and tend to reenact earlier occasions for that sort of emotion—our adult loves to pick up on our infant loves and so on. Perhaps it would be more correct to say that these primal experiences of emotions on the human range set the agenda for later occurrences of that sort of emotion, sometimes by repetition, sometimes by violent rejection of earlier values. Is there a primal shoulder shrug, a primal mocking laugh? None of us began by finding it a joke to deface a gravestone, but we may as children have giggled at solemn funeral services, as an outlet for confused emotions. So we can, up to a point, understand the strange and offensive behavior of the cemetery-wreckers, even of those who rejoiced at the suicide terrorists' spectacular successes. To them, as to us, death matters, has emotional charge.

For most of us the question will be not if anything matters, but rather how much various things that may compete for our attention matter. The relative strength of our reflective feelings about them, what I have called our feelings of chalance, what we give weight to, and what we shrug off, will decide that. This subjective feeling, or its absence, will not settle what if anything really matters, only what matters to us now. And as Descartes wrote, "What is it to us that someone should make out that the perception whose truth we are so firmly convinced of may appear false to God or some angel, so that it is, absolutely speaking, false?"[19] What matters to us is what we and those we can be in touch with take to matter. My concern here has been our everyday feelings about what matters, and our communication of such feelings. I offer for your attention what we accept or reject as having weight, what we, not Atlas nor Sisyphus, let alone Zeus or Jehovah, shoulder or shrug off.

---

[18] Baier, "What Emotions Are About," in J. E. Tomberlin (ed.), *Philosophical Perspectives*, iv: *Theory and Philosophy of Mind* (Atascadero, Calif.: Ridgeview, 1990 (Ch. 9 in this volume)), discussed and criticized in Lilli K. Alanen, "What Are Emotions About?" *Philosophy and Phenomenological Research*, 67/2 (Sept. 2003), 311–54.

[19] *The Philosophical Writings of Descartes*, trans. John Cottingham, Robert Stoothoff, and Dugald Murdoch, 3 vols (Cambridge: Cambridge University Press, 1984), ii. 103.

10

Demoralization, Trust, and the Virtues

Hume famously wrote that "we must look within to find the moral quality."[1] He took the inner moral qualities of persons and their actions to be lasting character traits, or virtues, expressed in their behavior, both intentional action and spontaneous reaction. Some have recently doubted that persons have such dependable traits of personal character, but rather claim that we all, uniformly, behave according to the situation we find ourselves in. So, for instance, we obey authority figures who order us to administer severe electric shocks to others or refuse help to the injured when we are late for an important appointment, regardless of our previous reputation for consideration or kindness. What is "within," on such a view, is uniform human nature, adapting itself to the particular situations in which particular persons find themselves. Such "situation ethics," as we might facetiously call it, eschews the attribution of individual character traits that purport to sort the generous from the stingy, the kind-hearted from the callous, the brave from the cowardly, the tactful from the blunt, the honest from the dishonest. Virtue ethics would then rest on a mistake, the "fundamental attribution error."[2] For all of us, regardless of how glowing the testimonials we may have received, it will then be true that only the grace of lucky circumstance keeps us from showing the worst that human nature can show—what it regularly shows in desperate battle, in enraged revenge, and in the callous torture chambers of overzealous "intelligence" services.

I am grateful to Karen Jones for drawing my attention to the topic of demoralization and to her and Kurt Baier for helpful comments on a draft of this essay.

[1] See David Hume, *A Treatise of Human Nature*, ed. L. A. Selby-Bigge, rev. P. H. Nidditch (Oxford: Clarendon Press, 1978), 477.

[2] For a good discussion of this debate, see Peter Goldie, *The Emotions: A Philosophical Exploration* (Oxford: Oxford University Press, 2000), 160–75.

It is certainly true that there will always be some conditions that threaten to rob a person of the good qualities she had been reputed to possess. These conditions include not just war, plague, and famine but also private shock and misfortune. The previously confident and cheerful person may become broken-spirited after personal tragedy, or gross betrayal, or violent assault. She may become demoralized, lose her moral nerve for a while, and need help if she is to recover her old self and its moral qualities. But this fact does not deter parents from trying to encourage children to be considerate, patient, brave, honest, and generous rather than violent, impatient, cowardly, and greedy. As long as we are not in a moral "state of nature," there will be normal conditions in which good habits of the heart can be cultivated and more or less survive. Even when these conditions fail, when a person is subjected to more than she can take, the broken habits may be restorable. Of course, it will still be a matter of luck that a given person was brought up in a way that gave her good initial habits, whereas another was not, or that she gets the support she needs after psychological trauma. We do not need the infamous Milgram experiments to convince us that it is always true that "there, but for the grace of God, go I" and so to curb our tendency to be unfairly judgmental of those who show unwelcome qualities.

I propose an analysis of good moral quality that takes it to lie in the mental attitude a person has, either on a particular occasion or on a succession of like occasions, to an ever present fact about our human situation, namely, our mutual vulnerability. I will speak as if there are more or less lasting character traits that show on these occasions; but since the crucial thing, on my analysis, is the sort of thoughts about oneself, others, and mutual vulnerability that are in a person's head on a particular occasion, virtue and virtues could in theory come and go rather than being habitual. What makes an attitude to mutual vulnerability virtuous, or morally welcome, I suggest, is its contribution to the climate of trust within which the person lives. A one-shot exhibition of great bravery and calm in face of danger by a normally timid person may make a great contribution, preventing dangerous panic, although usually it will be dependable, lasting traits that do this job of maintaining interpersonal security, a climate of trust that combines due caution with some willingness to give as well as to meet trust. The moral "mother thought," I suggest, is the thought of our power over each other, for good or ill.

When I say that it is thoughts about mutual vulnerability and mutual protection that count when virtue and vice are the issue, I do not intend to overintellectualize the virtues. The thoughts I am concerned with are what Hume would call "lively" thoughts, giving content to desires, emotions, and intentions.[3] Nor do I intend to require an explicit thinking of some particular form to go on in the head of, say, the brave person or the generous one when they display their courage or their generosity. Often the thought of power and vulnerability will be implicit only; sometimes virtue will show in its silencing. My thesis is that the moral virtues regulate, sometimes by increasing the volume of, sometimes by silencing, some variant of the mother thought of our power over each other, for good or ill, and that the point of such attempted regulation is improvement and maintenance of a climate of trust.

This role for trust does not reduce all virtues to trustworthiness, let alone to willingness to trust. To see where we properly trust, we must map the contours of our distrust.[4] Due vigilance, especially in those responsible for the safety of others, will be a virtue, just as much as helpfulness and friendliness. No reductive project is afoot here; indeed, part of my aim is to get an account that can do justice to the full variety of morally excellent traits (a variety I can here only gesture at). There is a sense in which what I am doing here is reexamining an old moral compass and its setting since I will be accepting a fairly traditional list of virtues. And we can turn to old Thomas Hobbes for suggestions about the plurality of attitudes that may require regulation. The thought of mutual vulnerability is "by divers circumstances diversified," and its due virtuous forms will be equally diverse.[5] Hobbes gives us marvelous analytical lists of passions along with the verbal forms expressing them, and he takes virtues to regulate our desire for preponderance of power over others and our fear of their power. He relies mainly on diversity of grammatical mood to get the variety of verbally expressed passions that may need moral regulation, but he rightly allows that words may be insincere and that "the best signs of passions present are in the countenance, motions of the body, actions and ends or aims which

---

[3] James Martineau, *Types of Ethical Theory* (Oxford: Clarendon Press, 1886), 468, called emotion "thought in a glow."

[4] Ajay Close's heroine, in her novel *Official and Doubtful* (London: Secker & Warburg, 1996), 272–3, is said to trust her lover "enough, which is to say she'd comprehensively mapped the contours of her distrust."   [5] See Thomas Hobbes, *Leviathan*, ch. 6, para. 13.

we otherwise know a man to have."[6] Virtues are regulated passions and intentions toward those whom we have some power to help or harm and who have that power over us. Their recognized presence or absence necessarily affects our mutual willingness to be in each other's power and so necessarily affects the climate of trust we live in. (I am here assuming that trust is the absence of apprehension when in another's power, confidence that the trusted will not use that power against us.)

Once we have our list of virtues, taken as regulated attitudes to mutual vulnerability, the question will arise of whether demoralization consists in loss of any of them or whether it is only some, such as fortitude, that are lost to the demoralized person. Fortitude may have a special place among the virtues, and there may be others—some version of faith, hope, and love—whose role includes staving off demoralization in stressful times, keeping us steadfast, and enabling us to endure. But before we can consider that, we need some list of virtues and some analysis of the varied ways in which they contribute to a climate of mutual trust by regulating the threats, promises, offers, orders, acceptances, and so on that we make to each other and what we feel toward them.

I begin with what, on this account, become central virtues: thoughtfulness and considerateness. The considerate person is appropriately aware of how her attitudes and actions affect those around her, and if necessary she alters them so as not to cause fear, hurt, annoyance, insult, or disappointment in others, particularly in those who hoped for cooperation or help. If she has more power over the other than that one has over her, she will not flaunt it or use it ruthlessly for her own ends. (She will, for example, silence any thought of the power her knowledge of facts about the other that he would not want made public gives her.) In conversation she will be courteous, willing to listen to others, and not force her views upon them. This is the old virtue of doing to others as we would have them do to us if roles were reversed. It is pretty obvious that its presence in people makes for a good climate of trust. Indeed, like its Christian and Kantian versions, this virtue threatens to swallow up all the others, leaving us with no need for a list.

However, a person can have this will to treat others as she hopes herself to be treated but not notice the particular vulnerabilities of those around her. If she is herself thick-skinned, she may not realize how hurtful some of

---

[6] Hobbes, *Leviathan*, ch. 6, para. 56.

her wit is to the thinner-skinned subjects of it. Or if she is intrepid in adventure, she may drag more timid companions with her on her escapades. She might desist if she were made aware of their distress, but she may fail to notice it. Such a person is thoughtless and imperceptive rather than inconsiderate. Rightly do those who know her come to distrust her moves, become uneasy around her.

The vice of cruelty, deliberately hurting others or threatening to do so, is of course a graver failing than lack of considerateness, thoughtlessness, and lack of perceptiveness. The cruel or malicious person relishes the opportunity and power to inflict disgrace, ridicule, and other more deadly hurt; and even a few such people around can, as anthrax scares have shown us, have dramatic effects on a climate of trust. When the hurt is inflicted in the name of some cause or as part of a "holy war," and when the one inflicting it is ready to share the fate of his or her victims, then fear will verge on terror, and the thought of our vulnerability will be loud and clear. The terrorist is clearly aware of her power to do harm and has made herself invulnerable by her will to martyrdom. It is difficult for us, whose religion respects its own crusaders, to find that the will to kill and to die for a cause is vicious; but there can be no doubt that it ruins a climate of mutual trust. The ruthlessness of the suicide attacker's determination to sacrifice lives, including her own, to her cause leaves us helpless and horrified. The horror is part admiration of such dangerous courage and determined devotion since we have been trained to admire such traits in our own crusaders and martyrs. We are nonplussed by suicide attackers, and that increases our loss of nerve. We look desperately around for some moral high ground, find only swamp, and so flail around. The terrorist planner knows this and so delights in imitating our own cultural heroes, and using, as refuge from our counterattacks, the underground tunnels we ourselves prepared, just as his suicide attackers show the military virtues we recognize in our own heroes: "He is bloody minded, and delights in death and destruction. But if the success be on our side, our commander has all the opposite good qualities, and is a pattern of virtue and good conduct. His treachery we call policy. His cruelty is an evil inseparable from war."[7]

The terrorist's violent, deliberate attack on our moral nerve and self-confidence must indeed, on this analysis, count, on the face of it, as especially

---

[7] See Hume, *Treatise of Human Nature*, 348.

vicious since it aims not to improve but to worsen a climate of trust. But if that attacked climate was a microclimate, that of a privileged group who ignored or refused to alleviate the distress of those outside it or profited from their oppression, then the moral status of terrorism alters. For moral purposes, nothing human can be alien to us, and the climate of trust we should be improving cannot have merely national borders. This does not condone the ruthlessness of terrorist action but rather points us to its causes, to the circumstances that propagate such desperation. The dreadful insecurity that may demoralize the terrorists' surviving victims is the normal condition of life for those on whose behalf some terrorists act. We cannot expect moral virtue from the homeless and starving. Such wretched or oppressed people are not so much demoralized by their conditions of life as never moralized. Morality and moral training presuppose some degree of security of life. If that is absent, then such pockets of security as more fortunate groups may have enjoyed must be at risk from the resentment of those outside their comfort zone. What is a national climate of trust without international justice but a conspirator's cell writ large? Demoralization is a disease of the morally fortunate, a bit like other occupational diseases of the affluent. It is a fall from a state of moral health that the really unfortunate never attain. Their activist groups may have superb morale, but that involves only a few virtues or apparent virtues, in particular courage, discipline, and solidarity. Demoralization may involve loss of these, and so include loss of morale, but it is a more general loss, just as moralization involves more than achievement of reasonably high morale. Morale is the approximation to morality that people in insecure conditions, such as battlefields and disaster zones, can possess. It presupposes a very limited trust, trust in fellow members of one's cadre. It nourishes selected virtues, such as dedication, loyalty, and endurance, but can be accompanied by cruelty, ruthlessness, and disregard for human life.

On this analysis, all moral virtues—those possessions of the morally lucky—contribute to a climate of trust. Respect for the lives and property of others, as virtues, makes a vital contribution to a climate of trust by blocking any thought of resorting to manslaughter or theft in those who might have motive to do so. Some awareness of how easily anyone can be harmed by such acts is proper, and vigilance for one's own security of person and property requires such awareness; but the person who sees every stranger, let alone every acquaintance, as a possible attacker, robber, or thief contributes, just as much as the criminal, to a climate of distrust. Those traumatized by terrible experiences may display such generalized fear and overvigilance; and children, such as those from Romanian orphanages, who have never known emotional or any other sort of security have an understandable habit of distrust that may be difficult to break. War orphans who had to scavenge to survive might also be less than fully respectful of others' property and have an understandable tendency to grab any tempting, easily taken good that lies to hand, even after their conditions of life have improved. Until they not merely are but also feel secure, skills for survival in a state of nature will continue to be exercised. And until they trust their human environment, they cannot be expected to be themselves trustworthy. The relation between trust and the virtues is a two-way dependence. A climate of trust must first exist before we can expect the virtues that sustain it. Aurel Kolnai wrote that "trust in the world ... can be looked upon, not to be sure as the starting point and very basis, but perhaps as the culmination and epitome of morality."[8] This seems to me exactly wrong. Some degree of trust in the social world is the starting point and very basis of morality.

Those who study the brains of traumatized or neglected children find underdevelopment of the frontal cortex, responsible for emotional regulation. The cingulate gyrus is apparently the brain locus of moral quality and will not develop unless some parent figure talks and plays with the infant. A trusting relationship must initiate the child into normal social interaction. Brain scans and cranial measurement show the lasting, but in principle reversible, damage of "adverse" infant experience.[9] Earlier I spoke of parents as "encouraging" their children to have the wanted attitudes to themselves and others; and if this sort of encouragement from trusted care-givers is lacking, then the developing child will literally lack the courage needed to function as a social being, the courage to let others control some aspects of his well-being, to cooperate, and to trust. He may not lack all forms of courage—he may be stoical in physical suffering—but what he will lack is what we could call social courage, the willingness to take the risks that relying on others always involves, the faith or hope that others will not treat

---

[8] See Aurel Kolnai, "Forgiveness," in Bernard Williams and David Wiggins (eds.), *Ethics, Value and Reality* (Indianapolis: Hackett, 1978).

[9] The research is being done by Bruce Perry, at the Child Trauma Academy in Houston, and Peter Fonagy, University College London, as reported by Jo Carlowe in *The Observer*, Jan. 20, 2002, 19–20, accessible at <http://www.guardian.co.uk/theobserver/2002/jan/20/life1.lifemagazine6>.

him badly. If his infant dealings with people have discouraged him from any trust in them, then he will, of course, be fearful and lacking in social courage.

Courage is a traditional virtue, but as Hume warned, we need to distinguish different versions of it. Military courage, the sort that gets medals, may contribute to death and destruction, not to a secure climate of trust. And that sort is shown as much by the terrorist as by the counterterrorist. (This is what high morale involves.) What the "girdle" around the frontal lobes of the brain gives us is a regulation of basic emotions like fear, which can be felt not only on battlefields but also whenever the perceived threat is another person, a social situation, or some other form of our human and human-made environment. (As a child of 9 or so, I was fearless in athletic activities and quite at ease in the classroom but terrified of shops and shopkeepers, and when sent to do simple household shopping, I felt as if I were struck dumb at the counter. To me the world of commerce was an alien and threatening place. Only after I, with my parents' encouragement, took a vacation job as a shop attendant, when I was 13, did my fear of shops begin to go away. Facing one's demons is the tradition-recommended way to banish them.)

The virtues of self-respect and respect for other persons, proper pride and appropriate modesty, can be seen as Hume saw them, as awareness of one's own strength and its limits, especially in comparison with the strength and power of others. These virtues are essential to a climate of trust in which, given a division of labor, each can count on the competence and good will of those whose competence is different from one's own and whose power to affect others is also different. Demoralization can lead to a feeling of total incompetence, helplessness, and loss of self-respect, along with an exaggerated respect, bordering on fear, of others and their power.

Patience with the common failings of others, with their lack of punctuality, tact, consideration, or good sense, is a virtue that allays expectation of anger and, like forgiveness of repentant offenders, restores a tolerable interpersonal atmosphere. Just when we should refuse to forgive and allow our anger expression is a question admitting of no general answer. We do deplore the overmeekness of those who let themselves be trampled on or abused, who forgive the same offense too many times, even when they do so out of love. Is this because such acceptance of wrongs by their victims encourages the wrongdoer, rather than deterring him? Protest at wrongs one has suffered is as much a duty to others who may suffer such wrongs as a matter of self-protection; and the virtue of slowness to anger must be accompanied by that of the courage to resist the abuser if our climate of trust is to be tolerable—at home, in police cells, or in the workplace.

It is fairly obvious how honesty in speech and in voluntary exchanges such as promises and contracts contributes to a climate of trust; indeed, the plausibility of contractarian theories of morality relies on it. As Hume pointed out, promises and contracts allow us to extend secure reliance on delivery of goods or services from simultaneous exchange to non-simultaneous exchange and future delivery. The whole of commerce and banking rests on this useful "artifice"; but to see the whole of morality as resting on it distorts relationships such as love and friendship—which do not rest on deals, fair or unfair—and equally distorts relations, such as that of benefactor to beneficiary, where the virtues of beneficence and generosity, not that of any sort of agreement-keeping, are shown. A tactful benefactor will allow for the pride of the beneficiary and not expect even gratitude in return for her help, or she will make her gift anonymously or somehow disguise it. This is not to deny that graciousness in acceptance of gifts and aid is a virtue and contributes to a climate of trust, but merely to recognize that the virtue of gratitude, as Hume and Kant agreed, is a hard one and in some conflict with that of proper pride. As feeding stray cats has shown me, the neediest are the likeliest to bite the hand that feeds them, out of understandable insecurity. It takes time for the really needy to come to trust the one who meets their need.

The virtues of fairness and a sense of social justice are also distinct from fidelity to promises and contracts and from generosity to the needier. These virtues should regulate what particular contracts get made and mitigate the need for people to depend on others' generosity. In a very inegalitarian society, where the gap between the rich and the poor is huge and blatant, there will likely be resentment, leading to theft, robbery, and other illegal acts by the poorest or those who act on their behalf, and a justified feeling of insecurity in the rich. A decent climate of trust demands some measure of equality, not just among citizens of one nation but among nations. Some redistributing of the earth's resources and wealth, rather than a jealous hanging onto what are often ill-gotten gains at the individual or the national level, seems a fairly obvious prerequisite for peace and any reasonable level of mutual trust. We know how, by graduated taxation, to redistribute at the national level, and it should not be beyond us to institute some form of international taxation. The individual virtues we need to cultivate in order to get greater equality are not merely a sense of fairness and the willingness to protest (and relinquish) unfair advantages but also the vision to design workable institutions, both national and international, or to extend existing ones in ways that improve our overall climate of trust.

Hobbes's third "law of nature," that men perform the covenants they have made, would be idle unless there is obedience to his first and second laws: that men seek peace and be willing, in certain conditions, to risk making a covenant, and so to renounce some right or power for the sake of peace. The virtue he called "justice" (keeping agreements) comes into play only after the prior ones of being peace-seeking and tractable enough to enter into a covenant have prepared the way for it. (His fifth law requires a more general tractability.) Such fundamental virtues obviously regulate our attitudes to our power over each other: power to attack, to refuse to renounce power, to wreck the efforts of peacemakers, and to be "stubborn, insociable, forward, intractable." A climate of trust that a person with the Hobbesian virtues will not, by his very virtue, make himself "a prey to others" requires that there be general cultivation of these virtues, that they be the rule, not the exception.

The virtue of conscientiousness, doing what others are counting on us to do, is close to but not the same as doing what one promised or contracted to do. Conscientious parents have not, in having children, contracted with anyone to rear their children carefully. Such duties as parental ones and filial ones are not founded on any sort of agreement, and not all duties of the workplace are taken on in a contract of employment. Others are always vulnerable to our discharge of such duties as we are, for whatever reason, expected to do, and the climate of trust is worsened if duties are neglected. In some conditions, such as industrial disputes or oppressive forms of marriage, the needed virtue may be the spirit to refuse to do what one is unfairly expected to do, but then fair warning will need to have been given so that innocent third parties to the dispute will not be harmed.

Discretion is also distinct, as a virtue, from keeping to agreements since not all of those who confide in us, trusting our discretion, ask for promises of secrecy, and the person of discretion may not always keep such confidences secret but rather show good judgment about when to divulge them. If in the confidence of a suicidal teenager, she may show her discretion in divulging her confidant's intentions to someone who can counsel and help, rather than in keeping quiet. Discretion is good judgment in what we do with sensitive knowledge we have about others. The gossip, the blabber-mouth who cannot keep secrets, the industrial spy, the blackmailer, all in different ways misuse the knowledge they have of others' private affairs.

It might be granted that cultivation of the virtues on Hobbes's and Hume's and other lists do contribute to a decent climate of trust without agreement that their very essence lies in this connection. What I am suggesting is that, as trust itself can be seen as the acceptance of vulnerability to the trusted—along with confidence that by trusting in this instance one will not in fact become the prey of the trusted—so each virtue regulates our attitude to some aspect of the mutual vulnerability that makes trust, distrust, and meeting and betraying trust possibilities for us, and does so in a way that preserves and improves our climate of trust. This thesis may seem more plausible with such virtues as fidelity to promises, veracity, and conscien-tiousness than with others such as respect for life, where, it might be said, the wrong done by the one without the virtue is simply manslaughter, not the inducing of fear for their own lives in survivors of the killer's threats or acts. The latter may be granted to be an ancillary evil done by the killer but not the main evil. What's wrong with murder, it will be claimed, is the taking of a life, whether or not that harms the climate of trust of survivors. But why, then, do we regard the terrorists' disregard for life with such pecu-liar horror? Lives were taken ruthlessly by those who bombed Dresden and Hiroshima, but they at least could say that they did what they did to hasten surrender and peace. Their commanders may also have intended to demor-alize, as a means to that end, and if they did, their killing is to that extent like the terrorists' in that the effect on survivors was essential to their intention. Admittedly my thesis that the moral evil of murder is the terror caused by the murderer, the fear of death rather than the death itself, is counterintui-tive. But the history of English criminal law shows that for a long time (until Henry II's reforms) murder was treated as disturbance of the king's peace and as loss of manpower to the victim's family, that is, as a kind of theft; so our common contemporary view that inflicted death mainly wrongs the one whose life is ended may rest more on indoctrination by right-to-lifers than on any insight into eternal moral truths. Respect for life is, of course, generally taken to regulate our attitudes to our power of life or death over each other, but to claim that it does so primarily to improve a climate of trust in security of life, rather than simply to protect and prolong life, is admittedly a controversial thesis. It has the advantage that the assistance in hastening death given to those terminally ill persons who request it can be seen as kindness, not wrongful killing. Once we give up the implausible view that cutting off a human life is always wrong, whether or not the one who dies wants to die, we can see how a climate of trust in hospitals and hospices would be improved, not worsened, if such assistance could be counted on. Of course, there are practical problems about ensuring that the patient's consent has been given, but provided proper safeguards were in place, there would be less, not more, to fear in hospitals were voluntary euthanasia an option. There are fates reasonably deemed worse than death, and continued life with severe disability, dependence, and suffering has a strong claim to be so judged. We should allow those who in their own case do so judge it the right to assistance in ceasing to go on living if our main aim is a decent climate of trust, including trust in healthcare workers. Respect for human life is respect for a person's opportunity to make something worth having of her life, and if the ability to do so is gone, respect for the person should include respect for her wish to die.

There are other traditional virtues besides respect for life and property that on the face of it do not seem to have much to do with a climate of trust since they seem to concern primarily the virtue possessor, not her fellow persons. How is our climate of trust the worse if I am greedy in my eating habits, or lazy, or unnecessarily morose? Of course, I will be worse company with such vices, but if I overeat, laze, and gloom away in secret rather than in company, what harm do I do to society? One answer open to me to save my thesis is "none—these are pseudovices." I do not, however, think that matters are quite so clear-cut since these "self-regarding" traits usually connect with other society-related ones. Indeed, eating disorders, inactivity, and depression can signal that demoralization that is fundamentally a loss of social confidence, of the courage to keep going as a functioning member of a group with a shared life. To "resign" from that shared life does affect others, and it will affect a climate of trust if too many become holed up, indulging their solitary vices. So my answer to this objection is not to deny that these matters are moral ones but rather to reject a sharp distinction between what concerns others and what concerns self. One might also explore the notions of self-trust and see self-respect as a sort of private climate of properly regulated self-trust, but I will not do that here.

Suppose it were granted that there is some plausibility in taking virtues to be essentially regulated attitudes to our mutual power and vulnerability, where the regulation serves to improve a climate of trust. What is gained by taking them in this way? A loose unity is thereby given to the virtues, making them more than a mere bundle but not reducing the variety to any one comprehensive virtue. We might even get a little structure into our bundle if some virtues serve to protect others against loss in adverse conditions, and others, those needed for good morale, can, unlike gentler virtues, be cultivated in bad conditions. I suggested that some strengthening "girdle" of social hope, faith, and love might provide the strength not to go to pieces when terrible things happen or the resilience to put ourselves back together, morally speaking, after a temporary collapse. Any virtue can be lost when we are demoralized: our courage, our self-respect, our self-control over fear and anger, our good sense about what to eat and how much, our sociability, our personal cleanliness, even possibly our honesty. In such bad times we tend to lose self-trust, as well as trust in others. We may need to be "retamed," as would an animal after a bad experience at human hands, and this takes extra patience, love, and tact in those who provide support.

I said that I was examining an old compass when I advanced my thesis about the role and essence of moral virtues, but the test of any such thesis is not merely "saving the phenomena" that are already recognized but pointing us to previously overlooked or not sufficiently looked-at ones, as well as relations among them. Do new virtues or new relations between virtues come into view once we see them as I have encouraged us to see them? Well, there is a special importance that accrues to the virtues of social faith, hope, and love, but that is an adaptation of an old thesis. Are there some new virtues protected by these special ones? One is the social inventiveness that enables some to design new trust-extending social "artifices" and to see what reforms of imperfect laws might improve society. Another is the diplomatic skill and understanding that allow some to become good mediators or peacemakers. Hobbes's fifteenth law, to allow mediators safe conduct, is without point unless some are able and willing to perform this vital role of facilitating agreement and peace. Then there is a virtue that as far as I know only Hume has noticed, namely, expressiveness, the complementary virtue to perceptiveness. And inscrutability does become a vice if we must rely on others' facial and other bodily or verbal expressions to know how they are affected by our own actions, expressed feelings, and intentions. John Banville, in his novel *The Untouchable*,[10] has his main character, a spy modeled on the art historian Anthony Blunt, observe that the poet T. S. Eliot had an immobile face, perfect for dissembling. With such people, we do not know where we are and so are uneasy and suspicious. But even with expressive people, we can go wrong in our assumptions about what thoughts and intentions their faces, body language, and actions show. If virtue is an inner quality, then one such virtue must be diffidence in judging others since we can never be sure what exactly was in their head and heart and we do not have infallible access even to our own.

Many virtues come in complementary pairs, like scrutability and perceptiveness. There are helpfulness and gratitude, trustworthiness and some willingness to trust, willingness to enter into mutually beneficial agreements and fidelity to them, willingness to apologize and try to make up for harms done to others and willingness to accept such overtures, self-respect and respect for others, perhaps respect for life and making the most of life, and respect for property and using one's property in a socially responsible manner (including the capitalist virtue of giving gainful employment to others). Putting the emphasis on our mutual dependence encourages us to note such complementarities, the virtue ethics parallel to the complementarity of the deontologists' rights and obligations. Some virtues, such as consideration for others, tact, gentleness, good temper, serenity, patience, and reluctance to condemn, do not need any complement, and new forms of them will come into play as conditions of life and technology change. (Good email manners are not the same as politeness in old-style letters.)

Taking the virtues to be attitudes to those to whom we are vulnerable and who are vulnerable to us is not so very different from taking virtue, singular, to lie in the "maxim" behind one's action or inaction. Taking the crucial thing to be a contribution to the climate of trust that we share is not so different from comembership in a "realm of ends." Hobbes, Hume, and Spinoza may be the more obvious sources for the view I have taken here, but I hope that no reflective moral philosopher is altogether alien to me, so I am happy to note this partial agreement with Kant. My debt to the utilitarians and contractarians is also clear. I have narrowed the aim of morality from the utilitarian's "happiness" to one vital component of it, a good climate of trust, since I do not want to include all personal traits that

---

[10] John Banville, *The Untouchable* (London: Picador, 1997).

contribute to human happiness (wit, musical and poetic genius, etc.) as moral virtues, nor do I want to restrict these latter to qualities of will. I have tried to generalize the contractarian's emphasis on reciprocity of contribution and yield, specified in a hypothetical agreement, to something more actual, our sharing in one climate of trust, which each can worsen or make better. Cultivating the virtues is making a contribution to a common good, although there is no way of ensuring that all will equally benefit from it, that none will exploit and damage it. Trying to more closely approximate equality of returns is one of the virtues we will recognize, and this requires vigilance against exploiters and wreckers of the climate of trust.

"Give me my scallop shell of quiet, my staff of faith to walk upon, my scrip of joy…my gown of glory, hope's true gage, and thus I'll take my pilgrimage."[11] We may need some secular equivalent of Walter Ralegh's faith and hope if we are to have his joy, his glory (in Hobbes's sense of confidence in power?), and his calm in a world where terror always threatens and death is a certainty. The world has always been like this, so we can use old moral compasses to set our course in it: those of Socrates, who taught us how to die; Aristotle, who taught us how much we need friends and gave us a useful revisable list of social virtues; the Stoics, who taught us serenity and highlighted vulnerability even while denying it; Aquinas, who saw the role for faith, hope, and love; Hobbes, whose perception of morality's main concern with attitudes to power I have relied upon here; Descartes, who taught us that *générosité* that makes us always courteous, affable, and of service to each other; Spinoza, who saw how an ethics of cooperation could show us how to increase our power and so show us how to live, as well as to die; Hume, who saw how vital to morality are those social institutions that enable an extension of mutual trust; and so on. With a little judicious tinkering and updating, these old compasses can still guide us.

I have in this essay sketched a method of taking familiar virtues in a slightly new way, as contributors to a good climate of trust. Since I have in other places defended an account of trust that sees it to lie in the attitude of the one who trusts to being in some respect in the power—sometimes but not always the voluntarily given power—of the trusted, and trustworthiness as the ability and willingness to use such power for the expected good, not the harm, of the one who trusts, I take the virtues to include good judgment

<hr/>

[11] Sir Walter Ralegh, "The Passionate Mans Pilgrimage."

about when to trust and willingness to meet such reasonable trust, but also to include many other qualities that affect such judgment and such willingness, all of them attitudes to mutual power and vulnerability. I take a climate of trust to be good to the extent that persons can safely trust others, including strangers, officials, makers of machines, builders, and those who issue licenses, control airports, and so on. Some may agree with me about virtues being contributors to a climate of trust but reject my presupposed account of trust, and so perhaps see the inner quality of what persons contribute to its climate differently. Others may more or less accept the account of trust but deny that a good climate of trust is the point of cultivation of the virtues. Some may reject or amend my incomplete list of virtues—for instance, ask how or if integrity and avoidance of hypocrisy fits into this account. (Are they part of self-respect?) Some may think I have quite misunderstood demoralization. There is much more work to be done to defend and elaborate the suggestions I have advanced, especially when it comes to the three descendants of the old "theological" virtues of faith, hope, and love, to which I have assigned an important role. I once did explore "secular faith," and those of us who have written about an ethics of care have to some extent addressed the sort of loving concern a secular morality needs to cultivate, but hope is for me a whole new territory to explore.[12] One of the good things about virtue ethics is that there is always something more to be said and that nothing, neither the list of virtues nor analysis of them, is ever final.

[12] On our bookshelves we have three so far unread German volumes about it by Ernst Bloch, so I have little excuse.

11

Sympathy and Self-Trust

> Whatever other passions we may be actuated by; pride, ambition,
> avarice, revenge or lust, the soul or animating principle of them all is
> sympathy.
>
> (Hume, *A Treatise of Human Nature*, 2. 2. 5. 15, SBN 363[1])

Trust and distrust are not among the states of mind that Hume says will
"languish" if not sympathized with, but I think he would be willing to
include them. One form of pride is pride in our ability to tell who is and
who is not to be trusted, and pride is among those states of mind which
Hume believes need sympathy, to "second" them. In the past I have taken
trust to be accepted vulnerability to the one whom one trusts, in the confidence that she will not in fact injure one, along with willingness to give that
one discretionary powers, in her care of something that matters to one.[2] It
is understandable, then, that I avoided saying anything about self-trust, and
have in fact continued to avoid it up until now, though I toyed with regarding
self-respect as a good climate of self-trust, in "Demoralization, Trust, and the
Virtues."[3] Can one be vulnerable to oneself? Can one give oneself discretionary powers in looking after something that one cares about? One seems
to need to split the self in two, one trusting, the other trusted, just as in
puzzles about self-deception one is tempted to divide the deceiver from the

---

[1] References to Hume's *Treatise of Human Nature* (henceforth *T*) are first to the *Treatise*, ed. David
Fate Norton and Mary J. Norton (Oxford: Clarendon Press, 2006), giving book, part, section, and
paragraph number, then to page number in the *Treatise*, ed. L. A. Selby-Bigge, rev. P. H. Nidditch (Oxford:
Clarendon Press, 1978) (henceforth SBN).

[2] As Karen Jones notes, in my later essays on trust, such as the Tanner Lectures, I tended to drop this
construing of trusting as entrusting, given in "Trust and Antitrust," in Baier, *Moral Prejudices* (Cambridge,
Mass.: Harvard University Press, 1995). See Jones, "Trust as an Affective Attitude," in Joyce Jenkins,
Jennifer Whiting, and Christopher Williams (eds.), *Persons and Passions* (South Bend, Ind.: Notre Dame
Press, 2005).   [3] The previous essay in this volume.

deceived.[4] But in fact, of course, we can indeed be vulnerable to ourselves, for example when we trust our own sense of how much alcohol to drink, of how much strain to put on ourselves, and, as Jennifer Whiting pointed out,[5] self-distrust is often warranted. She also questioned my assumption that we must trust our friends. If Aristotle is right, they are second selves to us, and I had foolishly assumed that self-trust was the norm. Here I want to approach these questions of trust in first and second selves, and in others, by considering whether we can sympathize with another's trust, including her trust in us, and with her self-trust or self-distrust. Self-distrust is important, for often we realize what we have trusted only when we come to lose that trust. So self-distrust is a good back-door entry into an understanding, at least a retrospective one, of self-trust. And others can sympathize with our self-trust or -distrust. We can also sympathize, or fail to, with our own past selves, and, as we age, distrust our future selves, when we put the control of some matters into younger and abler hands. We may even sign over enduring powers of attorney, so little do we trust our future selves.

Sympathy, as well as trust and friendship, connects us closely with others, and like love makes us vulnerable to others and their troubles. Trainee nurses have to be careful not to let themselves become too deeply identified with their suffering patients, as this could impair their ability to care for them. But equally, lack of any sympathy amounts to callousness. Hume saw our capacity for sympathy as a most important fact about us, and realized that it could be more or less "extensive" in the time stretch of the other's experience which is considered, and more or less "deep" in its delving into the reasons there are for the other to feel as she does. I shall explore the possibility that a suitable other's sympathizing fairly extensively and fairly deeply with our trust, and our sympathizing with hers, could be taken as a variant of the expressibility test I tentatively proposed for trust, in the final part of "Trust and Antitrust." This test is that we be able to trust the one we trust, or who trusts us, with the reasons why we trust, and meet trust. The sympathy test shares with the original test the limitation that it applies only to trust between pairs of individuals, not to networks of trust, and it remains true

---

[4] I discussed self-deception in "The Vital but Dangerous Art of Ignoring: Selective Attention and Self Deception," in Roger Ames and Wimal Dissanayake (eds.), *Self and Deception* (New York: State University of New York, 1996), and there tried to avoid this division of the self into two.

[5] See Jennifer Whiting, "Trusting 'First' and 'Second' Selves," in Jenkins, Whiting, and Williams (eds.), *Persons and Passions*.

what I said when I proposed it, that it may destroy some trust relationships to subject them to this test, since it may be so painful to come to realize what it is in oneself that the other is relying on, or that enables one to rely as one does, that one rejects that image of oneself, and ends the relationship. I then suggested that only when there are already suspicions would it be wise to use this test—best to take non-suspect trust on trust. It is possible that the sympathy variant of the test is less hard on the main parties, that the detour through a third party can soften the pain of the self-knowledge that the test would require, if directly applied. For a sympathetic other may see what each party to a trust relationship is relying on, in the other, when they themselves are not fully aware of it. As Hume pointed out, we may feel sympathy with those about whose situation we know more than they do. I shall return to this possibility. But for understanding self-trust, the fact that the test does not work for networks of trust is no bad thing, since however complex self-trust may be, it surely does not involve a whole network of inner sub-selves, trusting or distrusting one another. Or might it? If, like Walt Whitman, we each contain multitudes, then we would need a test for a climate of trust, such as that which Denmark supposedly has,[6] to test any self-trust, not just a test for an individual trust relationship. I certainly think there are a multitude of abilities and skills within us on which we rely in daily life, and in some of which we may come to lose trust, especially in age, or when demoralized, but I do not think that there are separate personalities going with these different abilities, which might display good or ill will to each other, and trust, as I have in the past taken it to be, does involve confidence in the good will, as well as in the competence, of the trusted. So it is unclear whether self-trust involves the attributed good will component of trust in others.

My account of trust made it a complex of beliefs and attitudes, including willingness to be in the power of the trusted. The test for morally healthy trust was that it survive awareness, on both parts, of the reasons for this willingness. Karen Jones has emphasized that trust is also an *affective* attitude. The belief that the trusted can be counted on, the willingness to be in the other's power, and the affective element, are all the sort of mental states that could

---

[6] Reuters, *Otago Daily Times*, *Focus*, Oct. 27, 2008: the article by Teis Hald Jensen, Copenhagen, reported that the Danes are the happiest people in the world, and have the best climate of trust. Pictures showed (unhelmeted) cyclists in the city, "Big on trust, high on happiness."

be communicated by sympathy, if Hume is right that not only emotions, but also beliefs and attitudes, can spread by sympathy, and if there are ways that we do show our trust and distrust, so others can easily be aware when we are trusting or feeling distrust. Whether it makes sense to speak of good or ill will to oneself, or of giving oneself, in some respect, discretionary powers, are other matters, to which I will shortly turn.

One case of sympathy Hume finds "pretty remarkable" is when "the communicated passion acquires strength from the weakness of the original" (*T* 2. 2. 7. 5, SBN 370). When we know the situation another is in, calling for some particular emotion, such as fear in danger, or distress in bad fortune, or possibly distrust, we may feel for the other, although he himself gives no sign of feeling anything. The stoic man in misfortune may express no distress, and, if Hume is right, this increases our sympathy with him, rather than obviates it. It is as if we have to feel twice as much, since he seems to feel nothing. Hume's other cases are when we blush for those who behave fool-ishly, although they themselves show no sign of feeling shame, feel compas-sion for the infant prince, captive of his enemies, and oblivious to his sorry situation, pity the sleeping victim of murder (murder is aggravated, Hume says, if the victim is attacked while asleep), and fear for the person asleep in a field, in the path of galloping horses. We might extend his examples to the case where another has reason to feel a degree of distrust that he does not in fact feel, where the trust relationship is rotten. Here we feel what we think the other has reason to feel, not what he is in fact feeling. Now in some of these cases, the sympathetic feeling, if expressed, could alert the person, say the shameless foolish one, to the reasons he has for shame, and cause him to come himself to blush, or alert the trusting one to the fact that he has reasons for distrust. Here the "rebound" of the sympathy may activate the so-called "original" feeling, belatedly felt.[7] This sort of rebound of sympathy could activate not merely belated embarrassment, but belated distrust, called into existence by another's expressed sympathetic distrust, or belated self-trust, called into existence by another's expressed sympathetic trust. In such cases the test for trust is that it be possible for a knowledgeable other to sympathize with it.

---

[7] Hume speaks of these rebounds when speaking of our esteem for the rich and powerful (*T* 2. 2. 5. 21, SBN 365). The rich get extra pleasure from their riches, he thinks, when others esteem them for their wealth and they are aware of this esteem, so the first pleasure has at least two rebounds.

If my old friend expresses distrust of my new confidant, finding him an indiscreet gossip-monger, and I note, and then come to have some understanding of and sympathy with, his expressed distrust, I too may come to lose trust in the new confidant, and also lose trust in myself as judge of potential confidants. Here, however, we have to be on the watch for that "principle of comparison" which Hume observes may drown out sympathy. My old friend may be jealous of my new confidant, so, however knowledgeable, may not be a trustworthy assessor of him. He may want to be the sole keeper of my confidences. So we will have to choose our sympathizer carefully, perhaps even trust them, at least on this matter, if sympathy is to be a proper test of trust. This is especially true when I let myself acquire trust, and self-trust, from others. If I ape a foolish trust-giver, I will myself become a fool.

If my driving teacher trusts me to drive safely, indeed puts his life in my hands when he leaves me in control, and sits calmly beside me as my passenger, my lack of confidence in my own driving skills may be slowly overcome, as I come to share his belief in me, and his calm. To call this "sympathy" with his trust in me, as Hume would, would sound odd to us, since we tend to reserve the word "sympathy" for condolence letters, for compassion, for our sharing of others' unpleasant feelings, and so we are more apt to speak of sympathizing with another's distrust than with her trust. My passengers in the car, when I was a novice driver, on my first time around in that role, would come to share my fear and distrust of my driving abilities, and this spread of fear and distrust was partly by sympathy, partly from my erratic driving itself. Distrust can spread from person to person, and so, in Hume's use of the term "sympathy," which is more like our "empathy," can confidence and trust. It may be rare for self-trust to be acquired, rather than just kept going, by sympathy or empathy with another's trust in one. But it can happen, and did with me when, in my seventies, having given up driving in my thirties after several accidents and complete loss of nerve, I began again, this time with a superb instructor, who, when I had, on my first lesson, told him I would not be able to drive at all fast since I was so scared, had me drive on a busy several-lane one-way city thoroughfare, and then gently pointed out to me that I was driving at the same speed as those around me, in a 60 kilometer per hour zone, so could, after all, drive at more than a slow speed. We were not in a dual control car, so he obviously trusted me to drive safely in traffic, and eventually he made me into a calm and confident driver. Good coaches in sports like acrobatics, swimming, and diving have this art of imparting not only skill but confidence in it. Theirs is a meta-skill, the skill of getting others to become skilled, and to have trust in their skills. Their expressed trust in those they train, like my driving teacher's trust in me, is replicated in the eventual self-trust of their charges.

Keith Lehrer has written about the self-trust we expect most people to have in their own cognitive powers, their ability to reason and form reasonable beliefs.[8] He concentrates on what he calls the "metamind," the self-critical ability that enables us to survey the beliefs we have formed, and "accept" some as reasonable, discard others as too carelessly formed. And Richard Moran has written of our trust in our powers of judgment,[9] that "natural ability" which Hume thought so much more important than a good memory, and which may come in when we engage in Lehrer-like reflections at the meta-level. La Rochefoucauld may be wrong that no one complains of his judgment. If Lehrer and those who learn from him can discard some of their own past beliefs, and judge them to have been too hastily formed and insufficiently checked, then old judgments *are* being complained of and revised.[10] The role of what Lehrer calls "acceptance" is to select which old beliefs and judgments to retain. We may trust our meta-judgment more than our lower-level judgment. But lower-level abilities too must be trusted, by ordinary knowers, the ability to observe and infer, to judge "what beings surround" us, as Hume put it, judge what moves we need to make to avoid "perishing and going to ruin," trust our ability to report our observations and inferences to others, and judge when to believe what they tell us. What Hume called "impressions" are those of our perceptions we cannot distrust, while we may distrust what he called our "ideas," which purport to represent things, and may misrepresent them.[11] The ability to observe, infer, and report what we have observed and inferred varies from person to person. Those losing their sight may lose trust in their eyes, and what they seem to see. Some of these basic abilities took some acquiring, and some of them were acquired only with someone else's help. A child

[8] Keith Lehrer, *Self Trust: A Study of Reason, Knowledge, and Autonomy* (Oxford: Clarendon Press, 1997).

[9] Richard Moran, *Authority and Estrangement* (Princeton: Princeton University Press, 2001).

[10] I discussed this crucial ability, to revise our judgments, in "Mind and Change of Mind," in Baier, *Postures of the Mind* (Minneapolis: University of Minnesota Press, 1985).

[11] I argue for this interpretation in "Hume's Impressions, and his Other Metaphors," in Baier, *Death and Character* (Cambridge, Mass.: Harvard University Press, 2008).

may pick up the language of those around her on her own, but usually needs some help in learning to read and write, do long division, and ride a bicycle. If her teacher communicates low expectations of her, that will not help. Calm confidence that she can do it, can learn to read and write, can balance on the bicycle, can be communicated from teacher to learner, and speed up the learning process. But it can also lead to false confidence, say when a child eggs on another to attempt some dangerous feat. The sympathy which is the test of trust must be adult and informed, not childish and ignorant.

This sort of confidence, to be communicated and duplicated, needs to be reason-backed, not blind optimism, if it is to spread from one to a reasonable other. And when it is spread from teacher to learner, the learner has to see not just that the other trusts her ability, but that she has grounds to do so. Otherwise it may strike her as mindless optimistic faith, with which she may have no sympathy. When my driving teacher asked me to drive past a road obstruction in a very narrow path, he showed that he thought I could do it, and so I could. I did not fully share his faith in me until I had actually done it, but then I did, and his confidence that I could do it was needed for me to actually attempt it.

It had to be more than hope that my instructor had, since I could have killed us both had he been wrong about my competence. Hope may be a splendid thing, and some element of hope may be involved in many trust-displaying actions. When I trust my cat up close to my face, I have to hope he will not feel an urge to hit out and scratch, as he does sometimes when I give him my arm to play with. I know I can trust his good will, but have to only hope he is competent to judge what play is too dangerous. What we hope for is more than the minimum that we trust we will get. Hope is for bonuses, but is not to be relied on for the basics. Talk of a "scaffolding" of hope,[12] supporting our trust, seems to me precisely upside down. It is our trust that must support our hope, when it is hope about how someone will behave, not vice versa. There may be an element of hope in the doubtful trust that some parents place in their adolescent children, when they leave them alone in the family home over a weekend, but in more robust trust relations we feel more assurance that the trusted is really to be trusted, so

[12] Victoria McGeer, "Trust, Hope, and Empowerment," *Australasian Journal of Philosophy*, 86/2 (June 2008), 237–54. The concept of "scaffolding" is taken from J. Bruner, who speaks of the young child's developing abilities having a scaffolding in the mother's hopeful confidence in her child. For more of my response to McGeer, see "Putting Hope in its Place" (Ch. 12 in this volume).

there is less room for mere hope. Trust does involve risk, but to say we merely hope it is a good risk would be to reduce trust to wishful ignoring of the evidence against trusting being sensible, in the circumstances we are in. Sensible parents do not leave their adolescent children unsupervised. And if they do, their hope, while away from the home where they have left their children, is likely to alternate with fear. The two emotional states are twins. Rightly did the poet Swinburne look forward to the day when he would be "from hope and fear set free," since hope is usually accompanied by fear that it will be a vain hope.

Sometimes we can sympathize with another's hope that things will improve, when we share that hope. At other times all we mean is that we know what it is like to hang onto hope, not to resign ourselves to the worst. We sometimes speak of being able to sympathize with another, because we have been through the same thing she is going through, where this may not mean that we endorse the other's reaction, to use Hume's word, that we "second" it. If you hope for a cure for your disease, although no cure is on the horizon, I will understand why you hang onto hope, while not myself sharing it. If I can recall my long-ago adolescence, I may in this non-Humean sense sympathize with an adolescent's misery and despair, while not wishing in any way to encourage her in it. "I know what it's like," I may say, "but believe me things will get better." It is the sympathy which "seconds" another's reaction, be it hope or despair, not that which merely understands it, which is the relevant sort for endorsing trust and self-trust. Usually we will then come not merely to understand what the person is feeling, and why, but to feel with her, have what Hume calls an "impression," not just an idea, of her feeling. If she is angry at some insult, we too will become angry at it. Sometimes our sympathy with our own past self is of this strong Humean kind, say when memory of a past sorrow at a loved one's death revives the original grief. But often we will sympathize with our past selves, say our adolescent selves, only in the weak sense. And sometimes we may refuse to sympathize in any sense with a past moment of extreme foolishness, instead feeling some antipathy for ourselves.

Not every case of a spread of a feeling from one to another by what Hume calls sympathy requires any "deep" sharing of the original grounds for the feeling. If I am low in spirits because my cat has just died, you, when you see me, may become sad, by sympathy, because I am sad, without even knowing why I am. And even if I tell you why, if you had not known my cat, you can scarcely be expected to mourn his death. Good cheer and gloom can spread by what Hume calls sympathy without any spreading of the reasons for good cheer or gloom.[13] But if you sympathize with my resentment, you must resent the same wrong to me that I do, and if you sympathize with my distrust of a certain person, we must have at least similar reasons for the distrust. If I distrust a particular dentist because he failed to diagnose my gum disease, and, after I have expressed my distrust to you, without telling you why I distrust him, you also come to distrust him, but, knowing that I am a coward, you surmise that he must be brutal, perhaps a sadist, and so fear him as such, the lines of communication between us have become crossed. It is not easy to show, by non-verbal expression, why it is that we fear or distrust someone, any more than it is to show why we feel resentment, or anger, or indignation. The cases Hume found remarkable are ones where we do see the reasons someone has for some feeling, see the situation that they, without realizing it, are in. We rarely see the reasons for a person's feeling from their expression, unless it is verbal expression. It is not even very easy to show, except by our words, when we feel trust or distrust, and it almost always takes words to communicate why we trust or distrust someone.

Is there a primitive sign of trust? Psychologists like Paul Ekman[14] have claimed that genuine emotions have a facial expression, across cultures, but such lists of emotions do not include trust or distrust. Taking another's hand is one sign of trust, which small children display, or refuse to display. Some shrinking away from the other, almost as if fearing him, is the behavioral sign of distrust, but what is that of trust? One reason why in my earlier writings about trust I, perhaps overinfluenced by Ekman (who neglects bodily expression from below the neck), did not say it is an emotion is that there seems to be no clear facial expression of it. Like love, it is more a complex of different responsive feelings in different situations, relaxation in the trusted one's presence, absence of anxiety if they are away from us, possibly taking something that we value with them, in their care, confidence they will return, not abandon us. But no one face is the face of trust. And neither Darwin's photos nor Ekman's drawings include a face for distrust. Suspicion

---

[13] See Annette Baier and Anik Waldow, "Conversation on Sympathy," *Hume Studies* (forthcoming), from which this example is taken.

[14] See my "Feelings That Matter" (Ch. 9 in this volume), where I discuss Ekman's views.

and distrust can show in the body in many ways: refusing a handshake, avoidance of eye contact. And even if we did agree on some range of bodily behaviors, voluntary and involuntary, as the expressions of trust and distrust of others, what are we to say about the face of self-trust, and self-distrust? If others are to sympathize with our trust or distrust, something about us must inform them of what we feel. Or do we have to tell them, for them to know when we trust, and distrust?

Self-distrust can show on one's face and body, by a questioning look, and a shrinking posture. But sometimes the lack of trust in oneself to do a particular thing may take other forms. Twice I have had to speak to huge audiences, while intending to say things that offended some of my audience. The first time, my 1990 presidential address to the Eastern division of the APA, I had no trouble addressing the enormous crowd, some of whom, among the women, wept with joy, while others in my audience fumed with anger. But then I threw up, for several days, as if unable to stomach what I had done. The second time, when I was to receive an honorary degree, then give a graduation address, in the Dunedin town hall, and had prepared a talk critical of the university administration at the time, I lost my voice, and made only squeaky noises, magnified so as to be audible and comprehensible. What I said did offend, and at the grand dinner following the ceremony, I, supposedly the guest of honor, was cold-shouldered by the administrators I had offended. In this last case, my self-distrust in my ability to give an address that would offend some of my huge audience showed in a psychosomatic disability. I had reason to distrust myself, after my own reaction to my oratory at the presidential address. This time I could stomach what I was saying, but had trouble actually saying it, then could eat a good dinner afterwards, easily avoiding eating it with those who were avoiding me. (There were plenty others there, more sympathetic to the sentiments I had expressed.) My psyche, when it resorts to psychosomatic ploys, is thorough: the loss of voice lasted for several weeks, as if to rule out mere pretending.

Was it my competence or my will that was lacking on these occasions, meriting my future distrust of myself as offensive orator? For trust is usually in both the competence and the good will of the trusted. The notion of good will to oneself is a little strained, but one can, in one capacity, say as self-critic, have good or ill will to oneself in another, such as challenger of the prejudices of others, or as prone to sarcasm. And for the loss of voice to occur, I think there had to be some ill will to myself, just as there was when I made myself sick by my presidential address. So it is not impossible to adapt the account of trust in others to the case of self-trust, keeping both dimensions, confidence in the competence of the one who is trusted, and confidence in her good will. Karen Jones thinks there must be confidence also in the trusted one's motivation to prove trustworthy, simply because one trusts her, but I had not required this, and do not think it always present, when we trust. The idea of being trustworthy to oneself because one is relying on oneself is one place where the extension of trust in others, if Jones is right about this, to self-trust, seems to me to break down. I can give some sense to giving ourselves discretionary powers, when we go on "automatic pilot" when driving, or trust our ability to speak a foreign language, so chatter spontaneously to a German taxi driver, rather than supervise our every sentence, as we might if speaking to a German academic. And we may sometimes regret such spontaneous behavior. I have learned that it is best to let my replies to email messages wait overnight, lest my off-the-cuff wit end incipient friendships. And there may be times when we should not drive on automatic pilot. Do we then let ourselves down? My quick email replies may have let down my friendship-valuing self, but mainly they hurt their recipients. We can speak of being true to our better selves and many of us were brought up on Polonius' advice to Laertes, "This above all, to thine own self be true. Thou canst not then be false to any man." Still, Polonius was a bit of a fool, and it is only in a strained sense that one lets oneself down, even when one acts in ways one comes to regret. If I drive dangerously, through inattention, I am a danger to others, as well as myself. When I spoke ungrammatically to the German taxi driver, I did not let my "grammatical self" down, since I have no such self (in German), and the taxi driver did not mind. Nor did I let myself down when I lost my voice, just in time for my honorary degree. I let down, if anyone, my audience and those who were honoring me. And if one of my enemies is right, I am an ingrate, so rightly put obstacles in my own way before attacking those who were honoring me, as earlier I had attacked many of those who had elected me as president. There may be some sense we can give to the idea that we can let ourselves down, but I think the best such sense is that we can and sometimes do feel sympathy with those who feel we have let them down. When an email correspondent breaks off the correspondence, offended at my hurtful wit at his expense, I may come to share his distrust of me as emailer, or quick emailer. Distrust from others can lead to self-distrust, both on grounds of our incompetence, and on grounds of our lack of good-enough will. I did not sympathize with those who were upset at my feminist mockery, in my presidential address, of the male emphasis on our upright stance and our dignity, nor with those university administrators who were offended that I criticized their running of the university as if it were a profit-orientated business. But I would sympathize with them if they resolved not to invite me, ever again, to give a graduation address, given how my vocal chords once failed to function.[15] (Actually I did later give another graduation address, in Auckland, and quite enjoyed it. Then I was not at all nervous, except when beginning and ending in Maori, as it is now politically correct to do. I recall looking around the Auckland town hall, from the podium, once safely into my own language, and thinking, "It's quite a small town hall, compared with Dunedin's," so some memory of my near-voiceless earlier address must have been with me. But it may be significant that there was nothing, apart from my halting Maori, to offend anyone in what I said on that occasion, so it took little courage.[16]) It can be by sympathy with another's distrust of oneself or others, or with one's trust in oneself or others, that one comes to feel self-distrust or distrust of another, or self-trust or trust in another, on some matter, though usually we will work our own way to these states. If Hume is right, we all need others' sympathy with our self-trust, and with any pride that we may feel, if we are to sustain such states. We have a standing need for reassurance. Few of us are like Medea, who, when asked who supported her, replied, "Myself, and that is enough."[17] (And few have sympathized with Medea's proud and vengeful acts.) Hume notes that we often do not sympathize entirely with another's pride, but sometimes regard it as arrogance or vain conceit, so it is especially

[15] This is no doubt because I can, as simulation theorists would say, see how a university might hesitate to invite someone prone to loss of voice.

[16] Adrian Piper in her e-book *Rationality and the Structure of the Self*, ch. 13, has criticized my anecdotal style, and also my overgeneralizations. Often I give personal anecdote both to show I have some experience of what I am talking about, and precisely to avoid making claims about all people. But she is right to complain that in past publications I have overgeneralized about women. So now I try to speak only for myself, but do assume I am not an atypical person, and still call on my own experience of trust and distrust, sympathy and the lack of it, to understand these important parts of all our lives. (Or is that a typical overgeneralization?)

[17] The reference is to David Hume, *An Enquiry into the Principles of Morals*, ed. Tom L. Beauchamp (Oxford: Clarendon Press, 1998), 7. 7. The page reference in the earlier edition by L. A. Selby-Bigge and P. H. Nidditch (Oxford: Clarendon Press, 1975) is 252–3.

important to check our pride, and our humility, against the sympathy for it that others give us. Of course, we do not always share their sense of what is worthy of pride, or of humility. I was recently interviewed by a journalist who described me as "unassuming," and quoted another local philosopher as saying I was "self-effacing," both of them meaning these terms, in Dunedin's puritan culture, as compliments. But to me they recalled one occasion when female graduate students in Pittsburgh gave their frank assessments of the three women philosophy faculty who taught them. One was too "butch" and aggressive, one was too flirtatious, and I was too apologetic, always saying "sorry." That criticism stung, and of course I immediately told the outspoken critic, "Sorry to set so bad an example." Not that I had prided myself on being modest, though perhaps I had assumed that arrogance was a vice. This frank woman student (who did not last in the profession, which does not tolerate outspoken women very well) may have increased my self-assertiveness, and certainly by the time I gave a presidential address I was assertive enough. So I had reason to wonder if I were backsliding in old age, when I read the report of the recent interview. We all need others' frank estimates of our perceived character traits, and of our faults, and our faults sometimes change from one extreme to another. I may have veered from undue humility to overconfidence, then back again. (My interviewer described me as "slight" and my living room as book-strewn, whereas I see myself as fairly large, and my living room had been tidied for the interviewer, so was a lot less book-strewn than it had been.)

All cases of sympathy with another's trust or distrust will be cases where we think we know and also share the other's reason for their trust or distrust, and maybe see further than they do into the reasons for it. What of trust in our basic abilities such as seeing, hearing, inferring? No good will to ourselves seems needed to trust the evidence of our own eyes, nor to trust our ability to make simple inferences from what we have observed. But maybe appearances deceive, on this matter. For there has been "scepticism with regard to the senses," and it may take some ill will to oneself as perceiver to indulge it. Hume indulged it in the first two sections of part 4 of his *Treatise*, and although he had begun the second section by saying that we must take for granted that our senses do tell us about lasting bodies outside us, he ends with a splenetic outburst against the "confusion of extraordinary and groundless opinions" which our faith in our senses leads us into. He knows we do show "implicit confidence" in our sensory powers, but he claims to have lost such confidence by the penultimate paragraph of *T* 1. 4. 2. In the last, he reverts, and predicts his readers will revert, by "carelessness and in-attention," to the usual implicit faith. Had his careful attention to the matter been motivated by self ill will? This is not the line most commentators take with this difficult section, but it may be worth trying.

Hume had begun his *Treatise* by saying that our "impressions" are where we must start, to understand where our ideas come from, what counts as evidence for our beliefs. I think that by an "impression" Hume means a perception that is doubt-proof or distrust-proof. It is not our sense impres-sions Hume comes to distrust, in his skeptical moments, but our usual construal of them as informing us of lasting external bodies. Such construals are not to be trusted, he argues, since we know that sometimes we can go wrong in them. Press our eyeball and our world doubles. There are sensory illusions, and hallucinations, and dreams, when what we seem to see, what seems to us at the time to be real things, are later decreed not to have been real at all. So skepticism can get a hold, when we recall our past revisions of what our senses seemed to tell us. As later philosophers such as J. L. Austin pointed out, if Hume had attended more to those later revisions, he would have had to grant that though we may sometimes be mistaken, we cannot coherently think that we could always be mistaken. (This principle, that what can happen occasionally should not be supposed to be able to happen always, is one Hume himself subscribes to.) When we see double by pressing an eyeball, we disable ourselves for normal sensory perception, disable ourselves from giving a reliable answer to the question of how many hats, shoes, and stones are present with us. It takes ill will to ourselves as perceivers to generalize from our abnormal and worst, and even from our deliberately disabled, performances.

Hume in book 2 of his *Treatise* gives us an account of how we can have "pre-sensations" of what others are feeling, from our reading of their invol-untary bodily expressions. We can in fact also tell, fairly easily, what they are seeing and hearing, if in the same room with them, though we have no mirror neurons to speed up that knowledge. The really shocking thing about "Of Scepticism with Regard to the Senses" is that, among the lasting bodies Hume claims we merely surmise to be there, are our own bodies, and those of anyone who might sympathize with our own feelings, including our convictions about what lasting hats, shoes, and stones are currently in our sensory field. Not only did Hume not consult the porter who opened the door, when he himself had only heard its squeak, he has denied that he had, and that we have, good reason to think that the porter had lasting rather than episodic existence. We are to regard the porter as "dependent" on our own seeing of him, and as "interrupted" in his existence as in his presence with us. If this is not ill will to fellow perceivers, what would count as it? Hume has not received much sympathy for his thoughts in this section, and nor does he deserve it, since the other people who might sympathize with him have been degraded, dissolved not just into perceptions, as he dissolves himself, but dissolved into the temporary objects of his own perceptions. His conclusions in this section rightly "languish" in the last paragraph, since they have been denied the "animating principle" of the sympathy of others. He has made himself into the "solitary monster" he calls himself at T 1. 4. 6. If this is not self ill will, what would be? And who is he trying to persuade? There is a joke on the Net about the young woman who proclaims, "I am a solipsist. I am surprised there are not more of us." The society of those who are skeptical of the existence of one another's lasting bodies is likely to be just as select.

It would be quite possible for us to trust our senses to tell us what color is before us, what sounds around us, what taste in our mouths, what shape our hands encounter, without trusting them to tell us about lasting bodies, independent of us. Berkeley gave his senses this minimal trust, while reserving maximal trust to the God whom he believed was the lasting active power behind the sensory phenomena, as if the world were run by a super-magician. Hume does trust his impressions, but has doubts about whether he should trust his spontaneous interpretations of their objects as giving information about lasting physical objects. His perhaps Berkeley-derived doubt is only section-long, and he cannot afford to doubt the lastingness of his own brain, as place of storage for his memories and beliefs, nor of the other people whom he expects to read his writings, and to sympathize with some of his sentiments.

When it comes to trusting our senses, we seem to have little choice, so it may, strictly speaking, count as reliance rather than trust. But we can construe it as trust in ourselves as sensors of our environment. As a dog must trust his nose, trust himself as sniffer, so we must trust our sense impressions, and most of our construals of them, and inferences from them, that is, we must trust ourselves as sensors, interpreters, and makers of inferences about our environment. Of course, we sometimes get things wrong, but mostly we get to correct those errors. Is this a matter not just of our innate competence, but also of our innate good will to ourselves? To say we count on ourselves as trustworthy sensors, interpreters, and makers of inferences seems true enough, but to say we expect ourselves as such sensors, interpreters, and makers of inferences to live up to our own expectations of ourselves, and to do so partly *because* we are counting on ourselves, seems to me absurd. We cannot collectively lose faith in these powers of ours, and we have nothing more reliable to use to try to catch them out in bad performance. Nothing would count as their always letting us down. If we pretend to skepticism about their reliability, that is what it will be, pretence. Just as the reason that would undermine reason has to "take shelter under her protection, and by making use of rational arguments to prove the fallaciousness and imbecility of reason, produces, in a manner a patent under her seal and protections" (*T* 1. 4. 1. 12, SBN 186), so it is by relying on what our senses tell us, with unpressed eyeballs, that we correct the wrong answers as to how many shoes were with us that our doubled vision gave us, and it is by confirming with touch what sight seems to tell us in the stick in water case, that we discover when our senses can mislead us, and what counts as normal conditions for their reliable use. That we have no choice than to trust our senses most of the time is not enough to show that it is not trust. Infants have little choice but to trust their parents. Their trust can be destroyed, and so might our trust in our senses, if, for example, LSD were put in our drinking water. The best reason not to call our reliance on ourselves as sensors and interpreters of what we sense "trust" is the difficulty of finding room for any notion of the good will that the sensing self would have to have to the whole self. I made sense of ill will to oneself for cases like Hume's unfair look at his own reliance on his senses, but there it was his argumentative powers, not his senses, that led to the bizarre temporary disillusionment. He had reason to distrust himself as philosopher, but not really any reason to distrust his senses. If we frequently saw double without deliberately pressing our eyeballs to achieve this result, or if we regularly forgot what we had just sensed so could not bring it to bear on the current sensory input, we might suspect something like a psychosomatic sensory disorder, which might indicate hostility to ourselves, and self-sabotage. And there are such syndromes, such as psychosomatic blindness or deafness. Whether they are caused by self ill will is for experts to tell us. Trust in oneself as sensor may lack the good will component of trust, and certainly lacks that possible component of trust, confidence that our reliance on the trusted will increase their motivation to fulfill our trust. This was not a component on which I myself put any emphasis, and critics like Karen Jones fault me for that. I agree with her that it is indeed there in many cases of trusting others. But need it be always there? (Could it be that all along I was secretly, unbeknownst to myself, preparing to give an account of self-trust?) When I trust professionals such as dentists to act competently, and in my interest, I do not expect their awareness that I am thus trusting them to make a difference to what they do. Indeed I regard the reminder "I am trusting you!" to be usually a bit of bullying, or moral blackmail, an indicator that the trust relationship is rotten, that the one who trusts is relying on the trusted one's fear of displeasing her to get her to be trustworthy. Normally those who are trusted know that they are, and do not need reminding. "I am trusting you to get this job done on time, and don't you forget it!" is a threat, not a contribution to a good climate of trust.

Does trust in ourselves as competent sensors of our environment survive the expressibility test? If the answer to why we rely on our senses is that we have no choice, will that knowledge destabilize our trust in them, bring on a skeptical moment? Descartes did manage, for five days' meditations, to withhold trust in his senses, but he managed this only by abstracting himself from his environment, doing only theology and mathematics. The moment he wanted to know about the things around him, the details of his world, as distinct from the status of the whole creation, he resumed trusting them, and had to. What had destabilized his trust in them, in the First Meditation, had been a bit of pretense on his part, that of the deceiving powerful being, and his awareness, in the Sixth Meditation, that he needs them to get the experimental evidence he needs, as a scientist, as well as to know how to preserve himself as an embodied mind, restores his trust in them, rather than destabilizes it. And, of course, we do have some choice about whether to trust our senses no matter what the condition they are in, or that we are in. It would be foolish to trust them after taking some hallucinatory drug, or when in bad environmental conditions for their use, such as trying to see things in the dark. Descartes, trusting the goodness of his creator, resolves to use his sensations of the secondary qualities only as an aid to recognizing poisonous berries, and other unsafe things, not, as a scientist, to treat color, warmth, taste, and sound as anything except a challenge, to find the primary qualities of what occasions our sensing of them. His Discourses on optics and on meteorology rely on sensory confirmation of his hypotheses, but do not need to rely on color vision, except to get the rainbow as a phenomenon to be explained. (And when discussing vision, he likens it to a blind man's stick.) So we do have a choice about how much to trust our senses, and sensible trust in them will take into account their known limitations, and the known conditions in which they malfunction. So I think they do pass the expressibility test.

I began by suggesting that that test for trust could be restated as the test of whether a suitable other could sympathize with our trust, once she knows why we trust the one we do. In the case of self-trust she likely will sympathize, if what we trust are the same sensory abilities that she also trusts in herself. If, however, I continue to rely on my eyes when my auto-immune disease is beginning to affect them, she, if well disposed, will not sympathize with me. If we trust the senses to work well even if we are drunk or drugged or diseased, she, if sober and healthy, will not "second" our self-trust. At this point we need to choose our sympathizer carefully, and the danger of what Virginia Woolf, in *Three Guineas*, called "unreal loyalties," comes up.[18] If the other shares the same false confidence I do in, say, our ability to drive when drunk, or in our powers as faith healers, she may "second" my self-trust as drunk driver or as healer, and we may both be deluded. It is not sympathy from just any person which should be the test for proper trust, but sympathy from someone like Adam Smith's impartial spectator, who sympathizes also with any possible victims of our foolish self-trust. Hume allowed that sympathy may be biased, felt more with those who are like us than with those unlike us. He thought moral judgment required both "extensive sympathy" and, because of its possible bias, its correction from a "general point of view," from which we can expect others who take it up to agree with us. So the sort of sympathy with our self-trust we might get from those with the same faults and prejudices that we have should not count as any sort of real test of its moral standing. Adam Smith required a judgment of "propriety" to precede our giving of sympathy, and it was to get this judgment that he invoked the judgment of the impartial spectator. If we want sympathy to provide a test for the appropriateness of trust, then we cannot first judge its appropriateness, before the sympathy operates. Should it then be the sympathy not of actual people, but of an imaginary impartial spectator?

[18] Jennifer Whiting refers to this in her "Trusting 'First' and 'Second' Selves."

This would make the appeal to sympathy "a needless circuit" since the real work would be done by imagining such a reliable spectator. The point of expressibility tests, including that of others' sympathy with one's trust, is to reduce a moral judgment to a hypothetical factual one, like Rawls's reduction of a judgment about a just social distribution to one we would find acceptable if behind a "veil of ignorance" of our place in the society in question. In this case, of the healthiness of a trust relationship, we seek to derive "You are right to trust as you do" from "We (but who exactly are we?[19]) sympathize with your trust." Would it do to require sympathy both with the one who trusts and with the trusted? This is more like the "extensive sympathy" with all parties that Hume makes relevant to moral evaluation. I think this does improve the test for trust, but it needs to be yet further extended to any third party affected by a given trust relation. Parents may trust each other with care of their children, and agree that sparing the rod spoils the child, so sympathy with the children too has to be brought in, if the trust relationship is to be fully tested. It is not just let-down of the trusting, and unfairly burdensome demands on the trusted, that constitute the pathology of trust; it is also oppression of those in the power of the trust-related pair.

If we extend the sympathy test for trust to the possibility of sympathy from someone who knows the reasons for trust, and for meeting that trust, and has no reason for her sympathy to be blocked, and require her sympathy with both main parties, and also with any affected third parties, who may get the fallout of the trust relationship, then to sympathize with my self-trust, say in myself as proofreader of my own writings, or as judge of the character of those I meet, or with myself as one who can balance on high ladders, she must sympathize with me both as giver and receiver of trust, and with those who accept my proofreadings, my confident judgments of character, and have to pick me up when I fall from ladders, once she knows why I trust myself in these roles. If I have in fact a very bad record for missing errors in what I read of my own writings, of sizing up potential confidants, and for balancing on ladders, I should not trust my proofreading, my judgment of acquaintances, nor any ladder ascents, and others, unless they are malicious, would withhold sympathy from any self-trust that I might show. But if I react to past disasters in these areas by excessive self-distrust, as may

---

[19] I return to this question at the end of this essay.

be appropriate after the first fall from a ladder, so now refuse to do the proofreading for my own books, and regard all new acquaintances as unknown quantities, possibly scoundrels, another may refuse to sympathize with my extreme self-distrust, not just because I am incurring unnecessary costs in having others do my proofreading, and doing myself out of possibly rewarding new relationships, but also because I am being uncooperative with my publishers, and unfairly suspicious of all new acquaintances. In the ladder case, it is unfair on those who have to pick up the pieces, as well as self-destructive, to take unnecessary risks. (I was once a confident climber of ladders, not dizzy in heights, but always had someone there holding the ladder firm. Now that I am old, and live alone, I forbid myself ladders. Many things it is safe to do with others are unsafe to do alone, and many that one could do in youth cannot be done in old age.)

In the case of distrust of myself as proofreader of what I have written, it is a case of distrust in my own eyes: I tend to see what I know I meant, not what is actually on the printed page. So there can be reasons to distrust what one thinks one has seen, even when one's eyesight is good. This is a case of wishful seeing, or reading. In the case of character assessment, part of what is being assessed by the judge-cum-sympathizer is my ability to judge whom to trust. If I have in the past been too trusting of others, I may in reaction become overly distrustful, distrusting both others and my own ability to tell if they are to be trusted. So sympathy or lack of it with meta-trust, trust in one's own trust, may be involved in this case, and in any case where I with-draw the self-trust I once had, say as ladder-user. Keith Lehrer may be right that it is our meta-mind, our revisionary mind, which we must trust, if we are to have any warranted self-trust in our cognitive powers. Sympathy with another's trust, in her givings and receivings of trust, including any self-trust, is sympathy with a meta-attitude. And if there is a "rebound" from such sympathy, from the original self-trusting one, sympathy with the other's sympathy with her, it will be meta-sympathy with meta-trust. But, as Hume notes, there can be too many ascents to the meta-level, so that we lose track, and the images and reflections of the original feeling become blurred, "by reason of their faintness and confusion" (T 2. 2. 5. 21, SBN 365). Reassurance of sympathy can be hard to distinguish from assurance of sympathy. And I think that such trust in our reflective revisions of our earlier trustings, although important, is not more essential than some trust in very basic, ground-level abilities, such as walking without falling, expressing our

SYMPATHY AND SELF-TRUST   209

thoughts in words, holding a cup of liquid without spilling it, keeping our balance on ladders, chewing and swallowing food. The tragic thing about old age is that these essential human skills can slowly go, and once they do we realize just how vital they were. Our higher-level abilities may last longer than these basic ones. By the accounts of Hume's death,[20] although he was able to receive and talk with friends until near the end, in his last twelve hours he could not speak. Had he any last revisionary thoughts, we cannot know what they were.

It is with some of these skills, such as talking in a foreign language, or driving, or even eating, that the notion of giving oneself discretionary powers does get some grip. If one becomes self-conscious, supervises one's own performance too closely, one can lose the ability in question.[21] To ask just what one's foot is doing, indeed must do, to move from accelerator to brake, is to court disaster, just as it would be to drive too long on automatic pilot. I can babble happily away to a German-speaker in what a tutor once called my "Strassen-Deutsch" as long as I do not ask myself if my grammar is correct. Then I fall dumb. There are many basic skills we do best on near-automatic pilot. Here trust in ourselves, willingness to give our spontaneous self-discretionary powers, is not merely warranted, its lack can be fatal. Of course, it would be better if I could not merely drive but teach driving, so know the theory of how the crucial foot should move, and better if my German were more grammatical, but for purposes of communication, and even for understanding and appreciating Rilke's poetry when my husband reads it to me, the faults in my German matter little. They would come to matter if I let my bad but fluent German loose on a German academic whose respect I wanted. (At lunch in the Berlin Wissenschaftskolleg I would keep fairly quiet, and supervise my sentences a little. Some kind German colleague would then gently correct my errors, and I would try to be grateful.)

It may be noticed that I have avoided talking about trustworthiness. Not only have I rejected the notion that one should be true to oneself, but I have

---

[20] I discuss his death and the accounts we have of it in "Hume's Deathbed Reading: A Tale of Three Letters," in Baier, *Death and Character*.

[21] I have a rare auto-immune gum disease which makes eating painful, and although there is nothing wrong with my jaw, or my teeth, I find I am losing the ability to chew normally, through too much care in the doing of it. If only I would just let myself chew, without thinking about what is happening, I would do better. As it is I may, like Zeno the Stoic, die of self-starvation.

not spoken of any demand for trustworthiness as part of what it is to give trust. Certainly it would take ill will to another not to take into account, in the way I act towards her, that she is relying on me, if she is, but the fact of this dependency is not enough to make the relationship healthy trust. It could be manipulative trust, unpleasantly cunning trust.[22] Of course, if the other is an animal, or a tiny child, her dependency does in itself create a reason for meeting it. But adults should not be so childish, or so cunningly pretend-childlike, and no one would ever let trust be given her if it included a demand for trustworthiness, or would ever give a promise, an institution designed for near-guaranteeing that the trust be met, if the penalty for breach of promise really is being branded as untrustworthy. Trusting a promise-giver to keep her promise is a form of trust, but a more penalty-dependent form than ordinary trust. The trusting are voluntarily in the power of those they trust, but trust should also be empowering to both parties, not a burden on the trusted one. My refusal to see there to be anything necessarily worthy in meeting trust, any obligation to be trustworthy, has been found a fault in my earlier writings about trust, by for example Adrian Piper, who like a good Kantian thinks the right question to ask is not when to trust, but whether it is ever excusable to fail in trustworthiness.[23] I am not a good Kantian, but, I hope, a good-enough Humean. I see trust as a fact about the way we live, and I see a good climate of trust, such as that Denmark seems to have,[24] as a social desideratum, but I see many virtues as contributing to that. Some of them will be forms of "trustworthiness," such as fidelity to promises, and to friendship. But I also see being "worthy" of the trust of oppressors as the vice of servility, of conniving in one's own oppression. The knowledge that someone is trusting us to do a particular thing does not always give us good reason to do it, and that is why I avoided making that motivation expected, in all cases of trust. Judicious letting down is sometimes the right

[22] I refer here to Philip Petitt's paper "The Cunning of Trust," *Philosophy and Public Affairs*, 24 (1995), 202–25. [23] Piper, *Rationality and the Structure of the Self*, ch. 13, pp. 29–30.

[24] See n. 6. In the Reuters report cited there, the OECD economist Justina Fischer is reported as noting the correlation between trust and economic growth: "If you trust someone in a market transaction then you have lower transaction costs. You do not even need to have a contract, because you trust his or her words. So you have no contract costs, you have no enforcement costs." A researcher at the University of Aarhus, Christian Bjornskov, is reported as attributing the Danish capacity for trust to their Viking blood, and inherited Viking norms. I spoke against the emphasis on contract in "Trust and Anti-trust," calling it a degenerate case of trust, but I did not realize that there were economic reasons to distrust reliance on it. Is it remotely possible that I have Viking blood?

thing to do. So I had reason to avoid dwelling on any trustworthiness except trustworthiness to sustain morally decent trust relationships.[25] Among adults these will usually be relations of mutual trust. Trustworthiness can be found in Mafia hit men. Conspirators and gang members expect it of one another. It is something we often claim we look for in politicians, but only because we are already assured that representative democracy involves an acceptable trust relationship between governors and governed. In order to tell which sorts of trustworthiness are morally acceptable, we must first be able to tell which trust relationships pass a moral test.

It is not *necessary* to bring sympathy into the test for appropriate trust, but it may make it more Humean, and may make the test less likely to kill the fragile plant it is testing. And it displays how our various capacities work together, the capacity to tell what another is feeling, and to feel with her, sometimes to see what she should be feeling when she is not, the capacity to trust and to meet trust, to judge which trust relationships deserve sustaining, and so which forms of willingness to trust, and of trustworthiness, are the ones deserving of our encouragement. This is as true of our self-trust as of trust of others. The sympathy of others with my self-distrust as ladder-climber in old age, or in my self-trust as walker, or as driver (as long as I do not try to theorize about just what my feet and arms are doing), or as continuer of old thoughts about trust, and about basic skills,[26] is the proper check on these self-appraisals. And we have reason to be willing to provide this service to one another, to let our sympathy be a sounding board for their self-trust or self-distrust. For others are affected by our self-distrust and self-trust. Indeed, for some things, such as driving, one needs a license. And even for walking, one may, in very old age, end in a "secure unit," locked in, or with an alarm mat, so any attempt to get up and walk is monitored. Old age can be very humiliating. One may come to need again the sorts of care an infant needs. Infancy is not humiliating, since the infant has no memories of having been more self-sufficient. Adolescence is more like extreme old age, in that there may there be the wish to be more independent than one is permitted to be. Just what in ourselves we should trust does vary with stage in life. Our ability to tell who to trust, and what in ourselves to trust, may increase with experience and sorry experience, and

---

[25] I discuss this meta-trustworthiness in "Trusting People," in Baier, *Moral Prejudices*, 187–8.
[26] I first discussed these in "Ways and Means," *Canadian Journal of Philosophy*, 1 (1972), 275–93.

this meta-ability may outlast the more basic abilities. It is not surprising if some of an old person's self-confidence in basic things like balancing vanishes, but she may still rightly take herself to know which of those who help her is to be trusted with what, and which ones are not to be so trusted. I doubt that anyone can stop a person, even in extreme old age, continuing her earlier thoughts, but it certainly helps if there is some sympathy with them.[27]

Do we sympathize with people in their display of vices? We all know what it is like to feel anger, to want to strike out, or to indulge in some self-pity. Hume thinks we need to feel sympathy with all parties before ruling on whether some trait is virtuous or vicious. Unlike Adam Smith, he did not think some human feelings beyond the pale. Violent passions usually get less sympathy than calm reasonable ones, and usually sympathy with the victims of expressed anger will outweigh that felt with the one who let his anger rip. Compassion is a virtue, but what of self-pity? If Hume is right, women are most prone to pity, and often imagine those to warrant it who in fact do not either warrant it or want it. It is in connection with compassion or pity, concern for another's misfortune, that Hume makes his remark about how sympathy can be strengthened by the weakness of the original feeling. Weak women may pity the one who in fact is arising above his misfortune. When they feel such compassion, Hume says, they "entirely overlook that greatness of mind which elevates him above such emotion" (T 2. 2. 7. 5, SBN 370). The emotion this admirable man is elevated above is self-pity. If he did feel sorry for himself, we women might feel with him, but perhaps not admire him. The "partial" sympathy which is felt with the great-souled person, if it became less partial, would be sympathy with effort to rise above his troubles, with his strength and self-trust. Of course, if his misfortune

---

[27] It was thinking about Humean sympathy, and whether it need go deep into another's reasons for her feeling, in connection with a discussion I was having with Anik Waldow, and disputing with Donald Ainslie whether Hume's "impressions" are images, that led me to bring together my thoughts about trusted sense perceptions, about sympathy, and about sympathy with trust and with self-trust. So whatever else I distrust in myself, my ability to benefit from discussion, and my eagerness to engage in it, are things about myself which I trust, and I have reason to hope that at least Anik and Donald will sympathetically "second" this limited self-trust. Not that they agree with my conclusions. Philosophers may be the only ones who welcome being shown to be wrong, who are not downcast by distrust of their conclusions, or rebuffed by others' refusal to sympathize with their argumentative moves. As Hume said, we may be disappointed if our argument fails, but "Our attention being once engag'd, the difficulty, variety, and sudden reverses of fortune, still farther interest us; and 'tis from that concern our satisfaction arises" (T 2. 3. 10. 10, SBN 452).

is extreme old age, and brings good grounds for loss of self-trust, it may be difficult for him to find any other part of himself to trust, to rise above self-pity. But some people, like Medea, are resilient. Some find, even in old age and disability, some core of strength to keep them going. The person whose sympathy with our self-trust or self-distrust would validate it had better, perhaps, not be one prone to womanish pity, but have a fairly pitiless gaze. He or she may not sympathize with Medea, since he will also have to feel with those she kills. In the case of self-trust, he must sympathize with both the trusting and the trusted (or distrusting and distrusted) self, do so "deeply," for the same or similar reasons as the one sympathized with, and not do so merely partially, so not be over-prone to pity. And if this one also feels with "third" (in this case actually second) parties affected by the trust (self-trust) relationship, then the feelings of any who help the disabled stoic (or even the self-pitying unfortunate one) will also be taken into consideration. If they are pleased to help, and we sympathize with their willingness, then the disabled unfortunate one's acceptance of what remains in himself to be trusted, what to be distrusted, is likely to be sound, seconded by extensive sympathy.

The select society of those who claim to rise above any self-pity, even in great misfortune or disabling old age, is unsurprisingly small in membership. And if they really do rise above it, then they are both saints and heroes. Adam Smith agrees with Hume and Malebranche that compassion, or "humanity," is a woman's virtue, but for Hume it is also the supreme one. To reserve it all for others, leave none for oneself, may be as perverse and unnatural as feeling nothing for others. At the very least, sometimes we might let ourselves sympathize with another's concern for us, just as we may come to sympathize with another's trust in us.

But, of course, we would first have to trust that other, as sympathizer. This sympathy version of an expressibility test for trust turns out only to be a test for whom *else* to trust, besides the sympathizer.[28] The problem I touched on with Adam Smith's impartial spectator's sympathy returns to bite me. Sympathy with one's trust may be not merely a "needless circuit," for testing trust, but a circular one too. I must trust myself enough to select

[28] It always was a matter of what else one can entrust to the trusted, besides what one has entrusted, in particular if one can entrust the knowledge of *why* one trusts, and bear the knowledge of why the other meets that trust.

trustworthy sympathizers, in order to use this test. Sympathy is involuntary, so not something one can easily refuse, but one can pretend to it, or attempt to hide it, when one feels it. Not very much good will is demanded of a trustworthy sympathizer, but both competence and lack of motive to resent the trusted is expected. My old confidant may not have been a trustworthy sympathizer with my trust in my new confidant, not because he did not know me, but because he may have been jealous. Need I trust the good will and the competence of the one who sympathizes with my *distrust*, and self-distrust, in order to check these by the sympathy test? My old and would-be only confidant would not be a trustworthy sympathizer with any distrust I feel in my new confidant. A sympathizer need not have good will to the one sympathized with, in order to sympathize, in Hume's sense, but may need it, to show their sympathy, and must not have ill will to the recipient of the trust which is being tested by the sympathy test. One may not be able to prevent oneself from showing sympathy, when one feels it. One may flinch when another is being hit, without having enough good will to want to prevent the blow. Hume does not expect sympathy necessarily to motivate, any more than he expects the moral sentiment always to motivate. To be merely a sounding board for others' feelings, one need not positively wish them well. But one does need to have no positive ill will, either for them, or for those they trust or distrust. Almost anyone non-autistic, and without malice to one, will do as a reliable sounding board for one's self-distrust. But a sympathizer with one's self-*trust*, who has no ill will to one, might well "second" one's overoptimistic self-trust, since self-trust is more comfortable to possess than self-distrust, so one might sympathize, in the sense of understand, the wish to avoid self-distrust. A true friend would fear for one, if the self-trust were overoptimistic, so not second such self-trust. Friends may be good sounding boards for self-trust, but not so good for trust in others, if jealousy can raise its ugly head in friendships. It is more difficult to find a suitable sounding board for one's self-trust than for one's self-distrust. I began by saying that self-distrust would be my back-door entry to a long-postponed look at self-trust. But now I have taken that entry, explored that approach a little, going perhaps in a few circles, I feel considerably more trust in what I have said here about self-distrust, than in any tentative conclusions about self-trust. So I retreat through the same door that I entered. Perhaps my title should have been "Pitiless Sympathy and Resigned Self-Distrust." If I do resign myself to fairly extensive self-distrust, does this mean I lack self-respect? No, since I am still respecting my own powers of selecting which sympathizers with my trust and distrust to attend to, and recognizing my need to consult others on the question of whether self-trust is warranted. Self-respect is hardier than self-trust. We do not trust all those whom we respect, either in Hume's sense or in Kant's.

12

Putting Hope in its Place

In this essay I consider what the proper place for hope is, in human life. I take it to be a conceptual truth that, when we hope, we hope for good outcomes in the future, when that future is, as the future usually is, uncertain. (We do sometimes speak of hoping, where what we hope for, such as that no one was in a house that has burned down, is in the past, and it is our ignorance of the past fact that makes room for hope. Then it is, strictly speaking, our finding out that there were no victims which is what we hope for.) It takes ignorance, as well as optimism, to make room for hope. This ignorance-cleared site for hope includes both matters quite outside our control, such as the weather tomorrow, and matters where we have some but not much control, such as when we are caring for someone, so have some influence on how well things go for that one, or where we are engaged with others in some public campaign. In the last case we hope that everyone does their bit, and that conditions favor the hoped-for outcome. When we are caring for someone, such as a young child, we trust our caring ability, trust the child with some matters, and have hopeful trust in her growing competence. Usually things go well, but in some cases the child fails to develop normally, or suffers some mishap, despite our efforts and our hopes. In both these cases, working together with many others and working with a child, there is a place for hope as well as some trust and self-trust. When we speak of trust, we think we do have reason to be fairly sure. Ignorance is not what clears the ground for trust, but rather some knowledge of the one we trust. When we do things on our own, or with one or a few trusted adult partners, to speak of mere hope of success in what we are engaged in doing would be too weak. Hope can be disappointed, and when we hope, we always risk disappointment. Trust if misplaced is more than disappointed: it is let down or betrayed. We take it we know we will succeed when we type a message or turn the car's steering wheel. Of course, we may be surprised and feel let down, if our computer or our car or our own hands malfunction. And when we intend to meet a friend for lunch, we can be pretty sure she will be there, unless something unexpected prevents her. Here we intend to meet, *deo volente*. That qualification has *always* to be put in; it is not special to actions with a trusted other. But to speak of merely hoping that these everyday actions, whether alone or with friends, will succeed in their intent would be to understate the assurance we need, in order to act with any confidence. We may often also have hopes, hopes that more will come of what we do than what we can strictly be said to intend. Suppose you and I plan to protest a local council decision with which we disagree, so write a joint letter to the local paper. What we intend is to give notice of our case. If, in so doing, we also get a great groundswell of support, that may fulfill our hopes. But we were not in a position to intend such support.

What we intend includes, at most, what we know we are bringing about by our action. Those who believe, as I do not, in the doctrine of Double Effect, exclude from our intention those things we know we are doing that we regret, and would avoid if we could. What we hope for is beyond what we can know we are doing, so beyond both supposed effects. And we do often have hopes as well as confident intentions when we act, especially when we act cooperatively, either with many adults or with a young child. But to make hope a frequent component of intentional action, something that "scaffolds" our intentional action, as some do,[1] is to confuse trust, and self-trust, with hope for the eventual outcomes which our and our coworkers' actions are aiming at.

When we act with many others, some of whom we do not know, as in any political campaign, we cannot be said to trust them to do their bit, since we are often in no position to judge either their competence or their will to support the cause. Talk of hope here is exactly right. Hope energized the Obama campaign. And it is a great force for desired change. But it is more than hope that should scaffold ordinary trusting action; it is confidence in our abilities and in the people we trust. It is too pessimistic to give hope the role that trust should play. We say "we can only hope," precisely when we have little confidence that we can ensure the coming about of the good that is hoped for.

---

[1] Victoria McGeer, "Trust, Hope and Empowerment," *Australasian Journal of Philosophy*, 86/2 (June 2008), 237–54.

We see most clearly what such confidence in what we are doing involves when we experience its loss. If we get to the point where the words we need to express our thoughts fail us, then we must only hope for them, when we open our mouth to speak. The deterioration of self-trust into mere hope is what many very old people experience. It is, of course, better to have hope than to have despair, but better still to have trust. Most of us in adulthood can trust ourselves to do what we set out to do, and each supporter in a joint campaign does have trust in what she herself can do, speak her mind, deliver leaflets, or whatever. Campaigners need hope in the success of their campaign, as parents need hope that their children develop normally, and the old may need hope that those who care for them will sympathize with their need and disability, and also hope that they can communicate, when they try. To be unable to communicate with those who might help one is a very sorry condition to be in.

When one acts with and for those who cannot act for themselves, be they very young or very old, one needs hope (sometimes to stave off despair), as well as trust in those one works with, and self-trust. And the very old have to hope for understanding, as well as hoping to be able to retain some self-trust, even if not in their dependable ability to say what they mean. They should be able to have trust that their relatives will make sure they are competently cared for. If I tell the head of the rest home where some relative lives, that she, the one needing care, told me that she found the way she was showered distressing, I have to hope my protest will be, not just listened to, but acted on. Relatives must trust those who work where the infirm live, or they would not arrange for them to live there, but hope is also involved. They should be able to trust that competent care will be given, but may have to "only hope" that it is also always kind and considerate.

This sort of case, where we act with those we have hired, is different from most cases where we act with others, since often in the latter there is no contractual relationship. But the place for trust, and for hope, is the same: with or without a contract, what we hope for is more than we trust we will get. When we act with others for some common goal, we have hopes that outrun our trust and confidence. We have merely to hope that efforts to control global warming will be effective, while trusting fellow campaigners to do their bit. It is less than a case of shared intentions, since we cannot be fully confident our joint action will succeed.

Victoria McGeer, when she writes about hope,[2] sees it to provide the scaffolding for much interpersonal trust. She takes the concept of "scaffolding" from Jerome Bruner, who speaks of the parental scaffolding loving parents give developing children. I accept the need for "hopeful trust" in the young in our care, and think it also there when we leave the care of the aged to professional care-givers. But to extend this role for hopeful trust from the extremities of life to its middle, and see it as involved in most cases of trusting relationships, seems to me to involve two errors. The first is simple: it confuses the scaffold with what it supports, the superstructure. Trust is stronger in its confidence in a good outcome than is hope, so must do the supporting, when support is needed. Hope is supported by trust, in trusting relations between adults, not vice versa. "Only hoping" is too wobbly a support for firm trust, which is usually self-supporting. The second error is a little less simple, but connected, since it concerns trust's steadiness. The so-called cunning of trust is that having trust invested in one can give one the motivation to fulfill that trust. Were this the main support for trust, then it would indeed be merely hopeful trust, not confident trust. I do not deny that the trusted may sometimes do what they are trusted to do, just because they are thus trusted, nor do I deny that when we trust children and young people, we may rely on their knowledge that they are trusted to prompt their trustworthiness, only hoping that they will prove trustworthy. When we do this, reminding them that we have faith in them, that we are counting on them, we subject them to moral pressure. As McGeer allows, trust of this strategic sort is manipulative.[3] Such manipulation and moral pressure may be excusable with the underage, but I think it is moral blackmail with adults. When we trust our friends, we do not need to rely on any cunning, since we take ourselves to know their character, and their competence, so know what and what not to trust them to do. If we know that a loved one is counting on us for some action, that will indeed give us some motivation to do it, but only if we had encouraged such reliance, and if the action is not itself wrong. Should a stranger ask me in an airport to mind his bag, telling me he counts on me to stay with the bag until he returns, I would, these days, be very foolish to agree—the bag may contain a bomb, and, for all I know, I may be a special target of that bomb. We do often trust strangers, for example when we ask them for directions in a strange city, but it would

[2] McGeer, "Trust, Hope and Empowerment."   [3] Ibid. 252.

invite deliberately misleading information from them if we were to say, "I trust you not to mislead me." This would be insulting. The stranger has no reason to mislead me. To be told, "I trust you not to lie" is, at best, gratuitous, at worst, moral blackmail. As McGeer acknowledges, trust can be a burden, and can be unwelcome. And even when it is not unwelcome, a normally self-respecting person will not expect the friend who trusts her to be relying on her knowledge that she is trusted to get her to meet the trust. Of course, she will meet it—surely her friend knows her well enough and would not have put trust in her, had she not been deemed a trustworthy friend. As I have said in other places, "I am trusting you!" is a threat, not an expression of hopeful trust. Just as, "Trust me!" is an invitation which, if it needs to be voiced, we should never accept, so "I am trusting you!" should be responded to with, "Well don't, as I do not accept the trust of those who threaten and insult me." So the second error in making hope the scaffold of trust is reliance on the wrong reason for trust, and trustworthiness. Strong trust need not rely on any cunning, and that cunning, when present, gives at best an extra reason, not the main reason, for doing what we are trusted to do. That extra reason may be hoped for, if there is a loving relationship, but if we want it to be the main reason why the trusted should do what we count on their doing, we would do well to have a contractual relationship with them: that is precisely the role of contract, and its cunning has long been recognized. The hope that the contract will not be broken goes with reliance on the other's fear of action for breach of contract, should it be broken. Contract does extend the range of trust; as Hume puts it, it extends it to "those who bear us no real kindness." Ordinary trust, such as trust in friends or even in strangers whom we ask for directions, is less coercive, assumes more kindness, and is less cunning.

In saying this I do not want to deny that others whom we trust may sometimes get extra motivation to prove trustworthy just from the fact that we trust them, and that we might hope that they will. But that is not the motivation we *trust* them to have. Usually when we act with trusted others, we share motivation to pursue some common interest. Even the parent who trusts the adolescent with the family home expects the care of that home to be of common concern to all family members. We do not enter trust relationships just for their own sake; they grow up naturally when we do things with others, with shared motivation. The parent may indeed have only to hope that the state of the family home matters to the adolescent who wants to party, or else hope that the fact that his parents are trusting him will matter to him. They can indeed only hope. Hope here outruns trust, but trust is firmer. It is not, like hope, twin to fear.

Others' hopes about how we might behave, and what successes we might have, can indeed energize and encourage us. But they should not come under the guise of hopeful trust. When I was young, I was well aware of my parents' ambition for my sisters and me, their pleasure in any success, and this helped us get ahead. They trusted us to do our best, and the hopes they had were that this best effort might win a prize or two, or be the start of a successful career. They did not burden us with the threat of their severe disappointment should we not win any prize, let alone with the thought that their trust in us might prove misplaced. That would have been not parental scaffolding, but the worst kind of parental bullying and under-mining. Of course, if a person has never been trusted in a particular matter before, they may indeed be grateful to be trusted. It is a curse to have a face which others instinctively distrust. Saul Bellow has a character who says, "There's something about the slenderness of my face and my glance suggesting slyness. People are not at ease with me, and sense that I am watching them. They suspect me of suspicion."[4] The apparently untrusting will not be trusted, any more than we trust those who are over-keen to be trusted. These we suspect of being con men.

I have denied that hope scaffolds trust. At most it is superstructure. What does scaffold our individual intentions and our individual trustings are some shared large-scale collective intentions, such as those we have for our local version of representative democracy, and shared intentions to protect our shared climates of trust, such as trust in those who offer certificates of competence to professionals (to medical doctors, dentists, police officers, lawyers, airline pilots, and all drivers). These are the vital social scaffolding of our individual ventures. We also have hopes for our democracy, that it can cope with the challenge of global warming, and also have hopes for our certificating agencies, that they tighten rather than relax standards. Here, as elsewhere, trust is in minimal competence and good will, hope is for luck and favorable outcomes of the trusted efforts. It is particularly interesting when, as in New Zealand now, there is a change in government. Those who did not vote for the party now in power have to have some trust that the

---

[4] Saul Bellow, *More Die of Heartbreak* (New York: Dell, 1987), 47–8.

new lot will function responsibly, and just have to hope they do not dismantle too much of what the previous government put in place to safeguard the environment. Trust in any government is in the minimum, and there is in such a case especially great room for hopes (and for fears).

Hope and fear are partners. Where there is room for one, there is always also some room for the other. Some voters in the recent US election said their vote was not cast for Obama, but against Palin. When there is a change of government, as now in New Zealand, there are fears that regress not progress will be made, for example on carbon emissions. Such fears are limited by faith and trust in constitutional safeguards, and in the good sense of individuals. And it is important, if such safeguards are to be dependable, that we take our fears as well as our hopes seriously. Distrust is to trust what fear is to hope, and we need to trust our instinctive distrust, as well as our instinctive trust. Parents who have hopes for their children also have to fear for them, in epidemics, and have them properly inoculated. They may have to fear that they will succumb to drug-dealers, as well as having hopes that they will not.

Both hopes and fears can be vain, but the vanity of hopes is a vice in them, while that of fears may come as a relief. When Antoninus, Archbishop of Florence, issued his *Promulgation Tridentina* in the fifteenth century, urging his flock not to let their fear of making a "bad confession" prevent them from confessing, the "vain fears" of such people were claimed to be ground-less ones. When Charles I spoke to those gathered at Heworth Moor, near York, in June 1642, he tried to banish their "vain fears" that the civil war would end in defeat for the royalist forces. Fears, like hopes, can be vain in the sense of groundless. But both fears and hopes can also be vain in another sense, if they rest on a false judgment of what is properly to be feared, what to be hoped for. For, as T. S. Eliot pointed out, sometimes "we should wait without hope | For hope would be hope for the wrong thing."[5] The fears of the York populace may have been vain in a sense their king did not intend, in that victory for the Roundheads would be a blessing for them, not a disaster. (The king's hopes were vain in the first sense, groundless, and the York supporters' fears for him proved not to be vain ones.) A good case of hope for the wrong thing came to my attention when the head of Air New Zealand was interviewed about his reaction to the news that an airbus

---

[5] *Four Quartets*, II: "East Coker."

belonging to them had crashed. He said that at first he had news merely of the crash of the plane, in the Mediterranean off Perpignan. The plane had been leased to a German airline, and was being tested before being given back. He said that he at that time hoped that no New Zealanders were on board. In fact five pilots and officials of the airline were, along with two German pilots. So his hope was vain, both in the sense of "to be disappointed," and also in that it was at least questionable if it should have been hoped for, questionable that it was worse for New Zealanders, rather than anyone else, to have been the victims of the tragedy. He may merely have meant that his grief, and his sympathy for relatives, was bound to be stronger if his own employees were the victims. But one might judge that he had hoped for the morally wrong thing, in this case.

In the past I have spoken about the pathology of trust, taking that to involve not merely trusting those who are not to be trusted, since they let us down, but also manipulative trust, and other trust relationships which would not survive the realization, on each part, of why the trusting one trusts, or why the trusted one meets that trust. In addition there is also the case where what is entrusted is itself bad. Some hit men are very trustworthy, if paid enough. Hope too has its pathology, and in its case the analogue of the last possibility, that what is hoped for, like that which was entrusted, should not have been aimed at or hoped for, since when attained it proves unwelcome, is especially strong. We often do hope for the wrong thing. Hope depends on uncertainty in two ways: not just on uncertainty about what will happen in the future, but on uncertainty about which eventuality would be best. Hopes and fears are subject to two kinds of vanity: that they may never be realized, and, if they are realized, that the hoped-for may prove bitter, the feared prove sweet. (As Oscar Wilde said, "There are only two tragedies in life. One is not getting what one wants. The other is getting it.") Maybe when Shelley spoke of hoping "till Hope creates | from its own wreck, the thing it contemplates," he meant that hopes which prove vain in the sense of groundless may, if they were also vain in the second sense, that is based on a false judgment about what would be good, led by their very disappointment to a state of affairs that turns out to be for the best. If I hope, when young, to become a writer of fine poems, but have my poems rejected as undisciplined by the editors of the literary journal to whom I submit them, and so concentrate on writing philosophy, where the discipline seems more inbuilt, and then prove to be fairly good at that, I may look back on my dashed hopes of becoming a poet without regret, seeing them to have been vain in both senses. They were not merely unrealistic, overoptimistic about my ability as a poet, they involved a mis-diagnosis of where my real talent lay. (Some critics of my philosophy who dislike my anecdotal style may think I should have tried short stories, before giving up on creative writing. Most of us have no way of knowing how well we would have done in a different profession.)

Hope has vanity as its occupational vice. What of fear? Its occupational *virtue* seems to lie in the fact that, even when prudently vigilant, it may prove vain in the sense of groundless. Fear if extreme can be crippling, para-lyzing, and, whatever its strength, it can be exaggerated, even paranoid. Oscar Wilde says that the basis of optimism is sheer terror, and that the pessimist is the one who, faced with a choice between two evils, chooses both. Clinging onto hope in discouraging circumstances may indeed be sensible, and Robert the Bruce was admirable in imitating the spider who when at first it did not succeed, tried again. If fear of failure stops one trying, then fear does tend to paralyze, where hope energizes, and Wilde is wrong about the basis of optimism. It may indeed be a reasonable fear of being paralyzed by fear that leads to trying again, but terror, extreme fear, demor-alizes completely. (I felt terror once in a fairly severe earthquake, and was literally shaking and unable to do anything, so I do not appreciate witticisms about terror.) But since hope of success and fear of failure do tend to share time in the realistic soul, the vices of hope and the virtues of fear tend to act as a control on one another. The thought to bear in mind is that both hope and its twin, fear, may be vain, in both senses, wrong about what is about to happen, and wrong about how we will like that. Vanity of vanities, said the preacher, all is vanity.

The place for hope is when some matter is out of our confident control, and we have reason to think it might come about, and would be good if it did. This is not to accept what McGeer calls a deflationary account of hope, reducing it to a combination of desire and belief that its satisfaction is possible. For the pessimist can have that, taking his desire to be fairly vain, and the chance of its attainment very low. Hope is dwelling on the good possibilities, so can affect agency. We can have hope in improvement of our own capabilities, not only in a better future but in our own better contri-bution to it. But such hope is more in place in youth than in age. In age the best one can hope for may be resignation to deterioration. To hope that all will be well, and all manner of thing will be well, where this includes not just one's own agency but that of everyone else, as well as good judgments about what to aim at, and good outcomes of all efforts, one would need some religious faith and trust to provide the scaffolding for such extraordinarily extravagant hope. Religious faith and hope do go together, along with love, as theological virtues. I have in the past defended the need for some secular faith, faith that cooperative efforts for our society will not prove vain, or counterproductive. But this can scarcely be hope that *all* will be well, and *all* manner of thing will be well. Modest hope will naturally accompany modest secular faith. If there is a scaffold here, I think it is faith which scaffolds hope. As for trust, it is more foundational than either of them. If our hopes are regularly dashed, we may become discouraged, and even lose trust in ourselves as ones who know where to place their hopes—in McGeer's term, to have good hope.[6] But if our trust is regularly let down, not only will we lose trust in ourselves as competent judges of whom to trust, we will lose trust in others as well. To be unable to give trust is to be really handicapped. To have given up hoping may merely be to look fate in the face, to be "from hope and fear set free." As Shaw's Caesar said, "He who has never hoped can never despair. Caesar, in good and bad fortune, looks his fate in the face." And when Lucius says, "Look it in the face then; and it will smile as it always has on Caesar," he gets the reply, "Do you presume to encourage me?"[7] Earlier in the play, after Cleopatra has ordered the killing of Pothinus, and after Caesar had heard his accusations against Cleopatra, then freed him, Cleopatra swears that she has not betrayed Caesar, and he gives her the cutting reply, "I know that. I have not trusted you." One sure way to avoid betrayal is to avoid trusting, just as one sure way to avoid disappointment is to avoid hope. (In my local paper today is the report of the award of $8,000 to a schoolteacher to attend a conference on thinking. He says that he had applied for the grant months ago, "but as a defense mechanism had put it to the back of my mind and forgotten about it so I would not be disappointed if I did not get it. It was a surprise and a pleasure when they announced I had won."[8] He maybe can teach the others at his conference about good defensive mental strategies. He said it

---

[6] See Victoria McGeer, "The Art of Good Hope," *Annals of the American Academy of Political and Social Science*, 592 (2004), 152–65.   [7] George Bernard Shaw, *Caesar and Cleopatra*, Act IV.
[8] Report by John Lewis about the award to Gary Tenbleth, *Otago Daily Times*, Nov. 26, 2008, 5.

was ironic that he had forgotten he had applied for an award to attend a conference on teaching improved thinking, but of course knowing what to forget, and what to ignore, are vital cognitive skills.) To avoid disappointment, it is often best not to raise or dwell on one's hopes. Living without hope is not the same as not looking on the bright side. Hume was not pleonastic when he wrote, in *My Own Life*, that he was "naturally of a cheerful and sanguine temper," so soon recovered from the blow that the cool reception of his *Treatise* dealt him. He cheerfully set about recasting its three books, and writing essays. One can be cheerful without being sanguine. But although some, especially if they are very old, may live wisely and fairly contentedly without much hope, one needs to be very powerful, indeed a Caesar, to live without any trust in others. Trust is the scaffolding, hope the optional superstructure.

When there is trust, there is someone trusted, but the hoped-for can be something quite impersonal, like sunny weather for our planned picnic. McGeer stresses the extent to which we do invest our hope and our "hopeful trust" in someone's agency, and thinks such hope and trust in others can pass the expressibility test I proposed for trust, that it survive the knowledge on each part of why the truster trusts, why the trusted proves trustworthy. Hope is not a relationship, so is not properly subject to such a two-person test. When it is another's action which is the object of one's hope, that creates a weak sort of relationship, but it need not be one that both parties are aware of. If I hope an old friend will reappear in my life, knowing he is to be in the city where I live, he may have no knowledge at all that I have hopes of seeing him. If I am disappointed, it will be fate, not the friend, who disappoints me. To write to him after he has left the city telling him I had hoped he would get in touch, but he had disappointed me, would be most unfair, if I had not written to encourage him to call. Others may indeed have hopes about what we will do, but that is their business, not ours. As we can be burdened with another's uninvited trust, so, even more strongly, if we know that others have hopes riding on what we do, that can be an unwanted, even a resented, weight on our shoulders. Others should not presume to have hopes involving us, unless we invite such hopes. The test appropriate for hope is not an expressibility test, for such tests are designed to sniff out concealed motives in maintaining some actual relationship, and hope does not create a real relationship. Hope resides in the one who hopes, while trust is between people.

McGeer speaks of our "investing" in the trust[9] and hopeful trust we place in others, and this metaphor needs some unpacking. What is the capital which is invested in hopeful trust, and what interest does one expect from such an investment in other people? Is it fair to invest in people? Slave-traders did, and those who place bets on how sports teams will perform. But do we really invest trust in our friends? It is true that there are opportunity costs to any friendship, since there is a limit to how many friendships one can sustain. Whenever we trust, we in a sense choose a particular person to trust, this one rather than that one, and what we hope to get from having given trust varies from case to case, but is always something which contributes to our good, as we judge it. Suppose the trust is betrayed, that the gardener we trusted to care for our garden while we were away did not turn up, so we return to a neglected garden. We will be a little annoyed, if he had agreed to come, and to wait until our return for payment. Have we invested anything in the delinquent gardener? At least in my city, it is very difficult to find a gardener, so it is just not true to say that, had I not "invested my trust" in this man, I would have done so in another, who might have proved more reliable. Trusting is not really investing, except in the rare cases where we have to choose from an array of eager candidates for our trust, and do expect some gain or profit from the relationship. Trusting is casting our bread on the waters, confident that it will return to us. The only way that ordinary trusting is like financial investment is that there can be the analog of market crashes, when the climate of trust deteriorates badly, so few feel safe in trusting others for anything. What we invest must be something we have a limited amount of, when we have a variety of options as to where to put it, in the hope it will increase there. We do have a limited capacity for trust, but what limits it is the number of people with whom we have dealings, and how well or badly we have survived past givings of trust. When I trust the people who run the rest home where my relative lives, I do not expect any "increase" from this trust. Maintenance of the relative's well-being is the most that can be expected. If things go badly, I may indeed wish I had chosen a different place for her, as I might wish I had bought different stocks when the ones I did buy lose their value. Where we really invest, we hope for return on investment, for interest. When we trust, the only return we expect is trustworthy responsive action, not for any analog of interest.

---

[9] McGeer, "Trust, Hope and Empowerment," 24.

Only with contract does trust advance what Hume, who understood his banking metaphors, called "the interested passion." Trust is not an investment, but can be seen as vesting powers in the trusted. We can transfer powers of our own to the trusted, let them do what we might ourselves have done.

Both the financial "investment" and the legal "vesting," or "vestment," are themselves dead metaphors, taken from the old French verbs *vestir* and *investir*, to clothe, surround, or cover something. To see trust as a sort of vestment we place on the trusted may be appropriate, since it does change the appearance of a person when she is trusted, but if the trust is withdrawn, the vestment removed again, she may be returned to her old self, and worse off than she was, if she has become accustomed to her vestment. Hope, too, may be vested in a person, but usually only if that person has invited us to vest our hopes on or around her, to cover her with our hopes. Unless someone wants our trust or our hopes to be placed on her, it can be presumption to cover her with them. They may be constricting, a tight not a loose vest, and in any case she may prefer to go vestless. Hope, if a vestment, is properly a covering for the one who hopes, often to keep off cold winds of despair.

Sir Walter Ralegh spoke of his staff of faith, his scrip of joy, his "gown of glory, hope's true gage,"[10] as if hope was indeed a form of clothing. Faith as a theological virtue is a staff to help one stand upright and move forward, hope a garment to cover one's possibly shivering body, and, in Ralegh's case, there was also a "bottle of salvation." Ralegh spent ten years imprisoned in the Tower of London, under sentence of death, so needed hope to stave off despair. He passed the time writing a history of the world, and after James I freed him, in 1616, to search for gold on the Orinoco, and the fiasco of El Dorado, his death sentence was reinstated. His pilgrimage ended in 1618 on the block, where he tested the sharpness of the axe, calling it a sharp medicine but a sure one for all ills. Hope's glorious gown is soon succeeded by "Our graves that hide us from the searching sun," which "Are like drawne curtains when the play is done."[11] The play of passion which is our life does have a place for hope, which can indeed be seen as a kind of vestment, but one worn by the hoping person, not, unless she shares her hopes, by those for whom she may have hopes.

---

[10] Sir Walter Ralegh, poem, "The Passionate Mans Pilgrimage."
[11] Sir Walter Ralegh, poem, "On the Life of Man."

The place for hope is when we face an uncertain future, and do not know our desires for it to be impossible of fulfillment. Hope keeps off the chill which foreknowledge might bring. The place for trust is quite different, since when we trust we take ourselves, rightly or wrongly, to have grounds for confidence that whomever it is we trust (ourselves included) can and will do what we trust them to. Hopes may accompany trust, when there is a chance of more good things than trust alone assures us of. Trust in others, doing things with them, means sharing fates with them, to some extent, and usually sharing some hopes as well. The two, trust and hope, are related, but if we get the relationship wrong we may understate the robustness of healthy trust, and overstate the supportive strength of hope. As pride goeth before a fall, so "hope deferred makyth the heart sick." Hope has to be cautiously placed, if sickness is to be avoided. Trust, too, needs caution in its placement, but since we place it on ones like us, not on the fates, we are better at judging whom to trust than at judging what to hope for.

I have denied that the expressibility test for trust is appropriate for hope, since hope need not involve any relationship, and it was a test for relationship. In the previous essay, "Sympathy and Self-Trust," I suggest that a gentler form of my expressibility test for trust may be that of whether it can be sympathized with, by one who understands why the truster trusts and why the trusted meets that trust. This gentle test is also a good one for hope. Would someone who knows why one is hoping sympathize with one's hope? If one's reason for hoping is to stave off despair, probably yes. If one's reason is that there is a good chance that what one hopes for will happen, and one's judgment that it is to be desired is sound, then whether or not the other sympathizes will depend on whether she shares one's estimate of the chances. But such an ideal sympathizer might sympathize most with those who try to live without hope, partly because hope may be hope for the wrong thing, partly because hope deferred makes the heart sick. It is important here not to equate living without hope with gloom. One could look for the best in what does happen, without indulging in hopes about what will happen. And a judicious sympathizer may sympathize more with the one who seeks out the best in what has happened and is happening, than with the one who places her hopes in the future, in which death is the only certainty. But, as I admit in "Sympathy and Self-Trust," one can only hope for a suitably judicious sympathizer, in order to test either one's trust or one's hope.

13

How to Lose Friends
Some Simple Ways

In order to lose friends, we must first have made them. Making friends is something children usually do readily and frequently, but the older we grow the less easy it seems to become to make new friends. As Aristotle points out, "Older people and sour people do not appear to be prone to friendship. For there is little pleasure to be found in them, and no one can spend his days with what is painful or not pleasant."[1] Even if the older person avoids becoming "sour," her company will often not be as agreeable as that of the younger person, so she will not make new friends easily. This would not leave her friendless, if the friends of her youth remained her friends as she aged, but typically only a few of them do.

We lose friends through death, through physical distance and neglecting to keep in touch across that distance, through change and the falling away of common interests, through increasing sourness, and occasionally through quarrel. Of course, children often punctuate their friendships with quarrels, either soon dramatically made up, or ending the friendship. They lose friends as easily as they make them, so that a turnover of friends is fairly normal. "I don't want to play in your yard. I don't like you any more. You'll be sorry when you see me, swinging on our garden door." It takes experimentation with a range of close companions for a child to find those she can continue to want as companions, and for her to develop the skills of friendship. By adolescence these skills are usually in place, and tastes in companions more confident and stable, so that this is the time when close, resilient, and fairly lasting friendships tend to be made. The young adult knows whom she does and does not want as a friend, and knows the demands of friendship, so,

---

[1] Aristotle, *Nicomachean Ethics* 1157^{b}14–17.

unlike the child, knows that these demands limit the number of friendships she can nurture. But the friendships of our youth do not always last, nor is it only death and distance that end them. My interest in this essay is with losing friends for other less inevitable reasons, losing them through some failure to maintain the friendship. Such failure is common. The ability to keep friends through thick and thin is as difficult as it is rare.

Friendship usually begins in shared beliefs, interests, and tastes, but, if it is to last, it requires some sympathetic sharing of the friend's interests when these are not, or are not at first, one's own. Nicholas Blake, in his novel *Room Temperature*,[2] has a great description of the difficulties of this project of keeping up with the other's changing tastes, when one reason for the change is the other's very success in coming to share what were one's own tastes. His pair are husband and wife, but the same situation can face any close friends:

And she too was at work on learning why the things that pleased me did please me, testing her progress against my reactions. This reciprocally crossed effort to master the other's interests meant a temporary subjugation of one's own, so that, for example, when Patty pointed out a beautiful book of photographs and engineering drawings of gears (sepia, gray, black) in a Rizzoli bookstore, not saying "Hey, here's something you'll like..." but rather "Oh, how beautiful these gears are!" as if an enthusiasm for mechanical engineering had been innate in her, I had to force myself back into my old technologically appreciative self and go "Oh Momma! Cycloids!..." when I myself had been scanning the same table of books to predict which one (*Blue and White China? Long Island Landscape?*) she might have exclaimed about had she not been trying to second guess my exclamation. And there we both reinforced a fixed earlier self with its simpler enthusiasms in order to reward each other for having seen and understood them, even when our more fluid present selves began adjusting to new admixtures, and we became proud of how far we had left those primitively in-character tastes behind.[3]

Mutual understanding becomes extraordinarily difficult, and full sincerity of response virtually impossible, when there is this never quite up-to-date effort to share the other's tastes. It begins to look miraculous that close friendships ever survive for long.[4] But few friends (and almost as few lovers)

---

[2] Nicholas Blake, *Room Temperature* (New York: Grove Weidenfeld, 1986).   [3] Ibid. 26.
[4] For more on this, see A. Rorty, "The Historicity of Psychological Attitudes: Love Is Not Love Which Alters Not When It Alteration Finds," in Neera Kapur Badhwar (ed.), *Friendship: A Philosophical Reader* (Ithaca, NY: Cornell University Press, 1993), 71–88; first pub. in *Midwest Studies in Philosophy*, 10 (University of Minnesota Press, 1986).

are quite as ambitious as Blake's pair about sharing each other's enthusiasms. Most friends are content to have some, but not all, their interests in common, and to show no more than some understanding of, and friendly tolerance for, the unshared interests. It is enough if one can correctly say, "Here's something you'll like"; not necessary that one like it as much oneself. Some friendships may fail through the impossible demand that all the friends' interests and tastes coincide, and the failed attempt to achieve this mutual mirroring, but more fail through too small rather than too great an effort to share, to some degree, the other's tastes and interests.

What friends do often expect each other to share are their enmities. "Love me, love my dog" is not as important as "Love me, hate my enemies." So one sure way to lose friends is to have made friends with those who become each other's enemies. Even if it is not necessary that "Your friends are my friends and my friends are your friends," one's several friends had better not become outright enemies if any of these friendships are to survive. For if one is caught between hostile parties, each expecting one's "loyalty" and support, either one chooses sides and makes an enemy of a former friend, or one plays the thankless role of would-be peacemaker, and likely offends both parties by one's incomplete identification with each's cause, or one tries to keep right out of the quarrel and so weakens or kills both friendships. As one chooses one's friends, one needs to be blessed with some prophetic powers as to who is likely to fall out with whom, if the friend-ships are to prove mutually compatible over the long haul. Maybe this is one reason why Aristotle advises that our friendships be "character-friendships."[5] Those of good character are less likely than others to get into quarrels, but it is surely not a sign of a bad character to have acquired any enemies. Ex-friends do not normally become enemies, but when the end of the friendship is due, directly or indirectly, to quarrel, there is the danger that in losing a friend one is gaining an enemy. At any rate, the peaceable will be ill-advised to make friends with the less peaceable.

A friendship can have a dramatic ending in a charge of treachery. The self-disclosure that is typical of friendship makes friends vulnerable to each's special knowledge of the other, and this, as Kant warned, can lead to charges of perfidy when this knowledge is perceived to have been misused, or shared

---

[5] See John M. Cooper, "Aristotle on the Forms of Friendship," in Cooper, *Reason and Emotion: Essays on Ancient Moral Psychology and Ethical Theory* (Princeton: Princeton University Press, 1998).

with unsuitable others. Friends can be lost through the perception of perfidy, on the part of one of the friends, and that loss may be good riddance, if the perception is correct, or even if it is not, if it reveals undue suspiciousness in the perceiver. Aristotle links the mutual self-disclosure of friends to their assistance to each other in the worthy aim of self-knowledge, and another less dramatic way that a friendship can die is through the fading of interest, on the part of one of the friends, in this Socratic project. To be reluctant to receive, or to fail to show sufficient interest in, what the other is disclosing to one, or to fail to offer any return disclosures, can put the friendship at risk. Aristotle advises us to end friendships with those whose character has changed for the worse, and Aristotelians will perceive a developing boredom with self-knowledge, one's own or one's friend's, as such a change. But, like increasing sourness, it may be a change that comes quite normally with aging. After all, if one does not know oneself by, say, age 60, one is unlikely ever to, and it is also possible that one has, by then, found more interesting things to get to know. But such developments, if not occurring in a coordinated way in both friends, are not conducive to the health of the friendship.

Fortunately not all friendships are based on this shared narcissistic concern to know oneself, and see oneself mirrored in one's second self. Youthful friendships may have such a basis, but mature friendships can merit C. S. Lewis's characterization: "We picture lovers face to face, but friends side by side."[6] Some friendships that are quite casual have an amazing resiliency, and can withstand lack of contact over years, or even decades, when this lack is due to physical separation, and even to the failure to keep track of the whereabouts of the friend. I have had friends of this sort, who reappear unexpectedly in my path, and the easy companionship resumes as if never interrupted. Had such friendships been of the intimate, intense sort, with confidences exchanged, they very likely would not have proved so immune to death through neglect. Is it that the less demanding the friend-ship, the hardier it is? We could call such reappearing friends "prodigal friends," and they have the special value the New Testament ascribes to returning prodigal sons.

It is not only loss of contact over long periods that some friendships can survive, against all reasonable expectations. They can also survive too close

[6] C. S. Lewis, *The Four Loves* (London: Geoffrey Bles, 1960), quoted in Badhwar (ed.), *Friendship*, 42.

contact with the friend's spouse, that is to say love affairs known to the "betrayed" spouse and friend. This may show as much about the amazing generosity of spirit of some friends as it shows about the tenacity of some friendships. There is as much to wonder at in the survival of some friendships as there is to interest the anthropologically inclined philosopher in other friendships' endings. And in both cases, the wisdom of the great philosophers fails dismally in helping us to understand which friendships survive, and why.

Kant writes that friends flatter themselves that, in case of need (and he is thinking of more vital needs than self-knowledge), they can count on each other's help, but that they will hesitate to ask for such help, since to receive it would put the recipient "a step lower, inasmuch as he is obligated and yet not reciprocally able to obligate," thus spoiling the equality of respect there should be between friends, and contaminating the mutual ties of friendship with one-sided gratitude.[7] Kantian friends are reluctant to have to feel gratitude, and preserve their friendship through carefully avoiding any threat to their equality of moral status. Each friend "is magnanimously concerned with sparing the other any burden, bearing any such burden himself, and, yes, even completely concealing it from the other."[8] Not everyone is content with merely Kantian kid-glove friendships; many of us expect friends indeed to be friends in need. I once endangered a close friendship by not phoning my friend, who was also my neighbor, at 3 a.m. when I was alone in my home, taken ill, and needing to be driven to the emergency ward of a hospital. Given the ungodly hour, I called a taxi. But there was no question of "concealing my burden" for long, and when the friend visited me in hospital I had to meet the reproach, "Why did you not phone me for help? Am I not your friend?" I did not lose this friend by my unwillingness to be a burden, but there was something to be forgiven, and something learned. I had never been much of a Kantian in my ethics, but I was even less a one after this inadvertent and unwise obedience to Kantian rules of friendship. These are more recipes for killing friendships than analyses of "true" friendships.

Another thing that Kant, repeating Aristotle, says that true friends expect of one another is frank criticism, when criticism is due. But mutual correction is not always a reliable sustainer of friendship, and one-sided correction

---

[7] Kant, *The Metaphysics of Morals*, pt. II, sect. 46.   [8] Ibid.

is, for adult–adult friendship, often fatal. Should one's friend be the one to teach one to drive? Only if the friend is a superb driving instructor, and if becoming a driver matters more to one than the friendship. And experience has shown me that, unless one intends to write a rave notice, a blurb rather than a critical review, it is very unwise to agree to review a friend's publications, even if one thinks that one would oneself have been able to take a critical review from that friend, or former friend. (One is likely to be self-deceived about that.) Nor need the review be sour in order to offend. Indeed, a witty review, if the wit is at the author's expense, is particularly unforgivable. A return unkind review from a friend earlier lost by a too frank or, heaven forbid, a sarcastic review from one's unruly pen can be, however, quite easily accepted as a sort of requiem for the friendship. Correction of judgment may be the end of life, as Kant would have it, but it can also be the end of a friendship. Friends respect each other's vulnerabilities, and it is difficult to overestimate the sensibilities of most authors to reviewers, especially when they know those reviewers.

One qualification to this gloomy estimate of the advisability of mutual criticism between friends, especially publishing friends, is in order. Publishing friends can be not just tolerant of, but grateful for, privately given criticism of drafts of what will later be submitted for publication, especially when they have solicited such criticism. What offends in an unfavorable book review from a friend, or even a friendly acquaintance, is the public airing of what it is felt, perhaps optimistically, would have been quite acceptable if communicated in private. It is even as if the offended author is charging the unkind reviewer with failing to make the criticism at the proper time and in the appropriate way, namely before publication, and tactfully. But if the critic has not been asked for private comments on the pre-publication manuscript, this charge is, of course, unreasonable. In theory, in publishing one is submitting one's writing to the critical scrutiny of anyone and everyone, and to the published judgment of whatever reviewer a journal chooses. But in practice, writers do not expect their friends to be frank about their writing's perceived faults, especially not in public. (I have lost at least three friends by too frank reviews of their books.)

Even when criticism is private, if unsolicited it seems bound to offend the touchy pride of writers. Recently I read a book about a long-ago acquaintance of mine, written by his son, who was an infant when his father died. I had never met the son, but I took the liberty of writing to him, expressing my appreciation for his book, but noting that his treatment of some of his father's deceased relatives and colleagues, all of them known to me, did not show that generosity of spirit that he had rightly attributed to his father. In reply, I received a letter from the author which, after thanking me for some factual details about his father that he had not known, went on to reprove me for passing any judgment on the generosity of spirit shown by the son, compared to the father, when I knew nothing, except his book, of the son. In this case, it seems, only a friend or close acquaintance was allowed to express a judgment, even in a private letter, about the personal attributes of the author, as expressed in his published comments about other people. (Not only am I prone to risk losing friends by published criticisms of their books, I also preclude new friendships by unsolicited unpublished criticisms of those I know only through their books.)

Writing memoirs of any kind is in any case a very dangerous business, as far as relations with those mentioned in the memoirs, or their friends, is concerned. Memories of the events related by the memoirist often diverge, or have been differently edited by different persons' selective and usually self-protective memories. Friendships can be put at risk when one of the friends puts on paper the way the shared past appears to her. It is nearly impossible to write non-self-serving memoirs, and almost as difficult to read non-defensively memoirs in which one figures. If one is asked for comments on such memoirs before publication, the temptation is very great to say "Not true!" whenever one remembers differently.

The fact that private criticism of a piece of writing has been requested is not always enough to make the criticism acceptable to a proud author. A German academic associate of mine, whose English was a lot better than my German, had an article he had written in English accepted by a journal on condition that he have some native English speaker go through it with him to eliminate some stiff and uncolloquial turns of phrase. He asked me to do this, and I was pleased, perhaps too pleased, to oblige, since he had been generous with his criticism of my German conversation. But it was no easy task to persuade him to alter any of his carefully composed, grammatically correct, but sometimes pedantic, sentences. Our tentative friendship was slightly strained by this requested but unwelcome reciprocity of assistance in use of a foreign language. Writers are naturally more sensitive than mere talkers to criticism of the words they choose, since the spoken word, or at least the word spoken in conversation, is not expected to last. Writers tend to have an unreasoning parental love of their written offspring. (This author graciously forgave me for correcting his English, and when we parted gave me a pretty little gift inscribed with congratulations on my progress in the German language, thereby, by Kantian rules, regaining the upper linguistic hand. Clearly the asked-for assistance had destabilized the delicate balance of the relationship. But then only someone with a proven track record of losing friends, and risking that loss, can speak knowledgeably about the topic that the editors of this volume on friendship[9] have agreed should be mine.)

A tendency to wit, sarcasm, and critical remarks can be something one values in one's friend, that makes her good company, even if one is sometimes the butt of her humor. But there is a time and a place, it seems, for cutting remarks. I was told recently of the distress caused in a group of old and close friends, when one of them, known for her sharp tongue, was dying, and kept up the habit of uncensored critical comments as long as she had breath. Her old friends were rallying around to help care for her in her final weeks, but were hurt by her apparent lack of appreciation, and by her acerbic words about their efforts to be helpful. One of them remarked that she would be lucky if she had any friends left by the end, to attend her funeral. Is one expected to change character when suffering and dying, so that one's sad and solemn friends not be offended by the tenor of one's remarks, even when that tenor is typical of one, and is what those friends once valued in one?

Does it matter, in any case, if one has no friends left to attend one's funeral? (The woman discussed in the previous paragraph in fact had a good turnout at hers, including all the offended deathbed helpers.) It is said that we die alone, so some last-minute shedding of friends, or apparent turning away from them, may be a sort of preparation for that, a turning of one's face to the wall. And some may begin doing this earlier than others.

So far in this essay I have been assuming that to live without friends is to be pitiable. But is it really true that, even if some choose to die without friends, no one would choose to live without them, as Aristotle, Hume, and a host of others have claimed? As Sebastian Barry's exiled, itinerant, and friend-pursued character Eneas McNulty reflects, "it is a mighty thing to

---

[9] This essay was first published in French in Jean-Christophe Merle and Bernard N. Schumacher (eds.), *L'Amitié* (Paris: Presses Universitaires de France, 2005).

enjoy the fact of a friend in the world. A mighty thing."[10] But this mighty thing is what in the end kills Eneas. Doubtless an entire life without friends is a poor life, but the one who has lost all her friends has of necessity once had friends. Should the loss of her friends have occurred through normal processes of attrition, that is to say through death, change, distance, and some failure to keep in touch across that distance, along with her not making new friends in her declining years, or even if some losses have occurred through her getting involved, directly or indirectly, in quarrels, or through too sharp a tongue or too little tolerance of a friend's sharp tongue, the friendless life need not be a bad life, for the friendless person. (I do not think it is necessarily worse for one's fellow persons, so worse morally, either. Even if there is a duty to associate, is there a duty of voluntary close association? Kant complained of the sentimentalists' overpraise of friendship, but contemporary moralists and virtue theorists too are in danger of overvaluing its moral status.[11] My main interest in this essay is in losing friends, as a natural rather than a moral phenomenon, and in the hedonic significance of such losses.) Friends are or were welcome companions. If they are physically absent, they can no longer be companions, and the pleasures of email are a poor substitute for talk, eye contact, body language, companionable silences, doing things together. Letters are better, but the art of letter-writing seems to be a dying one. So if one is without friends-as-companions, even if some old friendships are still intact, would it be so much worse to become friendless? At this point we are in the danger Socrates purported to find himself in, towards the end of Plato's *Lysis*, of associating friendship too closely with the useless. And that, as Socrates says, would strike a sour note. But memories of friendship are never useless. As long as one has the memories of good times with one's then friends, and is at peace with oneself, one's own company can be not so bad. (I have found that I notice and so enjoy the beauties of nature more on solitary than on accompanied walks, when attention to conversation can distract from looking and seeing. As John Updike writes, "Aging calls us outdoors... in truth all views have something glorious about them. The act of seeing is itself glorious..."[12] The pleasures of solitude are not to be despised. Nor need one resort to the inner eye to

---

[10] Sebastian Barry, *The Whereabouts of Eneas McNulty* (London: Picador, 1998), 77.

[11] See Lawrence Blum, "Friendship as a Moral Phenomenon," taken from his *Friendship, Altruism and Morality* (London: Routledge and Kegan Paul, 1980), in Badhwar (ed.), *Friendship*.

[12] John Updike, *Self-Consciousness: Memoirs* (London: André Deutsch, 1989), 235.

discover the bliss of solitude: the outer eye too can have its vision improved. As Updike wisely remarks, "People are fun, but not quite serious or trustworthy in the way that nature is."[13])

Reading, and for that matter writing, are for most people solitary activities, so their pleasures are little affected by friendlessness. (This is not to deny that one needs critics for one's writing, but friends are not necessarily the best such critics. Nor is it to deny the special, but these days rare, pleasures of being a member of a group who listen to and perhaps discuss what one of them reads aloud.) Listening to music is another pleasure that survives well in solitude. Even if some of one's best memories of times with friends are of attending concerts together, one does not need a fellow listener to enjoy the music itself, as distinct from the talk before and after it. (This is especially true of recorded music, but even live music can be enjoyed as much by single as by accompanied concert or recital goers, and some people, even if accompanied, shut their eyes during the performance to block out distracting stimuli.)

Some philosophers, Kierkegaard for example,[14] have suggested that close friendships might interfere with one's less exclusive ties, those of neighborliness, and humanitarianism. And, as E. M. Forster famously pointed out, one may have to betray one's country to avoid betraying one's friend. It seems to me unlikely that the friendless person will be a better neighbor, or better citizen, or better humanitarian, than the person with a circle of close friends. If a person has come to value the pleasures of solitude, she is in some danger of becoming antisocial, so is not very likely to be joining all those community associations that do good to her fellow persons. She may still support them financially, but if she seeks out the company of her neighbors and fellow do-gooders, she is likely to acquire friends from among them. As Emerson and C. S. Lewis say, friends see the same truth, engage in some valued joint activity.[15] So even if one is not, at first, close friends with the other members of one's community improvement group, or the local Save-the-Little-Blue-Penguin or Hands-Off-the-Greenstone-Valley group, if one meets regularly with them, one is choosing companions who see the same truth, and so, unless one is very prickly company, one acquires at least potential friends.

---

[13] Ibid. 245.   [14] Kierkegaard, *Works of Love*, pt. 1, ch. 2B.
[15] Ralph Waldo Emerson, *Friendship*, vol. ii of *The Complete Works of Ralph Waldo Emerson* (Cambridge, Mass.: Riverside Press, 1883); Lewis, *The Four Loves*.

The person who has lost her old friends and not made new ones does not, however, inevitably become antisocial, let alone a recluse, simply because she enjoys the admittedly insidious pleasures of solitude. She need not become a glutton for such pleasures. She can still enjoy passing encounters, and conversations with those she meets as part of a normal life, with her family (who are closer than friends, and do not cease to be her family when they or she become sour and bad company), with shopkeepers, with the plumbers who unclog her drains, with those who sit beside her on public transport, with those who attend the lectures that she attends, and with strangers who, during the interval at concerts, engage her in conversation about the quality of the performance. (The upper balcony at Carnegie Hall is a particularly good place for such brief musical encounters.) She can still have a host of friendly relationships, one-shot or recurrent, when she has lost her close friends. And she can still enjoy the company of, and even conversations of a sort with, her intelligent, charming, understanding, and communicative cat, Clara, who, though wonderfully responsive, and not without ideas of her own, is blessedly unverbose. (Indeed she has a Luddite tendency when it comes to word processors.) Is this what Solon meant when he advocated that the friends we need to keep are our children, our trusty steed, and a host abroad?

Friendship may indeed be a mighty thing, a crown of life and a school of virtue, but there are other fine things, other crowns and other schools.

I seem to have turned from my topic of how to lose friends to the related topic of where one is left, in terms of quality of life, if one loses all or most of them, as if my title had been "The Consolations of Friendlessness." I now return very briefly to my official topic to add an irresistible postscript: one final way to lose any remaining friends may be to write an anecdotal essay about losing them.

14

Alienating Affection

Alienating affection is a kind of theft, in which the responsibility for the transfer is shared between the thief and the one whose affection is at issue. It is as if a burglar, instead of entering and taking the silver, instead stays outside with a magnet, and attracts it out an open window, without any breaking and entering. My bad record for alienating affection seems to be continuing into my old age. As a young woman I was seen by some unkind critics to have alienated the affection of several of my married colleagues from their wives, and now, long past any risk of doing that again, I seem to be collecting my neighbors' cats. First one old retired tom moved in, with the eventual consent of his former owners, and soon his young female friend was spending most days at my home, rather than staying where she officially belongs. She even sleeps over, now and then, and letting a caller sleep over is, in alienators of affection, the very worst sin. A third cat has now taken to visiting, despite having a perfectly good home of his own. What is it about me, or about my home, which attracts these unfaithful types? Is it some character fault in me? It is not as if I, like the burglar with the magnet, actively lured any of them, and I never was of more than average attractiveness, in person. But I may not have done enough to positively discourage these acquaintances from transferring their affection to me, and, at least in the case of the cats, I have come to fully reciprocate it.

Smell is said by the experts to have a lot to do with attraction, and it has to be admitted that one of my affectionate cats seems particularly fond of the smellier parts of me, liking to lick my toes and nuzzle into my armpit. But in the human case, one would think that pheromones must have been at work in attracting the husbands to their wives in the first place, so that theory did not explain their movement in my direction. Or does the magic of the pheromones wear off, with familiarity? (Will the cat get tired of my toes?)

Is it that I provide better food than these straying ones got at home? Do they come for the refreshments? That could not be said of the husbands, whose wives were all very good cooks, a fact I had proof of, during the time when I was still invited to their dinner parties. With the cats it may have some truth, but surely there must be more to be said.

I sing to the cats, and they seem to like that, and we go walks together. With the husbands, too, music certainly played a role, although I never sang to them, merely met them at concerts, or listened to records with them. And I suppose I did go walks with some of them, but, as I remember things, it was the drives that played more of a role in cementing the relationships. (The cats all prefer walking to driving.)

Leaving one's door (or catflap) unlocked must also play some role. But locking uninvited callers out seems a desperate measure, and, in any case, a boorish thing to do. I do plead guilty to making my visitors welcome, and I liked (like) their company. As far as the cats go, it is the fact that I am at home a lot, now that I am retired, while their owners are out at work during the day, that partly explains their coming to me. They like company. With the husbands, all colleagues, it was at work that I got to know them, and perhaps the fact that I lived near our place of work made my home a welcome haven for them. Was I just a convenience to them? I undoubtedly am a convenience to the cats, if also a bit more, at least to the old tom. He follows me round like a faithful dog, and at the beginning howled on the doorstep until I took him in. (None of the husbands ever did quite that.)

What the second and third cat come to my place for is as much cat-company as my company, so perhaps it is the charming old tom who is now doing the alienating of affection. But then the husbands also were, at least to begin with, friends with each other, and were on occasion all together at my place, after work. Usually, however, I entertained them serially. Indeed, one sour observer accused me of letting myself be passed from one to the next, but this was quite unfair. None of them favored polyandry, only polygamy. The cats do not demand exclusive affection, and that makes some things easier. They do not fight over me, as one or two of the husbands eventually came close to doing.

If one alienates affection, one must expect some uncomfortable confrontations with those whom one has wronged. In my experience, such victims feel more hurt than indignation. "She clearly likes your place better than mine," said the owner of the young female cat, sadly, after she had slept over with me, and then, brightening slightly, went on to ask, "What brand of cat food do you buy?" "You will be better for him than I am," said one noble wife, relinquishing her right to her husband. "You have more interests in common." In both cases, I was a bit lost for a reply, though I did in the feline case manage to mutter the name "Purina One, Healthy Weight Control Formula." In the human case, the wife's noble act of renunciation may have been well calculated, as it did rather make me wonder if I really wanted a pre-loved husband who could be given up with so little fight. It has to be admitted that the former owners of my devoted old tom (who still had another eight cats at home, several of them his progeny) seemed relieved, not at all offended, when I gave up attempting to return him to them, and officially took him on. Oddly, that easy transfer of ownership did not devalue him in my eyes.

Perhaps I just like cats better than men. In the end I successfully returned all the husbands, but I still have the cats.

15

Faces, and Other Body Parts

Faces

Why have we, and so many other animals, evolved to have faces? A face is a portion of the head on which are found forehead, eyes, eyebrows, nose, ears, cheeks, mouth, and chin. Why are they all together? The fact that eyes, ears, nose, and mouth are close together on our heads seems to have something to do with the efficient working of these different senses. To be able to see and smell what we are eating, to smell what we are breathing in, is useful, perhaps essential. But we do not need our ears to vet what we eat and breathe in. Having both eyes on one plane was needed when we were hunters. Owls are advantaged that way over other predatory birds. That eyes and ears should be close to the brain makes good sense, but if our ears were on our shoulders, we would manage. If our eyes were on stalks, like crickets', we would also manage, but if they were on our knees, as imagined by Lawrence Shapiro,[1] it would be very difficult to manage. Shapiro points out how we need two eyes, and two ears, and the ability to move our heads around to vary what we see and hear, to get the information we do get from pairs of eyes and pairs of ears, and their distance from each other also matters for that (eyes' distance from each other gives us bifocal vision, and ears' distance from each other affects how much we hear), but he does not tell us why ears need to be near eyes.

Faces are on the front of heads, which contain foreheads, and we define "front" as where the face is, forward as where the forehead faces. (It is also important that the feet project in the same direction as the forehead faces, so our natural movement is forward.) The head, containing face, brain, and protective skull, is in charge of the body, as is the head of a school or a corporation.

---

[1] Lawrence A. Shapiro, *The Mind Incarnate* (Cambridge, Mass.: MIT Press, 2004), 186.

These other senses of "head" are metaphors, taken from the literal case of an animal head, given its role in controlling the animal's life.

In a novel I recently read, one character, a vegetarian, has as her rule of what and what not to eat, "Not if it had a face." So fish and crickets are out, but eggs and shellfish allowed. Faces do matter to us, and not just to us. My cats like to have eye contact, from time to time, and we sit happily gazing into each other's eyes, with some meaningful blinks on their part. They groom each other's heads, and sometimes try to groom mine. When they greet each other, it is nose to nose. The face is for facing each other, as well as facing the world. Faces are expressive, and from them we can tell if others are angry, upset, joyful, pensive. Cats' faces can show aggression, and their ears are more expressive than ours. So faces are important in the communication of emotions. Other parts of the body can help in this—fist clenchings, shoulder shruggings—but faces bear the main brunt of the expressive task. So it is not so unreasonable to refuse to eat any face-possessor, however different its face from one's own. I have never gazed into a fish's eyes, and birds' faces are a bit pointy for seeing all of them at once, but a face is a face, however beaky or fish-faced. Insects are more of a problem, but few of us are offered them as food. Would my fictional vegetarian eat witchetty grubs? Do worms have faces?

We take the face to be the mirror of the soul, and not only may we hesitate to eat something whose face we knew (a pet lamb, for example), our attitudes to killing human beings depend a bit on whether their faces have been encountered. Jeff McMahan points out that we regard infanticide as a crime, but allow the killing in the womb of viable fetuses.[2] Those whose faces have been seen, even if they are badly deformed, and premature, are those who count as fellow persons. The fact of birth itself can scarcely be the deciding factor, one would think, but the fact that someone has as it were "met" the infant, while no one has met the fetus, seems to affect our emotional reaction to the death of that being. It may be irrational, but it makes a kind of emotional sense, to care more about the death of those who have faced us and the world than those who have not, even when their faces are just as fully formed. And in places of mistreatment of prisoners, such as Guantanamo Bay, the victims are hooded, so that their torturers are spared having to face them. For faces can accuse, reproach, and beg. Those who did

---

[2] Jeff McMahan, "Infanticide," *Utilitas*, 19/2 (June 2007), 131–59.

saturation bombing were spared the sight of their victims, and this made their task easier. Faceless victims are less likely to haunt one than those into whose faces one looked as one killed them. Of course, for a person of any imagination, the knowledge of what one is doing when one drops one's bombs may be not so different from facing those victims, but not everyone has much imagination.

It is clearly unreasonable to be more willing to kill those whom one has never faced than to kill those one faces, including those who are blind-folded, when facing a firing squad. "Facing a firing squad" is still apt, since although eyes matter much, there is still a partial face for the killers to recall, when they have killed blindfolded people. If we know they have faces, that we could have faced them, looked into their eyes, then they should matter to us as much when those faces are not visible to us as when they are. But is it so unreasonable to regard those who have never faced anyone, or had their faces seen, except possibly on a scan, that is those still in the womb, as in a different category from those whose faces have been wiped and dried after birth? The miscarried or aborted fetus will often have a face, but not one that has screwed itself up to scream, or looked into another face. The mother usually does not see what has miscarried, or been aborted, but doctors and nurses do. Once when as a student I worked as a hospital cleaner in a maternity hospital, a bundle in a trash can I was emptying came undone and there was a tiny dead baby. That it was a baby, and not just "once-living human tissue," was very clear to me, partly because I saw its tiny face. Never after that could I agree with those who defend abortion by refusing to call what is aborted a small human being. Maybe sometimes killing it is defensible, but not because it is not a human being. Because its little face never faced anyone, it may not be deemed a person, but that it has a face is undeniable. It is considerate of medical practitioners to keep their sight of what they abort from being shared with the mother, and it would be considerate if they also kept it from those who clean up after them, but we should not deceive ourselves about what it is we are killing. Killing those with human faces is not like stepping on worms. And nor is killing a cat or a dog like stepping on a worm. If one has had a loved pet on one's lap as it is given a lethal injection, and gazed into its eyes until they glaze over, one knows that faces matter.

Sentimental nonsense? I do not think so. The combination of features on a face is an important and expressive combination, and more important as a combination than if one just added up their single contributions to the usual life of what has that face. To lose an arm is a great loss, but if one's face is badly disfigured, that is worse. One's mouth serves not just to ingest nourishment but to scream, and to speak. To have no voice, or no hearing, or no sight, is a terrible deprivation, but if one still has an expressive face, one is still a communicating person among persons. With today's methods of communication, we often exchange messages with those who may to us be faceless, but I find this very unsettling, and try to get hold of some photo of all my unmet email correspondents. Only then can I feel I am speaking *with* them. However distinctive their communicated thoughts, if they are to me the thoughts of faceless thinkers, they lack reality. It is not for no reason that we want representations of Socrates, Plato, Aristotle, Descartes. Even misrepresentations are better than none. Masks are better than facelessness. And that we have chosen to make masks is an interesting fact about us. We also have a long, if disputed, tradition of physiognomy, of finding significance concerning character in faces and heads. In China it is called Siang Mien, and its secrets have been passed down for over two thousand years.[3]

Most of us recognize familiar faces, and those who do not, the prosopagnosiacs, are almost as handicapped as those who lack normal faces. Not to recognize the faces of those one knows, to need their name given to one before one knows who they are, is socially crippling. One person I know with this disability copes with it, in a room full of people, some of whom she knows, some not, by approaching everyone with exaggerated cordiality, risking being too friendly to strangers rather than unfriendly to familiars. Her ear for voices is better, but not so good as not to need a name to be given, to be sure whom she is speaking with. Her beaming face would be a good illustration for what deserves the German *Antlitz*, the English "countenance," so deliberately composed is it, so ready to face whoever is there not just with courtesy but with sustained pleasure.

As I write, I have, above my desk, a copy of the portrait of my husband's face as a young internee, done by fellow internee Erwin Fabian, the original now in the Australian National Gallery. When I look at it, I know what mattered to me when I first saw that face, what character, endurance,

---

[3] See Lailan Young, *The Secrets of the Face: Love, Fortune, Personality, Revealed the Siang Mien Way* (London: Hodder and Stoughton, 1983). Thanks to my doctor, Marjolein Copland, for loaning me this book, despite her skepticism about the secrets it reveals. And thanks to Emilio Mazza for reminding me of the European tradition of physiognomy.

humanity it showed, along with a wonderful wild beauty. (Both Kurt and his friend Erwin were, at the time the portrait was made, rather ravaged by their trip on the hell-ship *Dunera*, taking them from Britain to Australia.) Faces are for facing the world, and the other people in it, and Kurt's face, in this old drawing, is both sensitive and fierce. He had bad experiences, but little resentment remains, so now his 92-year-old face seems not at all fierce. He faces his restricted future quite philosophically, and welcomes one of our two cats on his knee, appreciatively. That one, old Tab, is used to being there, while the new one, Shy Blackie, takes longer to be so at home. But since the two cats trust each other, and each trusts at least one of us, full mutual trust is to be expected. So it is with all of us; who trusts me trusts those whom I trust. Those whose faces I welcome, them my intimates also welcome.

The most enigmatic face I know of is Spinoza's "face of the whole universe." But if that supreme totality is a thinking being, as it must be to include all reality, then that it should have an expressive face does stand to reason, I suppose. It would take Spinoza's third kind of knowledge to know that face, and intellectual love of God to appreciate it. The New Testament promises us that the pure in heart shall see God, and all religious people live in that awesome hope. As I age, I find myself less and less inclined to scoff at human attempts to talk about God, and never was at all inclined to scoff at Spinoza's. I agree with Hume that dogmatic certainty and religious zeal have wrought great horrors, but still, there is something, the true religion, without which our lives become brutish. Kant's "starry heavens above," and something divine within some human spirits, make me occasionally want to worship the whole of which we are a part, despite the undeniable horrors, some of them man-made. Faces can be evil, and some actors, such as Javier Bardem, in the Coen brothers' film *No Country for Old Men*, can impersonate great evil with their expressive eyes and striking faces. Faces can radiate both good and ill will, and calm relentless purpose.

Of course, bodily stance can also show purpose very clearly. One does not need to see the face of a stalking cat to know what it has in mind. But our prime means of knowing each other's minds is by the expressions on our faces. Our mirror neurons tell us what another's look would mean if on our own face, so we know what to expect from that other. Malice, envy, derision, all tend to show on the face, unless an effort is made to prevent that. Even then, the shifty or frozen face will itself alert us. We are adept at reading faces, and need to be. Inability to read faces would be even more crippling than inability to recognize whose they are. What they reveal is more important than whose they are.

We find faces in the moon, and other odd places. "Faces in Places" is a website specializing in these read-in faces in machines and other inanimate places. We speak of clock faces and typefaces, as if wanting to share our animal privilege of a visage with timepieces and cold type. We urge each other to face up to things. We define "forward" as the direction we are facing, backward as the opposite. Faces are for facing what is coming towards us, whatever it be, for seeing it, hearing it, smelling it, maybe tasting it, and reacting with our facial muscles to that, maybe grimacing, or gritting our teeth. Faces are for facing things; what else would they be for?

Hands

After faces, hands usually are the parts of ourselves that most express ourselves. Some people have manicures, just as some have facials. What our hands are doing is observed as carefully by police interrogators as what our faces show. Restless hands show nervousness, just as clenched hands show anger.

My hands show age and arthritis, despite having been voted, when I was 14, the most beautiful hands in the class. (This was a sort of consolation award, given to one not positively disliked, if she had failed to be "most popular" or "most likely to succeed.") At the time of this award, my hands were a pianist's and a writer's hands, so fairly flexible, and usually ink-stained. I valued the award, as I myself found hands important, in my friends. Dürer's *Praying Hands* was a favorite piece of art work. Young people getting to know each other hold hands before other bodily intimacies take place. To touch another's hand is to invite intimacy.

Hands can play a part in other bodily intimacies, and their dexterity and sensitivity make them important in such close encounters. They are involved in love, and in most work. Manual labor is the usual kind of labor, and in skilled activities, like pottery, surgery, typing, and soothing fevered brows, hands are essential. They also are used, through fingerprints, to identify us.

There is handiwork, and there is handi-play. Playing footsie is also possible, but the foot is clumsy, for most of us, compared with the hand. Cards designed by the handicapped, with the mouth and foot, may be admirable, but artists draw, shape pots and statues, with their hands. Musicians perform with their arms and hands.

Most other animals have at best front paws, not hands. In Basil Pao's beautiful book of photographs *Hands: A Journey Around the World*,[4] one lovely photo (p. 360) has someone holding a kitten ocelot, from the Amazon, whose front paw rests on the human hand. Paws can stroke one's face, just as hands can. Apes have hands, but not opposed thumbs, so lack some of the dexterity of human hands.

Hands are handy; what else would they be?

Shoulders, and Other Joints

Only those who at least occasionally have an upright stance have shoulders. Or, for that matter, buttocks, surplus flesh where the legs join the torso. My black cat has beautiful shapely hips and haunches, and maybe a rump, but no buttocks, and only incipient shoulders. Animals with tails, even if they can stand upright, like kangaroos, seem to have no room for buttocks. Horses have rumps, and magnificent tails. Do we have buttocks to make up for our lack of tails? Some can swing them, just as a cat can swing its tail. "I wish that I could shimmy, like my sister Kate. She can make them wobble like jellies on a plate." Other animals are round-shouldered and flat-bottomed, compared with us. Maybe Nebuchadnezzar, when he went on all fours like the beasts of the field, lost both shoulders and buttocks.

Elbows, too, seem more important to us than to cats, since we need to flex and bend our arms in different directions, to get things and do things. Many animals can kneel, so knees are of quite general usefulness. We are the only ones who use them to beg.

What are shoulders for? Because of their protuberance, we can hang bags from a shoulder, and some carry heavier loads on them. Shoulders can be squared, and shrugged. The shoulder shrug is a very expressive gesture, showing that we regard some matter as quite unimportant. I have, in "Feelings That Matter,"[5] suggested that lowering the shoulders indicates a readiness

---

[4] Basil Pao, *Hands: A Journey Around the World*, foreword by Michael Palin (London: Thames & Hudson, 2006).   [5] Ch. 9 in this volume.

to take something seriously, possibly, as when we square them, to take on some new responsibility.

We can also turn a cold shoulder, an important ability, to deter those who might want to put too much on our shoulders.

As elbows are for elbowing, shoulders are for shouldering; what else would they be for?

Navels

Navels are perhaps the only thing that distinguishes us from all other animals, yet are given little attention by, for example, philosophers who treat our upright stance, shared at times by gophers, as symbolically significant. (They have also neglected buttocks.) Other mammals bite off the umbilical cord of their newborns at birth, so no navel remains to remind the animal of its early dependence on its mother. We have that reminder, and some now decorate their navels with rings and jewels. I doubt they do this to indicate their indebtedness to their mothers. Belly-dancing is an old art form. Recent fashions, for young women, display the navel in public in ways formerly unthinkable, but navel-gazing, in private, has always been allowed.

For navels do merit attention. We do not spring forth, fully formed, from any field of Ares, but are slowly formed and nourished in our mothers' wombs. And, unlike cats, we do have midwives and doctors who tie the umbilical cord, so the traces of its presence do not disappear, as in other mammals. Our upright stance makes birth more difficult for us than for cats, so helpers are needed. Our navels show us our dependence, both on our mothers, and on those who assisted them at birth.

The Greeks gave the earth a navel, the Omphalos, as Spinoza gave the universe a face.

Navels are for reminding us of our ties, for navel-gazing; what else would they be for?

"The best picture of the human soul is the human body" (Ludwig Wittgenstein).

16

Other Minds: Jottings Towards an Intellectual Self-Image

I take the concept of "intellectual self-image" from Neil Gross, in his book about Richard Rorty.[1] My self-image is of a self-questioner, and a resident alien, as I was, in fact, for so much of my professional life.[2] My first remembered utterance, at age 2, was "I don't like being me." This, I find, shows a nice awareness that I was one among many, and that some may be in better positions than others. I was the second child of a very intelligent father and a very devoted and sympathetic mother, younger sister of a bright and bossy elder sister, observant elder sister to two very different younger sisters. We lived at the end of the earth, in New Zealand, a country whose poets, when I was growing up, thought "distance looks our way,"[3] and certainly themselves looked distance's way, mainly back to Britain, which was still referred to as "home." All this helped me reflect on what it was to be a person, and one different not only from my sisters, but also from my Polynesian fellow citizens, from the swag men who would come to the door for leftover food during the depression years, and from those superior beings who lived where our ancestors had come from, in Britain, or in Europe. For as long as I can remember, as a child I had a dream of going, in the words of the title of a children's book we read, "beyond the hills," beyond the limits confining us to where we were, to other lands, other ways of living, other visions of life. This dream was realized when, after completing my university studies

---

[1] Neil Gross, *Richard Rorty: The Makings of an American Philosopher* (Chicago: University of Chicago Press, 2008).

[2] I once wrote an essay called "The Virtues of Resident Alienation" (*Nomos*, 34 (1992), 291–308).

[3] The phrase comes from a poem by Charles Brasch, "The Islands," first published in John Lehmann's periodical *New Writing*, later *Penguin New Writing*; repr. in Brasch, *Collected Poems* (Auckland: Oxford University Press, 1984). The phrase "distance looks our way" has since been used for book titles and titles for art exhibitions in New Zealand.

at Otago University, I traveled by ship to Britain, to study at Oxford. The ship's journey, around the world, through Ceylon, Bombay, Aden, Port Said, Naples, Marseilles, was itself an education. Trying to fit in with British ways, once in Oxford, was another, and adapting to life in Aberdeen, in my first job, yet another. But when I look back, these dislocations seem to me to be what enabled me to reflect on different ways of living, different climates of trust, different reasons for distrust. And in each place I met intelligent people in fields other than my own—on the ship to Britain I was given a crash course in biochemistry by Dick Matthews, later to become a member of the Royal Society, who was then on his way, with wife, Lois, and baby daughter, Sue, to Cambridge to do research with people like Francis Crick. Dick, met for the first time on that ship, and to be a close friend thereafter, could not understand why I would want to study philosophy, rather than do science. In Oxford I met mainly philosophers, American as well as British, but also some New Zealanders in other fields, John Child in economics, Graham Johnston in English literature, my old Otago University friend Hugh Templeton in history, Marianne Fillenz in neurophysiology, and Dan Davin from Oxford University Press, who more or less presided at the New Zealand club. Throughout my life, I have always valued friendships with those in other disciplines.

At home as a child, I had absorbed a little astronomy, and much general knowledge, from my father. He had left the Hokitika high school at age 15, with *Sartor Resartus* as a prize, to begin work as a clerk in the Justice Department. He had great intellectual curiosity, and a retentive mind. He was a keen amateur astronomer, and would show us the craters of the moon and the rings of Saturn through his telescope on cold clear nights. For years, every evening in the scullery, he ground away at a ship's glass porthole to make a reflecting lens for a large telescope, at the same time taking great interest in our school homework, especially once we were at high school. He was widely read, and keen to learn new things. We had a *Children's Encyclopedia* at home, and he consulted it as much as we did. We also had an old edition of Gray's *Anatomy*, which he had acquired from a hermit astronomer friend in Oamaru, Mr Garvie, and I would pore over it, especially the chapter on the brain. Neil Gross puts forward the thesis that the children of intellectuals are more likely, from the start, to see themselves as intellectuals than others who study at universities. Illness had prevented my mother from having any high school education, and my father was not an intellectual, but had a very enquiring mind. Both my parents had high hopes for their daughters, so it seemed quite natural to me that I should aim to get to study at a university, then, once successful as a student, to hope that I could find a lasting place there.

I was blessed not just with very supportive parents, but also with a series of great schoolteachers, who encouraged a questioning spirit. When I was 15, at high school in Hawera, I was taught by Tracy Gibson, who, while officially teaching English literature, in fact taught critical thinking. From him I learned about Socrates, and what sort of questioning he had encouraged. Then, at the University of Otago, I read Plato's dialogues, under the guidance of Denis Grey, and was introduced to Hume's philosophy by David Daiches Raphael and later by John Passmore. This started me on the way that I would continue on, for the rest of my life. Plato and Hume may sound an odd combination, but in my case, a good one. At Oxford I continued my studies of both of them. Denis Grey was an Oxonian, and seemed to us students in Dunedin like someone out of *Brideshead Revisited*, with his face makeup and exaggerated mannerisms. He played us Bach on the piano in his office, knew Japanese, and started a group where about five of us tried to learn Russian. He was my first encounter with someone quite different from the familiar. Studying Plato with him, and learning ancient Greek, was an entry into new magic worlds. In Oxford I studied Plato with Elizabeth Anscombe, and with Gwil Owen, fine scholars but a lot less exotic than Denis. He is my "other mind," par excellence. At Otago I had won a prize for an examination on John Wisdom's *Other Minds*, my first exposure to Wittgenstein's influence.

In Oxford, Ryle was the great guru at the time, and took a fatherly interest in all B.Phil. students, since the degree was his invention. His *Concept of Mind* certainly took the mystery out of the idea of other minds, made one's own just one among others, but I wanted others to have minds which were interestingly different from my own, and had a little mystery to them. For me in Oxford, my supervisor, J. L. Austin, was the dominant other mind. His wonderfully witty lectures, his great learning, his formidable critical powers in exposing and demolishing pretentiousness and silliness, his lack of concern about whether or not his shoes showed evidence of his recent trip to see how his pigs were faring, at his home in Old Marston, his helpfulness and friendliness to me, and his enthusiasm about my thesis topic, all made a deep impression, but I never felt I really knew him. There was an English reserve about him, as there was also about Peter Strawson, but it seemed lacking in Paul Grice, who was very approachable. Philippa Foot, at Somerville, was also a very helpful adviser, though one piece of advice she gave me was to beware of the influence of two German-speaking Australians who had been around Oxford, Kurt Baier and Peter Herbst. (Kurt in fact was already on his way to Cornell when I arrived in Oxford.)

I was lacking in confidence, feeling very much a provincial, but Austin went out of his way to encourage me. My B.Phil. thesis was on "Precision in Poetry," in those days a fairly unusual topic, and one that delighted Austin, who himself was famous for pointing out how much more we do with words than describe things. He "played old Harry with the true/false fetish" and enjoyed helping me play old Harry with the literal/non-literal one. We looked at the time it took metaphors to die, and relished the fact that "This is a live metaphor" is itself a dead metaphor. This sort of study linked up with my undergraduate studies of English literature, and fascination with William Empson's *Seven Types of Ambiguity*. I did not at the time link it with the philosophical texts I was reading, and it took me a long while to attend enough to their metaphors. Hume should have been more interested than he was in the precision of the metaphors he used, and Plato knew the power of poets to lead or mislead. During my two years in Oxford I learned much, not just about philosophy and philosophers, but about life, and forms of life. I had my first marriage proposal, from a young Spanish engineer, whom I had met in Paris when on vacation there, and who wanted to take me to his parents' bull ranch near Salamanca. Even imagining life with him was mind-stretching. He was desperate to save me from what he saw as my approaching fate, as a spinster teacher in despised England. He was my first encounter with a traditional enemy of Britain, good training for meeting the Viennese, when five years later I married an Austrian. Kurt himself had fled from Nazi Austria, since his father was Jewish, but his Aryan mother, half-brother, and most of his other relatives had stayed. His brother and stepfather had to serve in the German army, and the former spent several very hard years in Russia as a prisoner of war. I think I found it daring to be close to people who had recently been my country's declared enemies. As a schoolgirl, after patriotically knitting balaclavas for the troops during the war, and giving the speech for the navy at the Hawera victory celebrations (written by Tracy Gibson), I had then organized the sending of food parcels to defeated Germany, and I had several German pen friends.

I was definitely attracted to aliens, but not only to aliens. I was taken up as a friend by Janet Vaughan, distinguished hematologist and Principal of Somerville College. She had pioneered the storage of blood for transfusions during the war, and had been one of the first British people to enter Belsen, after the fall of Germany, as a medical adviser to the British liberators. Her brilliant mind and intense presence, and the privilege of her friendship, lit up my life. At her homes, in Oxford, in London and in Surrey, I got to know her two daughters and her husband, David Gourlay, and met other brilliant people. I spent one Christmas with the family at Plovers' Field, their Surrey home. When I graduated, Janet wrote me a testimonial saying that I would be at home in any company, and I felt flattered and overwhelmed. My Somerville friends saw me as one of the Principal's "special girls." She gave me an antique emerald brooch when I left Britain for Auckland. I was an innocent in sexual matters in those days, but I was aware of an undercurrent of something like passion on the occasions when I was alone with her. When I visited her on later occasions, as I did whenever in England, she would tell me about her blood research, and I would try to tell her about my feebler philosophical researches. I wrote about my last visit with her, for the Somerville magazine, after she died. She was still driving, in her nineties, and being her passenger was still thrilling, as it had been when she would drive me from Oxford to Plovers' Field, decades before.

My jobs, after Oxford, were in Aberdeen, then Auckland. In Aberdeen I froze, physically, but had good experiences, intellectually. Bobby Cross, the professor in the logic department, was a great person to talk to about Plato, and Bednarowski, the logician, introduced me to the liar paradox and other delights. I attended his advanced class in logic so as to learn enough to teach the introductory class. Early on he put to the class the problem of the road to Larissa,[4] which I solved fast enough to pass muster, and we became good friends. With some young Swedes who were experimenting on what could be made from codeine, and with those in the psychology and psychiatry departments who were conducting experiments on mescalin, I had my first (and only) consciousness-changing experiences. My hallucinations are documented in Peter McKellar's book on the imagination.[5] I did not benefit

---

[4] One comes to a crossroad while trying to reach Larissa. At it stands one of two guides, one who always speaks the truth, one who always lies. One does not know which of them stands before one. What question should one ask to find out the way to go?

[5] Peter McKellar, *Imagination and Thinking: A Psychological Analysis* (New York: Basic Books, 1957).

from those experiences, since they made me talk about Plato's dialogues while under the influence, and I never afterwards trusted my thoughts about them. It was then that my main attention began to shift to Hume. We read the second book of his *Treatise* at a reading party at "The Burn," and after I left Aberdeen and returned to New Zealand, to a job in Auckland, Hume slowly became one of my main interests. The professor in Auckland, Dick Anschutz, with whom my relations had been stormy, gave me a first edition of Hume's *My Own Life* as a farewell gift. A very generous one, but he was really glad to see the last of me.

The voyage home from Britain was just as important to me as the voyage out, since on it I met the charming man who became father to my daughter, born at the end of my first teaching year in Auckland, and adopted at birth, since her father was back in Britain, and our relationship was over. Neither my superiors at the university, nor anyone else there, knew of my pregnancy, and the fact that, if known, it likely would have counted as the "gross moral turpitude" necessary for dismissal, fueled my developing feminist thoughts. I was tall and big-boned, and did not "show" much. Since gowns were then worn for teaching, I could hide in my gown. One of the courses I was teaching was an introduction to ethics, a huge class in which there happened to be David Lange, later Prime Minister of New Zealand. Sarah was born during the study break between the end of lectures and examinations, when I returned to supervise my classes' exams. I led a very solitary life that year. Afterwards, life went on, with me considerably the worse emotionally speaking, but career-wise, none the worse.

After my very lonely first year in Auckland, I overcompensated in the next two years, and not only became good friends with bachelor colleagues like Jack Golson in anthropology and Andrew Packard in zoology, but became too involved with several married men, some of them quite senior in the university. My own professor, Dick Anschutz, became incensed, as good friends of his were involved, and I myself, after a brief engagement to marry one of these men, whose noble wife came to tell me that I would be a more suitable wife for him than she had been, soon thought better of that, and decided it would be best if I moved away. So I applied for, and got, a job in Sydney. Then, or about then, I met Kurt, and we married at the end of 1958, just after I left Auckland. The fact that we had been in each other's company only about fourteen days in all, since we had met at a conference in Christchurch earlier that year, did not deter us, and we have had a very happy marriage. We enjoy the same things, except that Kurt had had too much music in the home as a child, since his stepfather played the cello, and string quartets met in the living room, while I, who had had piano lessons as a child, could not get enough music. My last piano teacher, Mary Frazer, in Dunedin, had sensibly taught me how to listen and enjoy as much as how to play. Kurt's and my philosophical interests overlapped, so we each could help the other in what we were writing, and we both laughed at the same jokes, very important in any relationship. Kurt had been interned as a friendly enemy alien during the war, after having to leave Austria, and so his self-image, as friendly alien, fitted well with mine as self-chosen exile.

The conference where Kurt and I met was organized by Arthur Prior, who arranged for Kurt and me to be house guests of Doctor and Mrs Bennett, parents of the philosopher Jonathan, who had been with me at Oxford, and of the writer Margaret, wife of Harry Scott, psychology professor in Auckland, and a good friend. Prior later claimed to have arranged our marriage, as did two other mutual friends. It appears that others (except for Philippa Foot) could see, even before we did, that we were meant for each other. Prior had earlier had a hand in my getting to Oxford, and later had a hand in my first publication, an encyclopedia entry on nonsense, so was a sort of philosophical godfather to me.

My emotional adventures are a story apart, but I think they did affect my views about what matters in life, and so affected my developing philosophical views. The ongoing pain of separation from my child, and my long ignorance of how she was faring, showed me something about the strength of the maternal tie. I already knew its strength, from my bond with my own mother. She was very proud of my academic success. She was ill at the time of my own pregnancy, and so I had not told her about it. She suffered from Parkinson's disease, then later contracted cancer of the esophagus, and died in 1972 after horrendous surgery to try to remove the growth. I came from Pittsburgh, where we were by then living, and was with her before and after the surgery, indeed with her when she choked on her own blood and died. I stayed a little while with my sisters and my poor bereaved father, who was to live on another fifteen years. His mind seemed to remain sharp to the end.

I taught at Sydney University for only one year, living in Double Bay, where Kurt would join me at weekends, from Canberra, where he taught. My boss was John Mackie, a fine philosopher and Hume interpreter.

My students were a pleasure, but many of my colleagues were a sexist pain. The "libertarian" ethos of the retired philosophy professor John Anderson reigned supreme, and he and his elderly secretary–mistress were occasionally to be seen in the quadrangle. His followers regarded "free love" as an obligation, and parties tended to develop into orgies. As a newly married woman, I found this distasteful, and in Sydney suffered not just sexual harassment but moralistic sexual harassment. So I moved to Canberra, where I had no job, nor much chance of one, with Kurt as chairman. Our friends there were in a variety of fields: Paula Brown in anthropology; Igor and Ines de Rachewilz, and Wang Ling, in oriental studies; the psychologist Daniel Taylor and his philosopher wife, Gabriele; Heinz Arndt in economics, and his wife, Ruth; the historian Manning Clark, his wife, Dymphna, and their six interesting children. Life in Canberra was pleasant, and the other minds one encountered were interestingly varied, so when the invitation to Pittsburgh came, for Kurt, I was reluctant to leave for the US. We had already spent one semester there, when Kurt had sabbatical leave in 1960, at the University of Illinois at Urbana. I had not enjoyed that, despite a lively and friendly community of philosophers. It was on that stay that I met Kurt's half-brother, Gottfried, an architect, and his wife, Lea, and their daughters, who lived in eastern Pennsylvania. Then, when we went on to Europe, before a term in Oxford, I met Kurt's parents in Vienna, and they made me very welcome. Once we moved permanently to the US, we saw them almost every summer, and Austrian culture became of great fascination to me, especially once I learned the language enough to appreciate the theatre in Vienna. Its music I had appreciated from the start. I had visited Vienna from Britain, earlier, but then I was a tourist, whereas now I was a foreign family member, a quite different experience. Kurt's mother was warm and loving, and keen to teach me Viennese cooking as well as the German language. Kurt's extended family, especially those on his stepfather's side, were a varied, colorful, even eccentric lot. I often felt like the family idiot in their company, as they were witty, cultured, and very articulate, while my German never became good enough. Kurt's cousin Peter, a writer and at one point director of the Konzerthaus, sometimes used me as a sort of ventriloquist's dummy for his funny stories for his adoring aunts. I was left, from this experience, with a compulsion to prove to him that, in my own language and field, I was no dummy. I would send him my books, once I published any, and they must have bored him silly. Eventually, to calm me down, he wrote a long letter saying that he saw Kurt and me as a sort of Leonard and Virginia Woolf. (Insincerity had never bothered him.) That did effectively silence me. But on the whole, my summer immersions in Austrian culture were enormously valuable to me, pointing up features of the other cultures where I was more at home which otherwise I would have taken for granted. Being a foreigner is very good for the soul, and for one's sharpness of vision of features of more familiar cultures. And it is especially beneficial for a social philosopher.

Shortly after our return to Canberra from Europe, after that sabbatical, I suffered a miscarriage, and Kurt and I were to remain childless, until Sarah was restored to me, much later. Once the decision to move to the US was taken, and we were in Pittsburgh, Kurt was overwhelmed with the task he had taken on, chairing a department in an unfamiliar administrative and national setting. We looked for a house, and I looked for a job, and after a few months both were found. I secured a part-time teaching position at Carnegie Tech, as it then was. It soon became Carnegie Mellon University, and was a very good place to teach, as far as getting bright students goes. There were also some brilliant professors, such as Herbert Simon, a great influence on many students whom I taught, and a friendly man. I was at first embedded in a history department, teaching only the history of philosophy, and liked having historians as colleagues.

The house we found was a modern town house, walking distance from both universities, on a steep wooded slope, with pleasant tree-framed city views. We lived there for over thirty years, and many a rollicking student party was held there, usually for some visiting speaker. The largest crowd we ever had was that for Noam Chomsky, when we feared the floors and balcony might collapse. But we also had parties for Donald Davidson, Elizabeth Anscombe, Dick Rorty, Daniel Dennett, Hilary Putman, Sydney Shoemaker, Bernard Williams, Harry Frankfurt, and many others. Several of these guests stayed with us, in our guest room, so there was breakfast conversation, as well as party repartee. The most memorable of the remarks of our distinguished guests was that of Elizabeth Anscombe, with whom my relations while in Oxford had been fairly discordant: she had summed up her findings after my term reading Plato's *Theaetetus* with her, to check if my Greek was good enough to take the Plato exam, "Well, there is nothing wrong with your *Greek*." Perhaps she felt she had a reputation for acid comments to live up to, for on her arrival in our home, she peered at an oriental rug on the floor, then said, "What an interesting rug. For a moment I thought it was genuine." It was not an especially valuable type of rug, only an Ardebil, but perfectly genuine of its kind, bought in a bazaar in Shiraz, and its value in my eyes rose, after Anscombe's put-down. Another remark of hers I recall, which puzzled me, was "It's fairyland here, isn't it?" By "here" she meant the United States philosophical scene, which was at the time very keen to have visits from famous British philosophers, so paid them more than they were accustomed to being paid. But I was an under-paid spouse–philosopher at the time, not finding it by any means a fairyland, but a very sexist and violent land, where people, including philosophers, kept guns by their bedsides.

Eventually, at Carnegie Mellon, my position became full-time, my rank associate philosopher with tenure, and philosophy was recognized as separate from history. Once Kurt had finished his stint as chairman, the University of Pittsburgh could consider hiring me. First they invited me to give one graduate course, and I had a good time teaching a course on intentionality. It was around this time that I talked and corresponded with Wilfrid Sellars about this topic. He was a brilliant teacher, some of whose courses I attended. His cryptic writings made much better sense once one had heard him teach. He and his writer wife, Mary, lived for a while, with their Siamese cats Shem and Shaun, in an old house in wooded land in the North Hills, north of the Allegheny River, and we would visit them, becoming more friendly with Mary than with the rather aloof Wilfrid. Then the marriage broke up, Wilfrid moved to Schenley Heights, close to the university, and Mary to an apartment quite close to us, in Shadyside. She was very unhappy, suffered from severe migraines, and during one of these shot herself in the temple with a pistol that Wilfrid had given her, having phoned him to tell him her intentions. He came to us after finding the body, and calling police. If he had been withdrawn before that, with us, he was even more so afterwards, associating us with that terrible evening. When I would meet him for lunch, it would be in the Athletic Club, near the university, where a local freshwater fish called brown spots figured often on the menu. Others who knew Wilfrid may associate his name with pink ice cubes, a favorite example when he spoke of primary and secondary qualities, but my association is with brown spots.

I had begun publishing on intention while still at Carnegie Mellon, and continued that for a while, before my thoughts turned to the other topics in the philosophy of mind, those included in my essays in *Postures of the Mind*.[6] One thing that changed my focus, a little, after joining the Pitt department was my awareness of what obstacles some of my women graduate students had had to overcome, in order to be such students, and of the bias still working against them, from some of my colleagues. I had never felt such bias. Fear of dismissal for unwed pregnancy in Auckland, and sexual harassment in Sydney, there had indeed been, but I had never faced sexist bias against my professional ambitions. So a feminist theme came into many of the talks I gave, and, once I began publishing in ethics, into the papers I published. As I see them now from this distance, they also show a preoccupation with the question of who rears the children, not surprising in one who left her daughter's care to others. The Pittsburgh department provided me with wonderful graduate students and stimulating colleagues. For a while there was a very companionable cluster of those of us with interests in the history of philosophy, John Cooper, Paul Guyer, and Alexander Nehamas. I developed a special interest in Descartes, and directed several Ph.D. theses about his views. When Lilli Alanen visited, I shared my office with her, and we had many good conversations about Descartes. In ethics I sparred happily with David Gauthier, whose office was near mine, and I soon had the good company of other women faculty, including Nancy (Ann) Davis, Jennifer Whiting, and Tamara Horowitz.

The years in Pittsburgh saw, I suppose, my growth and blossoming as a philosopher, and that was due in part to my stimulating colleagues, in large part to my graduate students, on whom I tried out my ideas, but also to seeds sown earlier. My very migration from culture to culture, from New Zealand to Britain, from Australia to the US, and my regular summers in Austria, all fed into my writings on trust, which culminated in my 1991 Tanner Lectures, and which led to much subsequent literature on that topic. Only a wanderer and an exile, I think, could have been led to such thoughts. Most of my previous publications had been reactive to what others were writing about, but when I first wrote about trust, I was a voice in the wilderness. And I think all my writings in ethics have been influenced by my first-hand knowledge of how life is lived in different places.

In 1989, the year Sarah and I were reunited, the year before the Berlin Wall came down, Kurt and I spent a year in Berlin, where I had a fellowship

---

[6] Baier, *Postures of the Mind* (Minneapolis: University of Minnesota Press, 1985).

at the Wissenschaftskolleg. There I encountered scholars in many disciplines and from many places, but what I most profited from were conversations with the German scholars there that year: Eike von Savigny in philosophy, and Christian Vogel and Wulf Schiefenhovel in anthropology, who read my essay on violent demonstrations in draft, and took me to a conference on trust in Bad Homburg. The anthropologist faces not just the problem of getting the trust of those he studies, but of not abusing it in the way he uses the information he has obtained, so hearing anthropologists discuss trust helped me focus my own thoughts. I was also helped by meeting the retired sociologist Dieter Claessens, who had taught Wolf Lepenies, the Rektor of the Kolleg. Germans had thought more about trust than others, and it was anthropologists and sociologists, not philosophers, who had led the way.

By the time I gave my presidential address to the Eastern Division of the American Philosophical Association in 1990, I had become more focused in my feminist aims. That lecture led to some indignation among the men who had helped vote me into my position as president. And it also made me sick for several days, as I did not take easily to the role of accuser. My unease was partly due to my awareness that I had not myself suffered from sexist bias, and I had a very supportive philosopher husband, but I spoke, I thought, on behalf of other women in the profession. And the claims I made about bias in the received version of what a person is went beyond any such practical concerns, but went to what had concerned me in my first recorded utterance, what it is to be a particular person, a person among other persons. I criticized the individualism of much of our philosophical tradition, but in advancing a social view of mind and person, I was not being in any way original, since both Kurt and others of my Pittsburgh colleagues had argued for such a social constructionist view. I had learned from the other minds around me, and was in agreement with many of them. What offended in that address was not the emphasis on social ties, but the mockery of male dignity. Dignity is important to Kantians, but we Humeans find the peacock's strut rather comic, and nothing to imitate. When I think back now to the male philosophers I had known, I think of the example of Austin, in his muddy shoes and chalk-dusty gown, making jokes about various illocutionary misfires, some of them raising questions about what part animals can play in what we do with words ("Would christening a chrysalis baptize the butterfly?" is one line I recall from a poem I composed as Austin lectured, and there were also questions about the ordination of mules.) Austin set a great example of non-pompous philosophy, and also of careful and collaborative philosophy, so I certainly did not intend to include all male philosophers in the group of those I mocked. My own husband was in the audience, one of the few who were laughing, not either fuming, as some men were, or weeping with joy, as some women said they were. Kurt and I have had our philosophical differences, but not on the topics I was addressing in that address. I have dedicated two books about Hume to Kurt, but more because I thought he needed to attend to his writings more than he has than because we shared a love of that magnificently undignified and sermon-avoiding writer.

My own reading in philosophy had long included more than Anglo-American analysts. European thinkers of a variety of sorts, from Sartre and Merleau-Ponty to Hannah Arendt, all interested me. I had set Arendt's book about the human condition for my students at Carnegie Mellon, in a course in which we surveyed different traditions in philosophy. So when the row about "pluralism" in philosophy broke out in the American Philosophical Association, my sympathies were with the pluralists, and it was to some extent their votes which had got me elected to the presidency. This fact made me a few enemies in my own department, but the whole thing was a storm in a teacup. For those of us who grew up in philosophy by the study of Descartes, Spinoza, and Kant, later Continental figures such as Husserl and Heidegger, Derrida and Habermas, were, of course, of great interest. It would be the height of provincialism to ignore them, and fear of being provincial was, with me, a driving force. But when I took early retirement, in 1996, after delivering the Carus Lectures, it was partly the unpleasantness from some of my Pittsburgh colleagues that made me glad to return to my original province, New Zealand. Like Charles Brasch, I returned from the wider world with a new appreciation for the place I had come from, for what, in his words about the journal *Landfall*, which he founded and edited, is "distinctly of New Zealand, without being parochial."[7]

Since retirement I have been able to spend more time than before with my daughter, my sisters and their husbands, my son-in-law, and my four grandchildren. These four young people excel at wonderfully different things. One is artistic, one a star hockey player, one is an accountant who runs marathons, and the youngest is studying ecology. For a while, after

---

[7] Charles Brasch, *Indirections: A Memoir* (Wellington: Oxford University Press, 1980), 388.

retiring, I left philosophy alone, and wrote up my husband's interesting life, from Vienna through internment in Britain and Australia, to Oxford, Cornell, Canberra, Pittsburgh, Queenstown, and Dunedin. This turned out to be providential, as, shortly after I had, with his help, completed it, he suffered severe memory loss, so the document, with its rich photographic illustrations, now serves for him as an external memory of his life. Then I went back to philosophy, mainly continuing to work on Hume, with whose mind my own had long been engrossed. At last I read his *History of England* from cover to cover. This has led to two more books about his views, where what he wrote in the *History* is taken into account. I also wrote several essays in ethics, and gave the occasional talk to the local Dunedin philosophers. I miss my graduate students very much, but keep in email touch with many of them, and we read each other's writings in draft form. I am blest with many fine minds for my own to rub up against, not just the great philosophers of the past, and friends and colleagues of my own generation, but also much younger minds, who often see things I have missed, and have a different take on some matters. Agreeable disagreement flourishes in our correspondence. The other minds I have been privileged to get to know, to learn from, and to work with have made for a rich and lively intellectual life.

I said at the start that I see myself as a wanderer from culture to culture, and as one who left her native land. But I also returned to it, even to my birthplace, Queenstown, where we have a house on the lakeside, and to my home university, Otago, which set me on my intellectual way. I returned enriched by the other cultures I have come to know, and better able to see both what is good and what might be improved in my native culture. What is good is its egalitarian outlook, the opportunity everyone has to get ahead, as I myself did from a humble home setting. What is also good is that women here have been in charge of government, the courts, big business. What is not so good is the frequent suspicion of intellectuals, and a shocking degree of drunkenness and violence, including violence against little children. We are a multicultural society, and that leads to some frictions. We also tend to be smug about what we perceive as our manifest superiority over other societies. We may indeed be unique in dating the birth of our nation to a treaty between the native inhabitants, the Maori, and the colonizing British, but that treaty was not very well kept, and is still disputed, especially its provisions about ownership of the shore and seabed. Still, it makes us self-consciously

Polynesian as well as British, and I think that, in my own case, getting to
know Maori students and their collaborative work habits, at Auckland
University, when I shared a kitchen and bathroom with two Maori students,
while I taught there, made me aware of the questionable individualism, and
emphasis on solitary accomplishment, rather than on what we can achieve
together, which prevailed in the Pakeha world, including the university.

"Pakeha." Now there is a good concept which I can incorporate into my
self-image—I see myself as a self-questioning Pakeha. The word means
"pale," and was used by brown-skinned Maori to refer to those pale outsiders who came from afar and took their land, and tried to govern them. I
am a pale outsider, and there are not so many of us left. Intermarriage
between Maori and Pakeha has turned us New Zealanders into a nation of
people in varying attractive shades of brown. My awareness in youth of the
difference between the two main cultures in my country prepared me for
the other cultures I later experienced, in England, Scotland, Australia,
Austria, the US. I try to be cosmopolitan, but, of course, roots count for
much. I am a wandering and returning Pakeha, still questioning how it is
best to live.

This week I shall be attending "An evening with Charles Brasch," as part
of Dunedin's heritage festival. Brasch, a great benefactor to our city, had
turned down my adolescent poems for publication in *Landfall*, the journal
he began in 1947, after his return to New Zealand after the Second World
War, from his own self-chosen exile in Britain, Russia, and Egypt. His later
diaries record that Kurt and I met him, by chance, at Mt Cook, when he
was there with Harry and Margaret Scott, shortly after our marriage, in
December 1958. Brasch wrote, in his memoir, *Indirections*, that when he
returned to England, as war broke out, and began writing the poetry for
which he is now famous, "It was New Zealand I discovered, not England,
because New Zealand lived in me as no other country could live, part of me
as I was part of it."[8] In New Zealand, Brasch had encountered anti-Semitism,
and his self-image certainly was of a Jewish New Zealander, with bookish
tastes. I feel I have become Jewish by marriage, as it were (not that my
husband ever was taught the Jewish faith, but he did have to leave Austria
because of his Jewish blood), so I resonate to Brasch's sense of being an
atypical New Zealander, in his case because of his birth into a wealthy

[8] Brasch, *Indirections: A Memoir*, 360.

Jewish family, and because of his intellectual interests. He wrote of this country, in his well-known poem "The Islands":

> Everywhere in light and calm the murmuring
> Shadow of departure; distance looks our way,
> And none knows where he will lie down at night.[9]

I am fairly sure where I will lie down tonight, but not of the places I may dream of. I often dream of Oxford, of Vienna, of Manhattan, sometimes even of Jerusalem and Persepolis, Angkor Wat and Borobodur. For I have wandered the earth, and am glad to return in my dreams to distant places, but most of my dreams take me back to Oamaru, the coastal town where I lived from age 4 until age 14, and where, once war broke out, we went on practice route marches inland in readiness for a Japanese invasion. Brasch was a boarder at Waitaki Boys' High School, in Oamaru, and I too went there, with the rest of us from Waitaki Girls' High School, for the yearly Scott Memorial services, when Frank Milner would read from Robert Falcon Scott's last diary entry: "I do not regret this journey..." My journey, too, has taken me far, but unlike Scott I have returned safely to base.

I have been fortunate throughout my life to enjoy fairly good health. An ovarian tumor had to be removed while we were in Oxford, in 1961, and Janet Vaughan visited me in hospital in Headington, warning me not to expect a fast recovery of strength. I thought of her when again in hospital in Dunedin in 2002, after a serious stomach bleed, which required eighteen blood transfusions. I am, of course, grateful to those eighteen strangers whose donated blood saved my life, as well as to Janet Vaughan and her medical colleagues, who first stored blood in milk bottles, and perfected the art of safe transfusion. A stomach tumor was eventually removed, and my spleen with it, so now I live a little more dangerously. I have been sustained throughout my life not just by others' minds, but by others' blood, and others' skills. But now, in old age, my body seems unsure what is other, and what is self. The rare auto-immune disease I now suffer from is unpleasant, but seems nicely appropriate for one whose self-image is as voluntary alien. The philosopher Yajun Chen says: "Moral progress is a matter of learning from the other, not taking the other to be a member of us."[10] I have learned

---

[9] Brasch, *Collected Poems*, 17.

[10] See the end of his paper about Richard Rorty in a volume about Rorty: Barry Allen, Alexander Groeschner, and Mike Sandbote (eds.), *Pragmatismus als Kulturpolitik: Beiträge zum Werk von Richard Rorty* (Frankfurt am Main: Surkamp, 2010).

46

from many others, past and present, some in other disciplines and cultures from my own, and my thoughts have become mixed with theirs, as my blood mixed with that of those eighteen blood donors. I have been so long an alien, have become so familiar with that role, that now it seems I cannot tell what is and what is not alien to me.

I am acutely conscious how difficult it is to speak honestly about oneself, without either overdramatization or self-deceit. Hume began his *My Own Life* by saying, "It is difficult for a man to speak long about himself without vanity; therefore I shall be short." This piece of mine, about myself, is just a little longer than Hume's, so is too long. I do not think it shows vanity, but that may not be the worst fault. Honesty is a hard virtue, and sometimes in conflict with discretion. If what I have said hurts others, then I have said too much, or in some cases, too little. These jottings are towards an intellectual self-image, so the others to whom I refer are mainly those who affected my thinking. The host of friends who have sustained me through the years, emotionally, have largely gone unmentioned, as did Hume's friends in his autobiography, but, as he said in another place, without love and friendship nothing else is worth having.

THE LEARNING CENTRE
TOWER HAMLETS COLLEGE
ARBOUR SQUARE
LONDON E1 0PS

Acknowledgments

The following essays have been published previously:

1. The Rights of Past and Future Persons
   In E. Partridge (ed.), *Responsibility to Future Generations* (Prometheus Books, 1981), 171–83.
2. For the Sake of Future Generations
   In Tom Regan (ed.), *Earthbound* (Random House, 1984), 214–4c
4. Can Philosophers Be Patriots?
   In *New Literary History*, 39/1 (2008), 121–35.
5. Why Honesty Is a Hard Virtue
   In O. Flanagan and A. Rorty (eds.), *Identity, Character and Morality: Essay in Moral Psychology* (MIT Press, 1990), 259–82.
6. Getting in Touch With Our Own Feelings
   In *Topoi*, 6 (Sept. 1987), 89–97.
7. How to Get to Know One's Own Mind: Some Simple Ways
   In Michaelis Michael and John O'Leary-Hawthorne (eds.), *Philosophy in Mind: The Place of Philosophy in the Study of Mind*, Philosophical Studies, 60 (Kluwer Academic Publishers, 1994), 65–82.
9. Feelings That Matter
   In R. Solomon (ed.), *Thinking About Feeling: Contemporary Philosophers on Emotions* (Oxford University Press, 2004), 200–13.
10. Demoralization, Trust, and the Virtues
    In Cheshire Calhoun (ed.), *Setting the Moral Compass* (Oxford University Press, 2004), 176–88.
13. How to Lose Friends: Some Simple Ways
    Appeared as "La perte d'amis" in Jean-Christophe Merle and Bernard N. Schumacher (eds.), *L'Amitié* (Presses Universitaires de France, 2005), 137–52.

Permission to reprint these essays is gratefully acknowledged.

Name Index

The names of friends and family mentioned in Essay 16 have not been included in this index. From that essay, only topics and names of philosophers and other thinkers who were not close friends have been indexed. It is a fine line to draw, between a philosopher-friend as philosopher, and the same person as friend. I trust my philosopher-friends will feel pleased, not offended, at their non-inclusion in this index.

Subject Index